Roy Poindexter

Golden Throats and Silver Tongues

GOLDEN THROATS
AND
SILVER TONGUES

The Radio Announcers

RAY POINDEXTER

Printed in the United States of America

RIVER ROAD PRESS
CONWAY, ARKANSAS

Contents

Preface

During radio's glory years, I must have been an unusual kind of listener. As a teenager in the 1930's and a college student in the early '40's, I often liked to hear the announcer more than I did the other members of a radio show. I even liked his persuasive, well-delivered commercials. I was greatly impressed by the rich voice quality, and frequently I tried to emulate the tone and inflection, both in the solitude of my room and while among friends. And how most announcers spoke with such clarity! At least, I thought they did. I was also amazed at their ability to project an appealing personality into the microphone so that it carried through the air and emerged intact from the speaker of a table model cathedral or a booming console set.

The announcer's introduction of a program established the proper mood and setting for that which was to follow. And at the close, he wrapped it up and tied it together in a neat package, leaving you believing it had all been worthwhile. He was the border, the frame, around the complete imaginary picture.

I depended on the reliable fellow in the morning who ran the musical-clock type program. After every pleasant song, he told me how long I had to make it to my first class or to some other destination. Often he would strike a musical chime to accent the correct time. ("My watch must be right," folks would say. "I set it by the radio this morning.")

Were the baseball games always as exciting as the play-by-play man made them sound? I was fifteen before I saw the inside of a major league baseball park. The real thing didn't seem as thrilling as the game I was accustomed to hearing.

Announcers appeared to enjoy such a carefree, happy-go-lucky existence. If they had any problems (and I know now that they did), they managed to conceal them while they were on the air. Mikemen were always on the go, switching from one station to another. They must have been nomads searching for the ideal broadcasting facility.

Then the war came, and the newscasters and commentators sounded so authoritative and knowledgeable. How did they know how to pronounce all of those big names? And each commentator had a different approach to the events of the day. He seemed to have an insight about the subject that others didn't possess.

During recent years, there has been considerable radio nostalgia—presented by radio, television, and the press; however, most of the recognition has been given to comedians, singers, actors, and musicians. Because of their tremendous contributions to early radio, this renown is justifiably deserved. But the announcers have been virtually ignored. Sometimes they receive a brief mention—most times, nothing. It is my purpose to portray, partially, the significance of the roles they played. The hundreds of announcers included here represent the thousands who were actually there.

—Ray Poindexter
1978

A word fitly spoken is like
apples of gold
in pictures of silver.

—Proverbs, XXV, 11

I

The Warm-Up

The tones of the human voice are mightier than strings or brass to move the soul.

— Friedrich Klopstock

Hello. This is Harry von Zell. In my earlier years with CBS, all of the programs to which I was assigned as the announcer were performed in a studio, and there was no "live" audience. It wasn't until later, when vaudeville was waning fast and star personalities of that medium began "moving out" and looking to radio as a place to carry on their careers, that the absence of a live audience became a factor. For awhile both NBC and CBS followed the practice of using "canned" laughter and applause for that purpose. However, vaudevillians accustomed to the reaction of live audiences complained on two counts: (1) they felt that the air audience would soon come to realize that the applause and laughter were being mechanically produced, and would not approve of it; (2) (and the most important to them) was the fact that lacking the spontaneous reaction of a live audience tended to "throw them off" in their timing, adversely affecting their performance.

NBC was able to respond to the situation, having available a very large studio which actually constituted a "theatre" which could accommodate an audience of a thousand or more, a stage big enough to seat a large orchestra, and of course, a control room setup equipped with multiple "mike" outlets. CBS, on the other hand, did not have a studio large enought to accommodate an audience of more than thirty or forty. They solved the problem by leasing an off-Broadway theatre.

Free tickets were made available to the public upon request, and the demand was heavy. Both networks made it known that seating arrangements were strictly on a "first-come, first-

1

served" basis, so ticket holders were inclined to come early. This presented a problem, to wit: what to do with the audience in that interim between their arrival and "show time." They just couldn't be left there twiddling their thumbs and growing impatient; so—came the idea. The announcer would do a "warm-up."

Some announcers had routines prepared for them by professional writers. In my own case, I decided against a set formula. I had no "gimmicks," no "jokes." I simply sort of kidded around with the audience—example: "Look at this! We have a full house! We ought to raise the pot. You know, on some shows they have somebody hold up a sign which says in large letters 'APPLAUSE,' and another sign which says 'LAUGHTER.' We don't do that here. If you intelligent folks don't know when to applaud and when to laugh, we're in trouble right from the start. So we just take our chances and 'play it by ear.' If we don't hear anything, we cry. Of course there's always the possibility that the show is no good. If that turns out to be the case, I suppose you'll just walk out—and I'll go with you."

That sort of light nonsense seemed to work well for me. I think it was the informality of my approach which carried the most effect. It made the audience "feel at home" and loosened them up.

On such shows as Fred Allen's *Town Hall Tonight*, Eddie Cantor, Ed Wynn, Phil Baker, and *Duffy's Tavern*, my stint was very brief, so that I could bring on stage the star and members of the cast. Between us, the warm-up was most effective.

In early TV, the *Burns & Allen Show* was performed live on a stage in the CBS theatre. My warm-up there consisted of kidding around a little with the audience, then recommending to them that they avoid becoming intrigued with the "mechanics" of the show—cameras, of which there were three; the technicians; microphones; etc., pointing out that if there was too much attention concentrated there, instead of upon the action and the dialogue sequences performed by the cast, the full import of the plot could be missed, which would adversely affect their enjoyment of the show.

The factor of "live audience" reaction posed a problem when George Burns decided to go on film. He was opposed to trying to film the show before a live audience; but, of course, wanted live and spontaneous audience reaction. The problem was solved when George leased a large RCA recording studio for Monday nights from 8:00 to 9:00 P.M. CBS made frequent "air" announcements that free tickets were available to people who desired to attend a "preview showing" of the *Burns & Allen Show.* Having completed shooting two half-hour shows, we were ready for an audience. Our studio could accommodate an audience of about 350, and we were filled every Monday night.

My warm-up there consisted of kidding around a little, and then concentrating on calling to the attention of the audience the microphones suspended from the ceiling, and explaining that they were there strictly for the purpose of picking up their reaction in forms of laughter and applause on the sound track of our film. I would say, "Don't force yourselves. If it isn't funny, that's our fault." It worked fine.

This is your announcer, Dick Joy. For my warm-ups, I borrowed some ideas from Ken Niles, the best I ever saw. Bill Goodwin was a close second. (I worked the "hitchhike" spot on the *Bob Burns Show* when Ken announced the Bazooka man.) He had a routine with two musicians about "laughing for radio." A meek, skinny violinist would titter at Ken's command. Niles would say, "That's O.K. for tea parties, but . . . " Then he'd cue a great big trumpet player, who would shake all over while bellowing hearty guffaws. "THAT'S the kind of belly laugh WE need." It always worked.

Ken also told the audience he'd "fade out" their applause by slowly bringing his hand across their range of vision, "so you won't all quit at once." For the applause, he instructed: "Take the palm of your lazy hand, cup it—then tattoo it rapidly with the fingers of your busy hand to produce a rapid, steady clapping sound. It's much more efficient than just banging your hands together haphazardly. As to coughing and throat-clearing, let's get that all over with right now!" All of these, plus brief explanations about the show and intros of the stars, worked wonders.

I followed Ken's lead and usually got good cooperation. Telling jokes gets tedious for audiences, especially when many of the same people keep coming back. During the five years of filming *December Bride,* there were frequent gaps while sets and wardrobes were changed and cameras reloaded. I hit upon the idea of having people in the audience ask members of the crew about their work. THAT went over big with fans AND crew

3

members. It was always enjoyed by everybody. Once I had to fill forty-five minutes on *Pantomime Quiz*, which was live on KTTV, Los Angeles, and filmed simultaneously for syndication. KTTV's transmitter "blew," so we couldn't go till it came back on, and the audience wanted to leave. I exhausted every story I knew and so did everybody connected with the show. We finally got the welcome word, "It's back on the air!" My average warm-up was about four minutes. I could get in all the facts about the show, the intros, and a bit of humor, plus the Niles-type instructions.

On my first audience show, *Silver Theatre*, I was told not to be funny—just welcome the people, talk briefly about the show, and bring out Conrad Nagel; he would briefly intro the stars. Then I'd do the thing about coughing NOW, and we'd leave thirty seconds for the orchestra tune-up. The time Clark Gable was on, he was worried (as all stars were) about the "live radio" thing. Gable blushed from being hot and uncomfortable and ran his finger around his shirt collar during that half-minute tune-up time. The audience, mostly women that day, reacted by laughing. We went on the air with our theme trying to drown out the laughter. Soon the twx from New York carried an inquiry from the sponsor: "What did the announcer do to make the audience laugh?" Yes, we were handy to have around for blaming things on.

On the *Danny Kaye Show* in 1946, Danny took over after my brief words and simply snowed those doting New Yorkers into clapping and laughing all-out. He promised them an "after-show" if they cooperated, and THAT was worth waiting for, believe me!

I worked *Burns & Allen* a few times (as a newscaster) when Bill Goodwin was their announcer. He was great. George and Gracie would take over, as Kaye did, and really "wow" those audiences. I never felt I was a comedian-type, and at first I feared doing warm-ups. But I soon learned to look for friendly faces and "play" to them. That spreads through most audiences, and it builds confidence in the warmer-upper—a bit of "togetherness."

Roger Krupp speaking. When I announced *Famous Jury Trials*, I used a little gimmick which usually got a few laughs. When the director would call out on the P.A. system: "Standby... thirty seconds before air time," I would walk out to center stage,

4

put my script on the floor in front of the mike, step back a few feet, then trot over the script and say to the audience, "I always like to run over my script before we go on the air." (Not so funny, huh?)

One time during the same procedure, but on a *Quiz Kids* show, I dropped the script and got the pages all mixed up. It could have been a near catastrophe except for the fact that all I had to say at the beginning was, "The *Quiz Kids* brought to you by Alka Seltzer! And now, here is your master of ceremonies (or something like that), Joe Kelly!" I had that memorized, of course.

Once the *Quiz Kids* show was broadcast from Washington, D.C., from the Mayflower Hotel—a very small stage and box seats for a chosen few of the elite, most of which were what you might include in the "dowager" class. Very prissy and the "Do-I-know-you?" type. After my brief warm-up, I called for "quiet please." Then I pointed to the gallery and said, "And PLEASE, ladies...NO whistling!" A couple of those old gals really shrieked with laughter. I thought they were going to fall out of their seats. They were still giggling when we went on the air.

It seems that in my case, the star of the show did most of the warm-ups. Al Jolson, Milton Berle, and a couple of others did their own and certainly much better than I could. Many of the old shows I announced did have an audience, but they were on a tour around Radio City in New York, and were all behind plate glass.

II

On the Air

Never is the deep, strong voice of man, or the low, sweet voice of woman, finer than in the earnest but mellow tones of familiar speech, richer than the richest music, which are a delight while they are heard, which linger still upon the ear in softened echoes, and which, when they have ceased, come, long after, back to memory, like the murmurs of a distant hymn.

—Henry Giles

If you're twenty-four and work in the advertising department of Westinghouse Electric in East Pittsburgh in late October 1920 and want to stay in advertising all your life and the boss gives you an unusual assignment, you carry it out. Leo H. Rosenberg did. The head of the advertising department told him to take some of the fellows up to a recently thrown-together shack on the roof of a nine-story building and have them take turns talking into a crude microphone that was really the mouthpiece of an upright telephone encased in a small box and connected to a rubber tube that led to nearby wireless equipment. A group of company officials would be there to listen and to choose the man they considered to be the most articulate. The activity was part of a hurry-up process to get a radio station on the air in time to broadcast returns of the Harding-Cox presidential election coming up November 2. Would the voters return another Democrat to the White House to succeed Woodrow Wilson or would they switch to a Republican administration under Warren Harding? The Westinghouse hierarchy wanted to inform the public of the outcome, at least that small portion of the public who happened to possess some kind of receiving set.

On October 16, Dr. Frank Conrad, Westinghouse assistant chief engineer, had made application to the Radio Division,

6

Bureau of Navigation, U.S. Department of Commerce, a department that was headed up by a man named Herbert Hoover as Commerce Secretary, for a license. The knowledgeable Dr. Conrad had already started station construction by placing a 100-watt transmitter in the shack and running a six-wire antenna from a steel pole on top of the building to the brick smokestack of a powerhouse. As early as the summer of 1916, he had begun experimenting with his amateur station, 8XK, located on the second floor of the garage at his home in Wilkenburg, five miles from the plant. All amateur stations were forced to cease operations when the United States entered World War I. The ban was lifted October 1, 1919, and Conrad resumed his broadcasts, playing phonograph records and making announcements. Listener response led Westinghouse officials to believe there was a vast potential market for the sale of receiving sets. With a station of their own, they could help to create demand.

Leo Rosenberg figured that since he was up in the shack anyway, he might as well talk into the microphone, too. It was a wise decision. His superiors judged his style as the most impressive, and he was selected at that first audition to do the announcing.

Like the hero in a William S. Hart western, the license arrived in time. It came on October 27, authorizing a station to operate on 360 meters, which was equivalent to 833 kilocycles, with the call letters KDKA, the first identification that had all letters rather than a number-letters combination.

Arrangements were made with the Pittsburgh *Post* to obtain election returns over a private telephone line. Broadcasting was scheduled to begin at 6:00 P.M. The night was stormy. Dr. Conrad wasn't certain that the new station would work. He was standing by at his home with 8XK, just in case. Four men were in the penthouse control room: Rosenberg, the transmitter operator, a staff member who would take returns over the phone, and a telephone company man in charge of the line.

Rosenberg sat at the mike. The appointed hour arrived. The speech process began—air flowing over vocal folds causing vibrations that were in turn resonated and formed into syllables: "This is station KDKA, Westinghouse, East Pittsburgh, Pennsylvania."

The style was standard, unaffected—not regional. The voice was steady and calm—not anxious or hurried. The enunciation was clear and clean—not slurred. It was natural—not pompous.

7

Rosenberg called the announcements "bulletins." A wind-up phonograph was used to play records between speech segments. Periodically, he announced, "Will anyone hearing this broadcast communicate with us, as we are anxious to know how far the broadcast is reaching and how it is being received." The only listening audience he could definitely claim at the time was a group of Westinghouse people and other local residents who were gathered in the main ballroom of the Edgewood Country Club. Two Navy horn speakers had been borrowed for the occasion. It was a very enthusiastic assemblage. Several times they called the station requesting "more news and less music."

When a vote count trend was established, Rosenberg reported: "The Republican ticket of Harding and Coolidge is running well ahead of Cox and Roosevelt. We'll give you the state vote in just a moment, but first we'd like to ask you to let us know if this broadcast is reaching you. Please drop us a card addressed to station KDKA, Westinghouse, East Pittsburgh, Pennsylvania." Broadcasting continued until noon the next day, although the outcome had been determined much earlier.

KDKA's first broadcast was a tremendous promotional success. Newspaper publicity was generous nationwide. Mail response was heavy. The signal had also been picked up at sea. KDKA was ready to get on with the serious business of continuous broadcasting.

The election returns had been broadcast elsewhere on amateur stations. In Detroit, 8MK, which had been established August 20 of that year by William E. Scripps, publisher of the Detroit *News*, carried the results. The amateur outlet would later become commercial station WBL and then WWJ. In St. Louis, Lester Benson broadcast the returns with a transmitter located in the basement of his home. His station would become WEB and later emerge as WIL.

Leo Rosenberg continued to announce for KDKA, working from 8:00 to 10:00 each night, in addition to his regular daytime duties in the advertising department. He was eager to get some relief. The station's formal opening came on December 21. It was about that time that a Westinghouse employee became curious about that which was taking place on the roof. It was a case of being in the right place at the right time.

Harold W. Arlin moved with his parents from La Harpe, Illinois, to Carthage, Missouri, when he was four. A two-room school was the site of his elementary education. After graduation from Carthage High School, Arlin entered the University of

Kansas and earned a degree in electrical engineering in 1917. Then he enrolled in the Westinghouse graduate student training course. Engineers are a curious breed. Twenty-five-year-old Arlin knew that the company was operating a radio station, and he wanted to know more about it. He was working as a time study supervisor in the firm's manufacturing division when he visited the wireless setup. Leo Rosenberg noticed his intense interest as he observed the equipment and the broadcasting routine and had a hunch that this man might be the relief he was seeking. He informed Arlin they were looking for an announcer. Would he like to try out?

"Yeah," replied Arlin, thinking he might work at it for a few weeks. Christmas was coming up, and he thought it could be an opportunity to earn a few extra dollars that would help buy his wife a very special present.

The audition revealed that his voice was vigorous and carried well. He was offered an hour or two on the microphone each night. He accepted. After January 1 of the new year, he was given the position of full time announcer, enabling Rosenberg to return to his desk. The station still had no studio. Arlin played phonograph records and brought in remotes from churches, hotels, theatres, and auditoriums. At first, when playing records he didn't announce song titles or artists' names. Listeners complained. The policy was changed, and music stores enjoyed a thriving record and sheet music business. Pittsburgh *Post* sports writer Florent Gibson was enlisted to give a blow-by-blow description of a prizefight from Pittsburgh's Motor Square Garden April 11, 1921. The station took another programming step May 19 when arrangements were made with the Bureau of Markets, U.S. Department of Agriculture, to broadcast prices of grain, fruit, vegetables, and livestock.

During the same month, the plant's auditorium was used as a studio, but the acoustics were unsuitable. Next a tent was pitched on the roof near the shack. This proved to be satisfactory most of the time when good weather prevailed, but there were exceptions. One night Arlin introduced a tenor. When the singer opened his mouth fully to reach a high note, an insect flew into his vocal apparatus. It was quickly evident that his words were not suitable for broadcast, and the operator wasted no time before pulling the switch. Arlin's nightly program was always interrupted at 8:30 by the whistle of a passing freight train. The unscheduled sound became a regular feature, regardless of the type of show on the air at the time.

Major Andrew J. White was the publisher of *Wireless Age*. He was also the acting president of the National Amateur Wireless Association. White was a formal, dignified type of person who often wore a monocle. When a decision was made to broadcast an important event, White's organization was called upon to make the technical arrangements and handle the broadcast. Although the century was still young, the event was billed as "The Battle of the Century." World heavyweight champion Jack Dempsey would defend his title July 2 against Georges Carpentier, the champion of France, in Boyle's Thirty Acres at Jersey City.

White and the National Amateur Wireless Association first had to obtain a transmitter. They learned that RCA was having a transmitter built by its subsidiary, General Electric, at Schenectady, New York. It had been ordered by the Navy. By then, thirty-year-old David Sarnoff was RCA's general manager. Only five years earlier he had expressed his vision of commercial broadcasting in a memo to his superiors:

> I have in mind a plan of development which would make radio a household utility. . . .
>
> . . . . This proposition would be especially intersting to farmers and others living in outlying districts removed from the cities. By the purchase of a "Radio Music Box" they could enjoy concerts, lectures, music, recitals, etc., which may be going on in the nearest city within their radius.

Sarnoff realized that broadcasting the fight could be a milestone in radio's very early history. The transmitter was promised to the N.A.W.A.

White and his staff considered the site of the event as a possible place to install the equipment. This idea was rejected because there was no way to string the antenna without building costly towers. After further searching, it was decided that the Lackawanna Railroad terminal in Hoboken, two-and-a-half miles from ringside, was the best location. The company agreed to the temporary installation.

In order to insure the best possible listening audience, considerable promotion was necessary. It was decided to make halls, theatres, and auditoriums available as points of listening for people who didn't have radios. Extra help was needed to make the arrangements. Because Dempsey's opponent was from France, the assistance of the American Committee for

10

Devastated France was obtained. Since the transmitter was being bought by the Navy, the Navy Club was also lined up for duty. Its president was the former secretary of the Navy and Democratic vice presidential candidate of the previous year, Franklin D. Roosevelt.

Admission would be charged to those who listened in the designated buildings, and each promoting group would receive financial benefits, which would be used for aid in the task of rehabilitating war-torn and devastated regions of France and for the establishment and maintenance of a home, hotel, and club for enlisted men of the United States Navy and Marine Corps. Members of each group traveled to sixty-one cities and towns and arranged for public listening. Some sites would seat as many as five hundred people.

The transmitter was shipped down the Hudson River from Schenectady to the railway area. It was placed in a metal shack where porters changed into their uniforms. J. O. Smith, an associate of Major White and a well-known amateur radio operator of station 2ZL, was in charge of installation. The four-wire antenna was strung between a 400-foot tower and the lower clock tower on the terminal building, a distance of 450 feet. The ground system utilized the copper roofs of train sheds and other low buildings, a network of tracks, and a pipe system that led to the salt water of the Hudson River.

A one-day license was issued. The Navy's 1600-meter wavelength was selected as the best frequency. The Navy agreed not to use it during the broadcast. The government's chief radio inspector urged amateurs on nearby wavelengths to remain silent during the fight broadcast. It was estimated that the 3½-kilowatt transmitter would have a daytime coverage of more than two hundred miles. Many people bought receiving sets prior to the day of the fight.

The final step in the preparatory process was the selection of a person who would be capable of describing the action. Major Andrew "Andy" White seemed to be the logical choice. Because remote lines were not available to carry White's voice from Boyle's Thirty Acres to the Lackawanna terminal, it was decided that he would report the action into a telephone at ringside, and J. O. Smith would repeat his words into the microphone in the shack. Train porters were disgruntled about being discommoded. Fearing that the equipment might be sabotaged, Smith slept in the shack the night before the fight.

11

On the afternoon of the broadcast, Major White squeezed into a coop-like spot against the ring. He hardly had elbow room. He wore a dark suit and a white shirt with a high, starched, stiff collar. The hot July sun bore down. Ninety thousand fight fans were jammed into the arena.

"Hello, hello, this is WJY, Hoboken, New Jersey, speaking." When the bout started, the spirited crowd made so much noise the announcer could hardly hear himself. His eyes strained to follow the action, but the fighters threw punches so rapidly he couldn't describe all of them. He gave only highlights, the blows that did damage.

In the fourth round when a Dempsey punch sent Carpentier reeling toward the canvas, the Frenchman was only a few inches from White's unprotected head. Only a single rope was between them. The announcer instinctively realized that he must continue to talk without interruption regardless of what might happen. Fortunately, Carpentier landed away from White.

"...seven, eight, nine, ten! Carpentier is out. Jack Dempsey is still the world's champion!"

At the shack, J. O. Smith listened carefully to the earpiece and parroted White's words. Almost immediately after the fight ended, the intense heat inside the metal building caused the transmitter to melt. Had the encounter lasted even a round longer, further radio coverage would not have been possible.

Based on the tremendous response, it was estimated that three hundred thousand people had heard the broadcast. On the boardwalk at Atlantic City, one enterprising individual with a covered cart charged people twenty-five cents per round to listen on earphones to the "wireless telephone."

Members of the Brooklyn Chamber of Commerce wanted to be better informed about the thing called radio. They arranged for a receiving set to be installed for one of their meetings. A forty-three-year-old public-minded citizen volunteered to go to Newark and talk over an experimental station so that they could hear him. Hans Von Kaltenborn was an associate editor of the Brooklyn *Daily Eagle*. He was interested in the new medium; in fact, he owned a crystal set himself. Kaltenborn had been called "Spiderlegs Kalty" as a youngster. He was the son of a Hessian military officer who came to America and settled in Wisconsin. Hans was born in Milwaukee in 1878. When he was nine, the family moved to Merrill, where he began his newspaper career at the age of fourteen as a reporter for the Merrill *News*. At the age of nineteen during the Spanish-American War, he ran away from home and joined the Navy. In addition to his military duties, he served as a correspondent for three Wisconsin newspapers. The conflict ended while he was still in a U.S. camp. After being discharged, he traveled to Europe, working on a cattle boat to earn his passage. He stayed on the continent for several years before returning to the United States and a job with the Brooklyn newspaper. Sensing the need for further education, he enrolled at Harvard, still working as a correspondent for several papers. He graduated with honors and returned to the *Daily Eagle*. Later he married a baroness whom he had met aboard ship.

On the air in Newark, Kaltenborn talked about the merits of a chamber of commerce and its services to a town. When he returned to Brooklyn from his broadcasting venture, chamber members informed him: "We heard you. Your voice came in as clear as a bell." Ether waves were already beginning to nudge the printer's ink in his blood.

In Cincinnati, Powel Crosley, Jr., was running the American Automobile Accessories Company, manufacturing several items of merchandise. One was the Insyde Tire, a tire reliner made from old tires. There was the Litl Shofur, a device which returned Model T Fords to a straight line after the driver had been shaken by a rock in the road. Other products included canoes and phonograph cabinets. Crosley's son had been hearing about radio, and he wanted a receiving set. They shopped for one; but father, being a good businessman, thought they were too expensive. Instead of buying a set, he paid twenty-five cents for a book on radio. Then he turned loose twenty-five dollars for parts and built one. It picked up KDKA. Crosley decided there was a future in radio and began manufacturing receiving sets bearing his name. His first radios sold for twenty dollars. As his knowledge increased, he was able to cut production costs and reduce the price to only nine dollars. Not a man to be content with the status quo, he decided to plunge into the sending phase. In the summer of 1921, he bought a 20-watt transmitter and began broadcasting recorded music over 8XAA, the forerunner of WLW.

In Pittsburgh, KDKA had already established a reputation for broadcasting remotes. Harold Arlin thought the station had neglected one important potential remote product—major league baseball. So he took himself out to the ballgame. The date was August 5, 1921. The scene was Forbes Field. The Pirates were meeting their intrastate rivals, the Philadelphia Phillies. Arlin had followed baseball as a fan and possessed a good working knowledge of the finer points of the game. With this play-by-play broadcast "first," he reported an 8 to 5 win for the home team.

Thomas H. "Tommy" Cowan held the distinction of being the first radio announcer in the Greater New York area. Westinghouse, pleased with the progress of KDKA, expanded its radio enterprise by establishing WJZ at their Newark plant. A duplicate of the KDKA transmitter was sent from Pittsburgh. The transmitter-shack-on-the-roof plan was used again. Announcer auditions were arranged for many factory people. Officials felt that it was very important that a man be selected whose personality was such that it would be pleasing and whose voice would be able to carry more clearly and distinctly than any other. The selection process was finally narrowed down to Tommy Cowan and Joe L. Watt. Cowan had some limited stage experience. When he was fourteen, he had worked as an extra at the Metropolitan Opera. He was chosen as the principal announcer, and Watt was assigned as engineer and assistant announcer.

By late September enough progress had been made for some test broadcasting. Cowan went on the air from the control room on the roof: "This is WJZ, WJZ, WJZ, the radio telephone station located in Newark, New Jersey. This is announcer Cowan, Newark."

There was no regular program. Cowan just talked. Even this brought a considerable amount of mail. Soon he stopped giving his name. Instead, he would say, "This is ACN." For the formal opening October 1, he decided to play some phonograph music. His first job had been with Thomas Edison at West Orange, New Jersey. He went to see the inventor to borrow some phonograph records. Supposedly, Edison didn't like radio, feeling that some of his discoveries had been used in its development. Nevertheless, he lent his former employee some records.

It took a newspaperman to come up with a good radio idea. Sandy Hunt was a reporter for the Newark *Sunday Call*. The World Series would begin October 5, matching both New York clubs, the Giants and the Yankees. The intra-city match-up was referred to as a "subway series." Hunt submitted a suggestion to WJZ to broadcast the series. His idea was approved, and Cowan began trying to obtain a remote line to both parks. The telephone company refused to make installations. As a last resort, it was decided that they would try to put into effect the Major White-J. O. Smith method. A box seat was purchased for Hunt; and after much persuasion, the company placed a telephone in the box.

A crowd numbering 30,203 packed the Polo Grounds on opening day. Among them was Sandy Hunt with his telephone. More radio broadcasting history was about to be made. Cowan anxiously clutched his phone back at the station in Newark. Although it turned out to be a low-hitting, low-scoring game with no home runs, it proved to be quite a trying task for Cowan. He gripped the receiver tightly in his hand and pressed it against his ear. He was so intense as he repeated Hunt's words into the microphone that when the game was over, he didn't even realize which team had won. (The Giants won the first game 3 to 0, but the Yankees took the series five games to three.) Cowan's hand was numb and his ear was extremely sore. Before the second game, he was given headphones. The World Series broadcasts pulled more than four thousand pieces of mail. This proved to company management that the idea had been sound although they hadn't wholeheartedly endorsed it from the beginning.

Cowan began bringing talent over from New York City. It was almost impossible for singers, musicians, and actors to climb to the top of the building. Some semblance of a studio was necessary. The only available space was a ladies cloakroom. A portion of it was converted into a small broadcast area. Repulsive red cloth was draped on the walls to help absorb sound echoes. Two old rugs were laid on the floor. An ancient upright piano was obtained. Narrow, unsteady stairs led to the improvised studio. It was adequate enough to influence many artists to make the trip through the Holland tube to broadcast on WJZ.

Tommy Cowan was especially elated when he arranged for an entire Broadway musical cast to appear. It was scheduled for Sunday night, November 27. His happy feeling of accomplishment soon disappeared. A barrage of protests stemmed from some of the show's risque material and the fact that it would be heard on a Sunday night. Company officials relented and canceled the show. Cowan was depressed. A night of programming was left unfilled. He went to the Pennsylvania Hotel Grill where Vincent Lopez and his Orchestra played. The bandleader noticed the announcer's mood. After hearing about Cowan's problem, Lopez volunteered to take his band to the Newark studio. A suddenly jubilant Cowan offered to rent two Pierce Arrow automobiles to transport the musical aggregation. The bandleader refused the offer and settled for taxicabs.

The studio was packed with musicians and instruments. Cowan suggested that Lopez do the announcing. When it was time for the show to begin, the leader stepped up to the microphone and said, "Hello, everybody. Lopez speaking."

Cowan had expected more. "Is that all you're going to say?"

"That's enough for me," Lopez replied.

The band began playing and the phone began ringing. Favorable comments prolonged the program to two and a half hours. After a few more radio shows, Lopez suggested that they broadcast from the Pennsylvania Grill. Cowan accepted the offer, but the telephone company contended that it wasn't feasible. Cowan wasn't to be stopped that easily. He thought of Western Union. Yes, they would handle it. WJZ ran announcements promoting the on-the-spot presentation, urging listeners to see an actual broadcast. Within an hour, phone calls to the Grill resulted in a sellout.

WJZ began a magazine-type program. It launched Charles Hodges on his radio career. He would later specialize in radio news.

A little radio activity started down in Nashville. Harry Leith Stone installed a 100-watt transmitter in the basement of the First Baptist Church and became the city's first announcer. The station would later be licensed as WCBQ and then WBAW.

Back at KDKA, the tent studio served well during the summer, but it didn't fare so well come autumn. A strong wind toppled it. The station's engineers had learned from the tent arrangement. Why not build a tent inside? Drapes were hung in the style of a tent, meeting at a point in the center of the ceiling, reaching across to the top of the walls, and hanging down to the floor. Acoustical sound board was also utilized in the new, impressive studio, which was ready for use October 3. One night the Little Symphony Orchestra was rehearsing prior to a broadcast. The operator became aware of strange, grinding, grating noises coming through the equipment. He notified Arlin, who began searching for the trouble. The culprit was the orchestra leader. He was munching cookies in front of the mike. Each night that special guests were scheduled to appear on KDKA, Arlin wore a tuxedo. He stood before a box-shaped carbon microphone, which sat upon a fancily carved wooden pedestal.

Arlin continued to pioneer radio sports coverage with the broadcast of Pitt's opening football game with West Virginia. The microphone he used for the football broadcast looked like a tomato can with a felt lining. He called it a "mushophone."

16

Arlin's second football game, which matched Pitt against Nebraska, proved to be the most memorable. After one touchdown, he got so excited and yelled into the mike so loudly the needle was knocked off the modulation meter. They were off the air for several minutes.

Major Andrew White and J. O. Smith teamed up again after the Dempsey-Carpentier experience. RCA started WDY at Roselle Park, New Jersey, December 15. They were assigned to operate it. The station was located about sixteen miles due west of New York City. The studio was the shape of a hexagon with blue and gold draperies forming the tent effect. Carpet and rugs carried out the same color scheme. The lighting also contributed to the colorful setting. A large chandelier, hanging from the center of the studio, emitted a soft, mellow light. On one side of the room was a Knabe-Ampico piano. An Edison re-creating phonograph was at the other side. Major White was in charge of programming. On the nights when WDY broadcast opera, he handled the narrative segments. Smith did all of the regular announcing. Hours of operation were 8:00 to 12:00 P.M. Time signals were presented at sign off. In February 1922, WDY was closed as preparations were being made to move the station to New York City. The transfer was never made.

Being in the right place at the right time has been an important factor in the radio success stories of several people. Joe Barnett enjoyed that good fortune. Joe wanted to be a singer. He was living in New Jersey and studying singing. It was April 1922, and he wanted his mother to hear him sing on the radio. This desire inspired him sufficiently to go to WOR, Newark's newest station, which had been put on the air February 22, and ask for a program. He found the station in a closely confined enclosure in a corner of the sports and radio section of the Bamberger & Company Department Store. Outside the door, a lady anxiously awaited a singer from New York who was scheduled to go on the air soon. When program time drew nervously near, she rushed Barnett inside. Oriental rugs covered the walls. There was a piano and one old desk. The microphone was a megaphone-type speaker connected to a telephone transmitter.

The woman instructed Joe to announce his songs himself. After singing a few numbers, he received a signal to keep going. When he displayed uncertainty about the adequacy of his repertoire, an employee of the store's music department hustled

17

in copies of sheet music. The carrier held them up one-by-one, and the singer nodded whether or not he knew the selection. The program continued for an hour. At the conclusion, the radio lady told him he could be a good announcer. She was sold on his ability to the extent that she gave him a full-time job as an announcer with the stipulation that he would also sing when a scheduled singer failed to appear. Joe's success was rapid; in fact, three months later he was appointed station manager.

Out in Omaha, the *Daily News* wasn't completely satisfied with the work of their sports editor, Gene Rouse, who had previously been an actor. They thought perhaps he would be better suited to their radio venture, WNAL. Rouse was transferred to that branch of the company. It was a wise move. There he found his vocational niche, soon achieving the status of an early radio personality.

In January 1922, a Navy radioman by the name of Arthur Godfrey was standing radio watch at 4:00 A.M. on a destroyer which was anchored in the Black Sea at Varna, Bulgaria. He picked up an SOS and answered with his 5KW spark set. He awoke the skipper, who determined that the distressed vessel was in the Atlantic, too far away to lend assistance.

Powel Crosley, Jr., ceased operating as an amateur and established WLW, Cincinnati in March 1922. He still broadcast from his home in College Hill. In addition to Crosley, Russell Blair was also heard on the air. The following September, the station was moved to Crosley's new manufacturing plant in Mill Creek Valley. The studio had the era's heavy drapery concept. The transmitter was in the room with the microphone, causing a cooling problem for announcers and entertainers. The mike was a large morning-glory-type horn speaker some eight feet long and three feet in diameter at the opening. The person talking had to poke his head inside for the voice to register. When music was played, it was horn-to-horn. Since the plant was in an industrial area, train sounds were so loud that often the station had to call "time out" until a steam locomotive moved away.

Robert Cooper and Robert Stayman worked as part time WLW announcers while holding regular jobs in the plant. A man named Smith had been out of the country for awhile. When he returned, he heard some of the radio programs and quickly formed some definite ideas about the new industry. Fred Smith called on Crosley and shared his thoughts. This led to his being hired as station director. Smith's announcing style was described as "melodious." He signed on each evening with: "Hello, hello, good evening."

Like most of the other early announcer-personalities, diminutive Lambdin Kay of Atlanta didn't plan it that way. Born in Brooklyn of southern parents, Kay went to Atlanta at the age of eighteen. He played football at the University of Georgia and later published a movie magazine and operated movie theatres. The editor of the Atlanta *Journal* had his eye on the enterprising five-foot, four-inch, thirty-three-year-old businessman for a new project he was planning. He was going into the broadcasting business. Kay was picked to manage WSB ("Welcome South, Brother"), which went on the air March 15, 1922. Kay, dubbed "The Little Colonel," soon gained national renown because of the humor he injected into his *Hired Help Skylark* program and his easily recognized voice. His drawling way of saying "At-lan-tah, Jaw-juh" was an identifiable trademark. He labeled WSB "The Voice of the South." He also introduced the three-note chime to radio.

H. V. Kaltenborn made the ferry trip April 4 from Brooklyn to picturesque Bedloe's Island in New York Harbor. He didn't go to visit the Statue of Liberty; instead, he went to do a radio broadcast on WVP, the station operated by the Signal Corps. It was one of the few government wireless stations that were used to broadcast general entertainment, speech, and music. Its wavelength was 1,450 meters, not the usual 360 meters used by privately-owned commercial stations. Kaltenborn spoke extemporaneously. He felt very self-conscious because the microphone seemed so impersonal. The apparent complete indifference of the operators behind the glass didn't help either. He discussed current events, analyzing the coal strike that was underway at the time. His talk lasted thirty minutes. After it was finished, Kaltenborn realized he was covered with perspiration. His discussion was reputed to be radio's first news editorial.

The General Electric Company of Schenectady, New York, thought it was time for them to enter the radio broadcasting field. In February 1922, they established WGY on the roof of one of their buildings. The usual search for an announcer began, but they didn't have to look far, only as far as their own publicity department. Their man was Kolin Hager. He had been a prize-winning high school orator in Albany. While attending State Teachers College at Albany, he departed the academic scene in

1917 and joined the Army. In France, he played the male lead in a service musical that toured camps. By the time he joined GE's publicity department in 1921, he had trained for the operatic stage and had become versed in languages—French, Italian, and German. Because of his musical, dramatic, and linguistic experience, Hager was appointed as WGY's chief announcer and studio manager. Radio fans considered his voice to be pleasing, often expressing that opinion when writing to the station. Robert Weidaw joined the station as an announcer in July of that first year.

In the fall of 1922, Kolin Hager, who was known as "KH" on the air, was called upon to lend his voice to the testing of a new process—the development of sound film. The method was called Pallophotophone. His well-known voice was recorded on film, and the announcement was beamed to an Edison convention being held at White Sulphur Springs, West Virginia. He reported that his voice was recorded by the new device and was not being played on a phonograph. He asked listeners to let him know whether it was coming through as clearly as live announcements on his evening program. Many wrote that they thought his voice recorded by the Pallophotophone was even clearer.

Schenectady didn't boast of an abundance of singers, musicians, and other talented artists. This situation made it more difficult for Hager to present radio programs. Since he had a background in drama, he came up with the idea of airing plays for the listening audience. He was successful in putting together a good local acting company. Complete stage plays soon became a regular WGY feature. They brought the station and the players much recognition.

In Detroit during this period, Cornelius D. Tomy had a very popular program on WCX. He called himself "Uncle Neal," and his late night show was the *Red Apple Club*. It featured famous personalities of stage and screen. Tomy was also the manager of WCX.

KDKA greatly improved its service to farmers beginning July 1, 1922. All farm programming was assigned to the *National Stockman and Farmer* publication. A young farm editor, Frank E. Mullen, was brought in from Sioux City, Iowa, to handle the farm broadcasting. His program was the forerunner of a future popular show that would be a national feature, *The National Farm and Home Hour*.

Tommy Cowan was enthusiastic about getting program publicity for WJZ. He arranged to have pictures of guest stars taken for use in publications. The project backfired one night. Burning specks of powder shot forth from the flash and set fire to the studio. Lost in the blaze were valuable Vocallion records and two pianos. A new studio had to be built, and it was greatly superior to the original. The walls were of thick asbestos brick, making the room soundproof. Heavy carpet on the floor and shirred monk cloth on the walls and ceiling eliminated echoes. New musical equipment included a Knabe-Ampico reproducing grand piano, a Victrola, and a Brunswick talking machine. The microphone was a standard condenser type. It was hung from a movable and adjustable stand. An Aeriola Jr. crystal receiver with a loop aerial was installed to use to check a program as it was being broadcast. Although women's speaking voices on the air were not well-accepted by listeners, a lady created a popular program series on WJZ. Miss Bertha Brainard called her show *Broadcasting Broadway.* She reviewed plays and reported other news of the theatre. Her opening was alliterative: "Bertha Brainard broadcasts Broadway."

Live sports coverage by direct wire became a regular WJZ feature. Tommy Cowan announced, "This is WJZ, the Radio Westinghouse Corporation broadcasting station at Newark, New Jersey. A blow-by-blow description of the Leonard-Briton bout will now be given from the ringside at the New York Velodrome. One moment please while we make connections."

"Hello, hello! Good evening. This is J. Andrew White speaking from ringside."

Where did they all come from? Everywhere, or almost everywhere. Even Hell's Kitchen, New York City? Yes, at least one did. Milton Cross spent his years as a youngster in the tough environment. By the time he was twenty-five, he was a tenor singer, singing as a second tenor for pay in several superior church choirs. He was also taking a music supervisor's course at the Institute of Musical Art under the direction of the renowned Dr. Frank Damrosch. Cross visited some friends in Newark one night, and they told him what he considered to be a fascinating story, a story about a friend of theirs, an expert electrician who had put together a device which picked up sounds from the air. Intrigued by the thoughts of this phenomenon, Milton insisted that they take him to see it immediately. They were received enthusiastically by the owner of the set, which had cost the clever

21

host only sixteen cents, with ten cents of that amount going for a glass tumbler to protect the mica from dust. The singer put the earphones on his head and felt goose flesh creep over him. From out of nowhere came the voice of a Newark politician telling listeners to drive carefully on the highways.

His friends talked about the great need for live talent on radio and suggested that he sing on WJZ. A letter to the station brought a reply from Tommy Cowan inviting him to visit. Cross went on the air with a group of songs. Cowan thought that his quality was professional and asked him to return the following week for another program. After several appearances, Cowan told him that they would soon need another announcer and, apparently impressed with his knowledge of foreign names and musical terms and his natural respect for good diction, offered him the job. It really wasn't what Cross wanted. He possessed a great desire to make it as a singer, and he thought announcing would interfere with his musical career. Besides, he wasn't getting paid by WJZ to sing, and he wasn't certain they would pay him to talk. He discussed these matters with Cowan. The announcer made an arrangement for him to receive a small salary, and he accepted. The amount was not sufficient to pay his tuition at the school of music. It was necessary for him to continue singing in choirs for pay as a means of livelihood.

Milton J. Cross went over to Newark four times a week. He was on duty from 4:00 until 10:30 P.M. Although he sang as a tenor, his radio speaking voice was in the baritone to bass range. In addition to his announcing duties, he continued to perform on the air as a singer. He also operated the Ampico organ, read the Sunday funnies, and recited "Uncle Wiggly." Since Cowan was using "ACN" as an identifier, he selected "AJN." His work was very acceptable to his employer. Soon he was making forty dollars a week.

Because the World Series broadcast the previous year had been so popular, WJZ made arrangements to carry the 1922 event. This time Tommy Cowan didn't get a sore ear. The Yankees and the Giants were again the rivals. Highly acclaimed New York *Tribune* sportswriter Grantland Rice was hired to handle the play-by-play. Rice and an assistant reported by direct wire from the press box behind home plate. In his column, he expressed his feelings about the new assignment:

> After the first pleasant shock, when we discovered that no one
> could answer back or cut in with a winning argument, the rest of it
> was something of a thrill, in retrospect at least.

After the first inaugural statement it was as simple as talking to one man, a dumb man who isn't deaf, as simple as asking for a cigarette or ordering a peck of potatoes over the phone.

WJZ continued its sports coverage from the Polo Grounds that fall with W. S. Flitcraft, a sports editor, reporting a college football game each week.

Leo J. Fitzpatrick was a Kansan, born in Wichita in 1895. He attended the University of Kansas. Later he served in the Navy. After being discharged, he was a performer on the chautauqua platform. In Butte, Montana, he took a job as a newspaperman. Fitzpatrick advanced his journalistic career by joining the Kansas City *Star* as a feature writer. He covered the American tour of Marshal Foch. He made the western train trip which turned out to be fatal for President Harding. The *Star* created the position of radio editor, and Fitzpatrick was given that job. Then the newspaper went even further into the wireless medium. On June 5, 1922, it put WDAF on the air. The studio was a burlap-covered room in the basement of the building. The owner put his finger on twenty-seven-year-old Leo Fitzpatrick to run the station because he could talk and sing and had a mind that was capable of coming up with new ideas. One of these creative outbursts resulted in a late-night program called the *Nighthawk Frolic*, which originated from the Plantation Grill of the Muehlebach Hotel. The show was broadcast from 11:45 P.M. until 1:00 A.M. The musical portion was furnished by the Coon-Sanders Orchestra, playing such songs as "Gallagher and Shean," "Maggie, Yes, Mam," "Stumbling," and "Always." Fitzpatrick emerged as one of the true character-type radio personalities of that era. Soon he acquired the monicker "The Merry Old Chief."

Membership cards were offered to listeners.

WDAF
The Kansas City Star's Nighthawks
"The Enemies of Sleep"
This is to certify that (name) is a member of the
Kansas City Star's Nighthawks and has been granted
an official charter from WDAF.
Signed Leo Fitzpatrick
Chief Nighthawk, The Kansas City Star

It was said that two million people enrolled as "Nighthawks."

Fitzpatrick kept two mikes at the remote spot in case one went dead. At sign off time, he would say, "Well, well, well, well, brother and sister nighthawks, that will complete our session for tonight. Tune in at 11:45 tomorrow night for our regular *Nighthawk Frolic.* This is WDAF (chimes), the Kansas City *Star* Nighthawks, the enemies of sleep, signing off. Mr. Phelps, call a taxi. Mr. Johnson, shut off the juice, and let's all go home. Nighty night."

Many early radio listeners regarded Fitzpatrick as a radio impresario. They were impressed with his humor, naturalness, and individuality.

John F. Parr was also a WDAF announcer. He was later listed among the most popular announcers in *Radio Digest.* One of his achievements was the development of *The School of the Air.*

A neophyte New York radio station instituted a policy in August 1922 that would in time be a financial boon to announcers. It started the business of radio commercials. AT&T put WEAF on the air August 16. The studio was on the twenty-fourth floor of the company's building between Walker and Lispenard Streets. The transmitter was in the Western Electric Building at 463 West Street. The station's parent firm didn't like the idea of a non-revenue business. Immediately, plans were formulated to change that situation. A member of AT&T's commercial department sold a ten-minute time segment to a real estate company for a hundred dollars. The institutional advertising message was broadcast at 5:15 P.M., August 25, but it was not read by the station's first announcer, Vischer Randall, an employee of the Long Lines department. Instead, he introduced H. M. Blackwell of the Queensboro Corporation, who urged listeners to live at Hawthorne Court in Jackson Heights, where they could enjoy "the recreation and daily comfort of the home removed from the congested part of the city, right at the boundaries of God's great outdoors, and within a few minutes by subway from the business section of Manhattan." The commercial ice was broken.

WEAF prepared a booklet to instruct their announcers and speakers on microphone technique:

A broadcast performance is as personal and intimate as one given to a small group of friends in your home. There is none of the annoyances and disturbances occasioned by large audiences. The studio is comfortable, quiet, and homelike. You need not raise your voice higher than you do in entertaining a group in a drawing room. Although the radio audience is large, broadcasting requires a minimum of effort. When speaking over the radio telephone, do not hurry. Use a quiet, clear, slow, and distinctive voice of the same pitch as addressing a group of five or six people seated around a table.

When radio stations began popping up all over the nation, the publisher of the Fort Worth *Star-Telegram* didn't want to be "left at the switch." He started WBAP in May 1922. The announcer slot had to be filled; and, as was often the procedure during the pioneer stage of radio, the hunt centered on the established portion of the organization. All of the paper's veteran newspapermen rejected the possibility of going on the air. Cam Arnoux (pronounced AR-noo) wasn't a seasoned reporter. His lack of seniority led to his being told, "You're it!" He soon became a capable broadcaster, once being described as one who "speaks in well-modulated tones and with perfect diction." It wasn't long until Arnoux had to go to the hospital for a minor operation, and the question again arose: "Who will do the announcing?" This time there was a volunteer for the temporary job.

Harold Hough was born in Mulvane, Kansas, in 1887. Later his family settled in Oklahoma City and Harold got a newspaper route. He and three other boys organized an alliance and almost sewed-up newspaper and magazine sales in the city. Harold lost à foot when he was dragged under a train. He transferred to an inside job, becoming the assistant circulation manager. In 1912, he read in a trade paper about the resignation of the circulation manager of the Fort Worth *Star-Telegram*. Immediately, he called the publisher for an interview and showed up in Fort Worth the next day. He sold Amon Carter on the idea that he was his man. He got the job and started at twenty-five dollars a week.

Harold Hough said that he would try to fill in as an announcer while Arnoux was away. He figured, "You don't have to have lace in your tonsils." He went on the air and projected a dry humor that soon boosted him into the role of a national radio personality. At first he identified himself as "HH." Listeners wanted to know what that meant. He responded that it stood for "hired hand," saying that he was just the janitor around there who was filling in until the regular announcer returned. Thereafter, he was billed as the "Hired Hand." When Arnoux resumed his mike duties, Hough also stayed on the air. A picture he had made for listeners showed him in overalls, work shirt, and cap. The two men planned arguments and phony feuds. Harold Hough would be at WBAP for a long, long time.

Being from Phillipsburg, Pennsylvania, could be an advantage if you wanted to be a radio announcer for WWJ, Detroit. It was for E. T. "Ty" Tyson. Bill Holliday, chief announcer and program director at WWJ, was a native of Phillipsburg. So was Tyson. Ty served in World War I and later went to college at Penn State. Holiday invited him to join WWJ as his assistant. Tyson learned fast. He arranged for a singing group to appear on the station, an aggregation known as Fred Waring and his Pennsylvanians. Tyson also did an early man-on-the-street program.

In St. Louis, Lester Arthur Benson was originating the city's first baseball and prizefight broadcasts on his station, WEB. He later moved the station from his home to a larger area in his radio store and changed the call letters to WIL.

WGU, Chicago went on the air in 1922 and soon became known as WMAQ. Judith Waller was the first announcer and manager. The station was owned by the Chicago *Daily News* and the Fair Store. It was located in a corner of the store. Miss Waller was responsible for the first broadcast of the Chicago Symphony Orchestra.

In Fort Smith, Arkansas, fifteen-year-old Jimmie Barry signed on WGAR at 5:00 P.M. each day: "This is WGAR, the *Southwest American* station, located at Fort Smith, Arkansas, the playground of America. We have just come on the air, and we wonder if anyone is listening." He would call names of various set owners and ask whether they were home yet. The telephone would ring, and someone would say that the program was coming in fine. When a person called and said that he was having trouble with his receiving set, Barry would announce that fact on the air and promptly lose most of his listeners. They would hurry to the home of the owner of the defective set to help with repairs.

There were novice announcers in 1922 who would stay in radio for a long period of time. Phil Carlin started with WEAF. Brace Beemer, the future "Lone Ranger," began his radio career as an announcer and actor in Indianapolis. J. Lewis Reid joined WJZ, Detroit after touring the country with entertainer Elsie Janis and her gang for a number of years. W. Gordon Swan, who was still a student, took a job at WGI, Medford Hillside, Massachusetts. A. W. "Sen" Kaney joined the staff of KYW, Chicago as announcer and studio director. Hoyt B. Wooten started KFNG in tiny Coldwater, Mississippi, and he and his brother, S. D. Wooten, Jr., broadcast programs. Later, the station was moved to Memphis, Tennessee, and the call letters were changed to WREC.

A Texas girl fell in love with an announcer's voice in Oklahoma City. After writing to him a few times, she made a trip to see him.

Radio announcing was a new speech form. It had no direct precedent. Since the age of the Greek orators, there had been dynamic speakers. In our own country, there were political spellbinders with compelling eloquence and hard-hitting debaters and chautauqua lecturers—each who often found it necessary to project his voice with great force to reach the last row in the upper balcony of an auditorium or a hall with bad acoustics, or from a stump in the open air without the aid of mechanical amplification, and they also found it necessary to over-enunciate each syllable of each word so that the message could be heard and hopefully understood. Too often during radio's early years ornate rhetoric was present at the microphone.

Mother McNamee wanted her son Graham to have a success-ful musical career. As a former singer herself, she hoped to continue her association with music through him. The youngster disliked taking piano lessons and resented being called from the playground by the sound of "Baby, come take your music lesson." The kidding he received from others engaged in a sports activity sometimes resulted in fisticuffs. On the way home, he took his time by doing such things as tossing rocks at birds sitting on telegraph wires.

Graham McNamee was born in Washington, D.C., in 1888, but was moved to St. Paul when he was only two. By the time he reached high school age, he was very active in sports, partici-pating in baseball, football, basketball, hockey, and boxing. At the age of eighteen, he switched from piano to singing and found that he really liked the vocalization. Graham first worked as a clerk for the Rock Island Railroad. Next he became a salesman for Armour and Company. His mother, who was by then divorced, insisted that they move to New York for the purpose of advancing his singing career. She had saved a little money. When he was nineteen, they journeyed to the big town.

After several months, he had not acquired any singing engagements. He was ready to take a clerk-type job, but she insisted that they keep trying. His first break came in a manner that could be considered an element of fiction. Mrs. McNamee was riding a street car one afternoon and was trying to open a window when another woman remarked that she couldn't be a New Yorker because a native would not struggle that much for fresh air. This led to further conversation, which included the difficulty Mrs. McNamee's son was having in his search for singing opportunities. The other lady stated that she was connected with several musical organizations and even mentioned that she needed a good baritone.

Graham followed through and soon enjoyed regular work as a soloist in church choirs. He continued to take singing lessons. Later he sang in a Broadway production. This was followed by a part with a grand opera company. After many more engagements and more study, he gave his own concert at Aeolian Hall. The critics treated him rather well. A concert season followed, which took him to most large cities around the country.

In May 1923, Graham McNamee was "at liberty" because the summer season didn't offer many musical engagements. Jury duty was paying him three dollars a day at the Federal Court and Post Office Building. After being dismissed one afternoon, he began walking and noticed a sign indicating WEAF at 165 Broadway. He had never listened to radio but was aware that they used live talent. He had a decision to make— whether to go and buy a fifty-cent lunch or visit the radio station. The latter won. After taking the elevator to the fourth floor, he entered the station, which had two small studios. He talked to the office manager, relating his training and experience as a singer. The manager was impressed. McNamee was offered a job as an announcer and a baritone soloist. He thought he would work there during the summer until he could obtain some concert bookings. The radio salary wouldn't be nearly as much as he could make when more singing engagements were available. He reported to work at WEAF at 6:30 the next night. His shift was from 7:00 to 10:00. Rehearsing was in progress when he arrived.

McNamee made his sportscasting debut with the Harry Greb-Johnny Wilson fight August 23. He had visited their training camps and had made notes of interesting points concerning each fighter. When the day of the broadcast arrived, he was nervous. The bout was scheduled for the Polo Grounds that evening, but the neophyte broadcaster showed up at the scene at 4:00 P.M. He observed the workers preparing the ropes and canvas of the ring. He chatted with the WEAF engineers as they installed the remote equipment. At about 7:00, he ate a couple of hot dogs and drank a bottle of pop. Sixty thousand fight fans filed into the seats, but he realized he would be talking to a million or more. A tap on the shoulder by an engineer told him he was on the air. What would he tell the people he couldn't see and who couldn't see the action? Would he just say that one fighter hit the other? He knew that wouldn't be sufficient. Because he had done some boxing, he knew something about the finer points. Suddenly, he capitalized on this knowledge, describing whether it was a left hook to the chin, a right to the head, a jab to the body, or a roundhouse swing that was blocked. He also included their movements—feinting, ducking, going into a clinch. He mentioned the expression on a fighter's face. When it was over, McNamee was as weak as a whipped fighter. It was difficult for him to stand up. It had been quite exhausting; but later when the station manager gave him an enthusiastic commendation for his handling of the broadcast, he knew it had all been worth it.

The summer months passed, and plans were being made for WEAF to broadcast the 1923 World Series. It was also the time Graham had planned to return to concert work. He was told he would be assigned to help with the important baseball event. That settled it. His concert days were behind him. The Series was another Giant-Yankee affair. William O. "Bill" McGheehan, sports editor of the New York *Tribune*, was to be the regular play-by-play man with McNamee adding color between innings. It was more than the writer wanted. During the fourth inning of the third game, McGheehan decided he would rather man the typewriter than the microphone and turned the complete broadcasting job over to McNamee. Mac quickly discovered that it was somewhat different from announcing boxing. There were more slow spots and then sudden, fast action. He felt that he had to draw upon his imagination. He was afraid that listeners would lose interest during the duller moments. He began to dwell on interesting sidelights in the stands and on the field—straw hats being torn up while fans wrestled for a foul ball, a movie star watching the game, the manager flashing signals, a pitcher warming up in the bullpen, a batter knocking dirt from his spikes with his bat. He must have done pretty well for a beginner. Seventeen hundred pieces of mail arrived at the station after the final game. Listeners liked the enthusiasm and excitement generated by the announcer. Some of the letters received as a result of his night programs were addressed merely "Good evening, Ladies and Gentlemen of the Radio Audience," Mac's salutation. A few were addressed to his closing, 'Good night all."

A very popular and enduring show had its beginning on WEAF in 1923, *The A & P Gypsies*. Phillips "Phil" Carlin was the announcer for the musical feature. In later years, Ed Thorgersen and Milton Cross would handle the announcing duties.

A master New York showman successfully transferred his stage technique to radio. Samuel L. "Roxy" Rothafel was manager of the Capitol Theatre. He began broadcasting *Roxy's Gang* over WEAF from the theatre for an hour and a half each Sunday night, presenting his troop of entertainers. Phil Carlin also announced this show. Those peppy concerts soon established Roxy's radio popularity. The weekly mail pull reached five thousand pieces. He was unable to understand or explain his success as a program host in the new medium:

> I just talk into that little black thing, and that's all there is to it, no applause, nothing to tell you what kind of effect you are making, not a response until you get the Monday mail, and Tuesday, that's the day when a big batch comes. Even from Havana.

H. V. Kaltenborn began a weekly series on WEAF in the fall of 1923. The half-hour program was heard on Tuesday nights and was sponsored by his newspaper. As he waited in the studio for the little red light to signal the beginning of his first broadcast, he paced back and forth, anxious because he didn't have a live audience. WEAF's announcers were amused when he called the draped studio a "torture chamber." He delivered the talk standing, fearing that if he sat he would relax too much and have dead air. He spoke extemporaneously from brief notes on cards, using broad gestures, which brought smiles to those who watched. He didn't mind their reactions because the physical action lessened his tension.

Kaltenborn commented on England's Lloyd George, comparing him to Theodore Roosevelt. Next he discussed prohibition. Then he talked about the bad conditions in the Rhineland. He didn't know that WEAF's staff pianist was standing by should he not be able to fill the allotted time. Usually, the musician was prepared to play something that would be appropriate to the speaker's subject such as "How Dry I Am" if he had talked on prohibition. Kaltenborn's style of speech was most often described as "clipped." To some listeners he sounded "foreign."

When he finished that first broadcast on WEAF and walked from the studio to the reception room, he was handed a radiogram from the captain of the steamship *George Washington,* which was sailing far away in the Atlantic: "We're listening. Good stuff. Keep it up."

He later expressed his feelings at that moment: "The thought of the mighty ocean, of the liner plowing the lonely waves, of some mysterious current flashing through the silent ether across thousands of miles of intervening distance, burdened with the cogitations of my little mind, made me feel at once humble and proud. I, too, was standing upon a peak in Darien."

Before his second broadcast, studio personnel placed his head in a frame, a device somewhat like that used by early photographers to keep the subject's head still. They wanted to prevent his mouth from moving too far away from the round carbon mike, the type with the small, round holes that formed a circle around the outer edge. They also drew a chalked square on the floor where his feet were placed, in the same manner as a baseball hitter in the batter's box.

As the broadcasts continued, there was some criticism along with the plaudits. One listener (a school teacher) questioned his authority for slighting the first "n" in government. A resident of Los Angeles telephoned and asked him to pronounce the name of the city correctly after hearing him use the soft instead of the hard "g."

Kaltenborn commented on the peculiarities of listeners:

Radio audiences are not only sensitive to what is said, but they are peculiarly sensitive to a speaker's manner and method. Sloven speech is much more offensive on the air than on the platform. Speakers who have been guilty of certain mispronunciations all their lives are likely to hear about them for the first time when they address an invisible audience....Radio speaking is an almost indecent exposure of the personality. Your audience hears you breathe, knows when you turn your head or turn a page, catches the whispered comment intended for one ear, and gets a shock from the blasting detonation launched into the ether as a half-suppressed cough.

Kaltenborn once danced with the wife of the mayor of Fairbanks, and she slapped him on the shoulder and declared, "Boy, you're some spieler!" But it was not that complimentary from the managerial side. He believed he had the same freedom to speak on the air that he had to express himself on the editorial page. He criticized the decision of a New York judge who was going to preside over an important case which would affect

AT&T, WEAF's owner. This brought a warning from the station. The next week he spoke against a strike that would, in his opinion, be detrimental to the public interest. It was pointed out to him that his comments were damaging to the company's labor relations. The secretary of state heard a broadcast in Washington and objected to Kaltenborn's criticism of the U.S. rejection of diplomatic recognition of the Soviet Union. The station cancelled his program. Mail response urging its return was heavy. The Brooklyn *Daily Eagle* offered to pay the station's regular rate of ten dollars a minute for the resumption of broadcasts, but WEAF refused.

Newspapers around the country continued to jump into radio broadcasting. The next was the Memphis *Commercial Appeal*, which started WMC, January 21, 1923. They also found their principal broadcaster on their own staff. George Dewey Hay was not a southerner, but his career achievements were mostly in that region. He was born in Attica, Indiana, in 1895. When the U.S. entered World War I, he was living in Chicago. In the Army, he served at a camp in Georgia, where he managed the Liberty Theatre. This experience helped to give him a feeling of show business, which he never lost. After returning to civilian life, he chose newspaper work, obtaining a job with the Memphis paper. First, he worked as a cub reporter. He was given an assignment that would be a major influence on his future career. He covered the funeral of a Marine hero in Mammoth Spring, Arkansas, which was adjacent to the Southern Missouri border. Hay later recounted his experiences on that trip:

> I sauntered around the town, at the edge of which, hard by the Missouri line, there lived a truck farmer in an old railroad car. He had seven or eight children, and his wife seemed to be very tired with the tremendous job of caring for them. We chatted for a few minutes, and the man went to his place of abode and brought forth a fiddle and a bow. He invited me to attend a "hoedown" the neighbors were going to put on that night until "the crack o' dawn" in a log cabin about a mile up a muddy road. He and two other old-time musicians furnished the earthy rhythm. No one in the world has ever had more fun than those Ozark mountaineers did that night. It stuck with me . . .

George Hay later became a feature writer, doing a column called "Howdy, Judge," composed mostly of the lighter side of cases that came up in police court in Memphis. His byline was G.D.H. "Solemn Old Judge." When WMC began broadcasting, he made his debut as radio editor for the paper and announcer for the station. He ran a late-night feature frolic which was designed to portray a night of entertainment on a trip down the Mississippi River. He used a miniature steamboat whistle to produce a sound effect, calling the device a "hushpuckiny." He wouldn't retain his newspaper position much longer.

Westinghouse began using short wave stations to boost KDKA's coverage. In Pittsburgh, 8XS was built and broadcast KDKA's programs several hours each evening. On March 4, 1923, short wave repeater station KDPM was established in Cleveland. On November 22, KFKX was placed into service at Hastings, Nebraska, near the geographical center of the country. Millions of listeners were able to hear KDKA programming. Lloyd Creighton Thomas was secretary-manager of the Hastings Chamber of Commerce. He soon convinced Westinghouse officials that some broadcasts should originate at KFKX. The studio was located in a room above a music and furniture company. Thomas knew a young man who sold pianos, musical instruments, and sheet music for the store and also directed the Methodist Church choir. He was twenty-six-year-old William G. "Bill" Hay, a Scotchman. Thomas arranged for Hay to be the announcer and program director. He took the job on the condition that he would be permitted to mention the name of the piano used on the programs. He traveled great distances in search of talent. As a result, KFKX became one of the nation's most popular stations, and Hay earned quite a reputation as an announcer. His brogue-style stationbreak itself was a good show: "KFKX, Haastings, Neebrrawska."

One day during the summer of 1923, the New York Yankees came to Pittsburgh for an exhibition baseball game. A newspaper reporter brought Babe Ruth to the KDKA studio for an interview. He had written a little speech for the baseball slugger. The Babe got mike fright as most celebrities did in those days and said nothing. Harold Arlin took the script and read it on the air. Later, the pioneer announcer received several letters saying what a good voice the baseball hero possessed. Friday night, June 13 was the date of the Dempsey-Firpo fight. Arlin received a report of the blow-by-blow action by wire and did a re-creation of the action from the studio. At one point, Firpo knocked Dempsey into the ropes. Just at that instant, the wire went dead. To avoid silence, Arlin switched without explanation to the farm studio. The next day the announcer met a friend who remarked, "Well, Firpo knocked Dempsey into the ropes, and hogs went up two cents a pound."

WJZ moved from Newark to New York. Radio Central was opened in Aeolian Hall May 14, 1923. Announcer Tommy Cowan was named studio manager. There were two studios on the sixth floor, one on the ground floor in the concert hall, and another at the Waldorf-Astoria Hotel. Major Andrew White was the WJZ sports announcer, covering boxing, the World Series, and football on a free lance basis.

That year a man named Edward Britt "Ted" Husing, who was a payroll clerk for a hosiery manufacturing firm, won a ten-dollar prize from the New York *Daily News* for the best letter of criticism of radio programs.

Joe Barnett was very busy over at WOR, Newark. He originated a morning gym class, which he called the *Daily Dozen* program. He started a series of eighteen operas, broadcast short versions of Broadway shows with original casts, inaugurated studio audiences, and broadcast remote control programs from French steamships moored to piers in New York.

Kolin Hager saw a need for some specialized training for announcers to achieve progress in radio speaking. He established an announcers school at WGY, Schenectady. Their pronunciation, air presentation, and other factors were covered. One newcomer to receive the instruction was H. O. Coggeshall. He had found a radio home.

W. Gordon Swan joined WBZ, Boston-Springfield October 2, 1923, moving from WGI, Medford Hillside. He would remain at the station for a long, long time.

Various announcers were gaining prominence in their localities. Elmer G. Johnson, a deep-voiced announcer at WJAX, Cleveland, was called "The Voice of the North." Stanley W. Barnet was announcer and program director at WOC, Davenport, Iowa. George S. Cruger served as the concert announcer at WOO, Philadelphia. Herbert Dwight Miller, "HDM," was a genial announcer with a keen sense of humor at WGI, Medford Hillside, Massachusetts. He was also an instructor of English at Tufts College. One night a singer didn't think the microphone would boost her voice sufficiently. Miller stated that he would get out the resonator. He didn't know what one was, but he found a drawing board and placed it beneath her on the floor. She was happy.

Out on the West Coast, A. McDonald and George S. Naill did the announcing for Earle C. Anthony's KFI, Los Angeles, located on top of the Packard Motor Building. They wore black coats and instructed guest speakers: "Speak in a natural tone of voice.

Don't hurry, and remember that every sound you make will be heard by thousands of people." E. J. Martineau had been a radio officer in the war and had sent out about twenty-five SOS calls during attacks by submarines. In 1923 he was sending out programs from KPO, San Francisco. In the Midwest, H. Leslie Atlass was talking on WBBM, which he started in Lincoln, Illinois, located in the central portion of the state. The station's future would be in the Windy City.

During much of his life, Dr. John Romulous Brinkley had license trouble—both medical and radio. He bought a medical license in Kansas City in 1915 for a hundred dollars and obtained a license for a radio station in Milford, Kansas, in 1923. His getting the medical permit directly led to his desire for the broadcasting facility. While working in the medical department of Swift and Company in Kansas City in 1916, he observed that goats had no diseases which were common to people. He arrived at tiny Milford in 1917 and set up practice, performing goat gland transplants for the purpose of restoring male virility. Business boomed and Brinkley prospered. A hospital was built. Harry Chandler, owner of the Los Angeles *Times* and KHJ, invited him to California to discuss his medical methods. Brinkley was very impressed with the radio station and decided that the medium would be the best way to publicize his work.

On September 23, 1923, Dr. John R. Brinkley went on the air in Milford with KFKB (Kansas First, Kansas Best). His low, authoritative voice sounded convincing to many listeners. His medical lectures gained wide listenership. He began receiving many inquiries about individual health problems. This led to his starting a radio program he called *The Medical Question Box*. He read letters from listeners who described their ailments. This feature resulted in his establishment of a lucrative drug company. He would refer listeners to "authorized" pharmacies around the nation with instructions to ask for a certain drug code number for specified cures. If a cooperative pharmacy was not available to them, he would dispense the medicine by mail. Dr. Brinkley was engaged in commercial radio in a big way, but difficulties loomed ahead.

WJZ, New York ran an ad in the New York *Times* in 1924 for an announcer.

Wanted: Announcer for Metropolitan radio station. Must be college graduate and have knowledge music terminology. Apply Broadcast Central, 33 West 42d Street, New York City.

From all the replies, seventy-four applicants were considered. One was Norman Brokenshire. "Broke" was born in Murcheson, Ontario Province, Canada, in 1898, the son of a minister of Scottish descent. Because of the church travels of his parents, Norman was often left with his grandparents or other families. While he was growing up, he lived in many towns in Eastern Canada and the United States. During his school years, he worked at various jobs—operating his own print shop, working a short time for a shoe factory, doing a variety of tasks in a lumber camp (where he lost part of a thumb), and driving a manure truck for a truck garden farmer.

After graduating from Arlington High School in Boston in 1915, he worked during the summer as manager of the garage of a resort hotel. Then he spent two years as an apprentice draftsman at the General Electric plant at Schenectady. When the U.S. entered World War I, he enlisted and was a trainee at the time of the Armistice.

Brokenshire became a YMCA secretary at Fort Totten, Long Island, aiding returning servicemen. A YMCA scholarship enabled him to enter Syracuse University in 1920. It was necessary for him to help support himself by doing some work. First he was employed as a hotel night clerk. The Near East Relief project needed someone to conduct meetings and show films. He took the part time position. After two years of college, he left for a good salary with the same organization. Later he worked in New York with the advertising department of a firm that had developed a new welding process. One day he was sent on an errand to West 42nd Street. There he noticed a sign on a door that read "Broadcast Central." He curiously opened the door and asked the girl at the telephone switchboard what the chances were of becoming an announcer. Her answer put the odds at a thousand to one. He went on his way.

A lapse in judgment led to Brokenshire's being fired from the advertising department. Reading the want ads seeking another job, he spotted the WJZ insert. Instead of applying in person, he wrote a letter. He had given up the idea of getting a reply when a post card instructed him to report for an audition. At the station, he was given a newspaper story, some regular announcements of varying moods, a foreign news story with difficult proper names, and an ad lib assignment of describing the studio. He noticed some men in the control room looking at what he later learned was an oscillograph, a piece of equipment that showed his voice vibrations on a screen. After the tryout, the manager interviewed him. Was he a college graduate? Well, Broke stated that he almost was—two years at Syracuse. What about his knowledge of music terminology? The interviewee declared that he didn't have the slightest idea what it meant and inquired whether or not the manager knew. No, he didn't. The executive, in turn, asked the station's musical director about it. He had written the newspaper ad. The latter produced a copy of the *Musical Courier* and turned to a list of many classical composers. Brokenshire confidently said that he could learn the list in five minutes. That's how much time he was given. The director read the names aloud several times. Then it was Broke's time to try. He raced through the names as though he knew them well. The manager told him he would get an on-the-air-tryout that evening at six, reading a five-minute summary of the Dow Jones report.

He was so excited that he went all the way to the eighties to tell his brother the good news. He didn't make it back to WJZ in time. Announcer Tommy Cowan had covered for him, telling the manager on the phone that Brokenshire was a little nervous and he had decided to put him on later. Instead of unemotional stock market news, Broke made his debut with a pianist, which gave him the opportunity to display some personality. He went on as "AON." WJZ didn't let announcers use their names at that time. His brief appearance resulted in a mention in a newspaper radio column the next day. The writer asked about the real identity of "AON" and noted that he spoke with "perfect enunciation and exceptional modulation." Brokenshire was hired for forty-five dollars a week. WJZ announcers in addition to Cowan were Milton Cross and Lewis Reid. Major Andrew White was not on the regular announcing staff, but he was retained to cover sports broadcasting and other special events.

Norman Brokenshire later credited his voice for his initial success: "For those crude mikes my voice was perfect. I could vary the tone, the speed, the expression; the engineer's control needle would scarcely waver."

He often had more difficulty with things pertaining to the equipment than he did with the announcing. One night he slammed the control room door, shattering the glass. The operator was so apprehensive about the possibility of something injurious happening to his expensive, unprotected tubes during the night that he stayed at the station until the door was repaired the next morning. On another occasion, the announcer was displaying his knowledge of the station to a friend. WJZ's antenna was on top of the building where the engineer was posted to listen to the station's output and to monitor a receiving set tuned to an emergency frequency for use by ships at sea. Brokenshire made some dots and dashes on a mechanism connected to the equipment on the roof. The engineer thought it was an SOS. The law compelled commercial stations to leave the air under such circumstances. He immediately cut WJZ off the air and listened two and a half hours for further distress signals. After the true story of the "emergency" was revealed, the announcer's paycheck that week reflected the loss of program time.

Once during the early part of his career, Brokenshire ran short of material near the end of a program. Raising a studio window, he said, "Ladies and gentlemen, the sounds of New York," and stuck the mike out the window. Mail response to this innovation was good.

During a later stage of his announcing career, he made a realistic commentary regarding the attitude of announcers of that early period: "Each announcer knew in his heart that he was God's gift to radio. Actually, each man was strictly out for himself."

Radio coverage of political conventions began in 1924. The relatively uneventful Republican Convention was held in Cleveland from June 10 to 12. Graham McNamee handled the reporting duties for WEAF, and Andrew White did the announcing for WJZ. It was a mere warm-up for the rambunctious, free-wheeling, drawn-out Democratic assemblage beginning in the old Madison Square Garden in New York June 24. McNamee was again WEAF's man at the mike, and he was assisted by Phil Carlin. Major White again received the WJZ assignment. His helper was Norman Brokenshire. The two principal announcers were stationed in small glass enclosures on the speaker's platform. Carlin worked from a temporary booth in the steel overhead structure high above the crowd. Brokenshire served primarily as a roving reporter for White. He was alert for inside information such as changes in delegates' voting and various human interest stories that occurred from time-to-time.

The political battle was heated. Sectional factions bitterly stumped for their favorite candidates. Sessions lasted as long as sixteen hours per day. The first week ended and the second week began. No candidate was able to muster a majority of votes needed to capture the party's nomination. The broadcasters were existing mostly on sandwiches and soda pop.

38

One day Major White left his booth to grab a little lunch, turning the microphone over to the neophyte, Brokenshire. While he talked, a fight erupted on the convention floor. The inexperienced announcer sensed an opportunity to give thorough coverage to the fracas. He gave his full attention to the physical exchange, giving a complete blow-by-blow description of the belligerent activity. Signs were broken over heads. Nearby properties such as chairs and decorations were crushed. At the height of the encounter, Major White returned. His face immediately turned the color of his name. Grabbing the mike from Brokenshire, he motioned for the operator to cut the broadcast. Then he telephoned the studio. The music director filled with piano music. White quickly explained to his assistant that WJZ had been given convention broadcasting rights with the provision that adverse circumstances would not be put on the air. Broke never understood why he wasn't told before convention coverage began.

During the long proceedings, radio made the state of Alabama a topic of national conversation. At the beginning of each alphabetical roll call, Alabama's governor would cast his state's votes for favorite son Underwood. His speech style of prolonging the words and his Southern drawl became a matter of universal humor: "Alabama casts twenty-four votes for Oscar W. Underwood!" That line was repeated thousands of times by listeners long after the convention ended. It took 103 ballots over a period of fifteen days for the delegates to reach a decision. At 2:30 A.M. on July 10, John W. Davis of New York finally received the nomination. The radio crews were tired but emerged considerably wiser about the techniques of remote broadcasting.

WJZ again chose to use the New York *Times* want ad section as a method of finding an announcer:

Radio Announcer—Must be young, married, conscientious, social by nature, college graduate, have knowledge of the terminology of music, and ability to say the right thing at the right time. Box X611.

It brought hundreds of responses. One was from Edward Britt "Ted" Husing.

Husing was born on Thanksgiving Day, 1901, over a saloon in the Bronx, a business that his father owned. Both parents had come from Germany. The nickname "Ted" was given to him by a childhood sweetheart. His father's work as a steward and head-

39

waiter moved the family to several places on Manhattan Island, including Hell's Kitchen, where the youngster learned the art of holding his own. He was a vigorous reader, keeping every book he bought to add to his lending library. He liked to learn and use new words. Ted imagined that he would like to become some kind of professional talker. He even envisioned having an office door with the word "Commentator" printed on it.

When his father took the job of steward at a Columbia University club, fifteen-year-old Ted began to gain an excellent knowledge of sports. He served as mascot for the school's football, basketball, and track teams. He especially listened to strategy that coaches passed on to the players. Low grades forced him from his high school football squad; therefore, he quit school. He and a friend hitchhiked as far west as Missouri, doing odd jobs along the way. One task called for Ted to be a shill for a carnival. Later, the two teenagers went to Florida to invest five hundred dollars of his father's money in real estate. The money was invested but not in tangible property. Places of amusement and entertainment were the recipients.

During World War I, Ted Husing enlisted in the New York National Guard under an assumed name. He was assigned to night sentry duty on some docks of the Hudson River. Believing that he sighted a submarine periscope one night, he immediately sounded an alarm. The object turned out to be the neck of a beer bottle. After leaving the service, he re-entered high school and later took courses at a business institute and at Columbia University. Then he applied for a job as payroll clerk for a hosiery manufacturer. One requirement was that the applicant must be a married man. Ted told them he had a wife and got the job. He began dating a young lady who had been a Follies girl. They were married in June 1924, a year after he went to work for the hosiery firm. His boss heard about the wedding and fired him for not telling the truth when he had applied. Some friends in Florida invited the couple to visit them.

On their way back home to New York, there was a train layover in Washington. Husing bought a newspaper; and since he was unemployed, it was natural for him to turn to the classified section. That's when he read WJZ's ad. He knew that was what he wanted. He was brash enough to believe that he possessed all of the requirements except the educational qualification. Quickly, he invented that facet and immediately sent a telegram stating that he had a B.S. degree from Harvard. At home he found a message telling him to report to WJZ,

Aeolian Building, 33 West 42nd Street the next morning. RCA had purchased the station the previous year.

That night he stayed up late practicing the pronunciation of names of famous composers. He also researched their works in an encyclopedia. He studied the most important story in a newspaper, the crash of a Navy dirigible during a thunderstorm in Ohio, memorizing all details. After a few hours of sleep, he was up rehearsing again. While hanging to the subway strap on the way to the station, he continued to rehearse, using low tones. This irritated some riders—one woman moving as far away from him as she could. When he arrived at WJZ, he found a mob-like scene, created by some six hundred applicants. Ted waited his turn for almost three hours. By then he was disgruntled and hungry. Finally, his name was called on the loud speaker. In the studio he stood on a plaform before a microphone, aware that some listeners were behind a glass panel in the control room. He was instructed to discuss music first and then to ad lib without using notes. As he talked, he avoided looking at the judges. It took about ten minutes for him to tell what he knew about music. Next he started telling the dirigible story, giving such details as the names of crew members and their hometowns.

Once when he looked at his watch, he discovered he had been talking for thirty-five minutes. Glancing at the control room, he noticed the people were gone. Thinking they had deserted him, he left the studio and went home. The telephone rang, but he didn't want to answer it. As a matter of fact, he didn't want to talk to anybody. He was exhausted. His wife finally picked up the phone as he went to another room. She quickly informed him that the station was calling. Suddenly he *did* want to talk to somebody. The caller explained that the judges had gone to another room to evaluate the auditions. The job was Husing's if he passed the interview with RCA general manager David Sarnoff the next day. He was to wear a dinner jacket for the meeting with the RCA boss. Ted rushed out and bought a used tuxedo.

On September 13, 1924, David Sarnoff looked Ted Husing over and gave him the announcer's job at forty-five dollars a week. Ted reasoned that he was hired because he could talk louder and longer than the others. On the WJZ staff were Milton Cross, Norman Brokenshire, J. Lewis Reid, and John B. Daniel. Andrew White was still under contract to do the sports broadcasting. Tommy Cowan had joined the new municipal station, WNYC, located in the Municipal Building, as studio manager and chief announcer.

41

While Ted was soaking up station atmosphere, Milton Cross asked him to read some market reports for him. Ted thought it was a practice session, but he wanted to impress the experienced announcer. After reading for fifteen minutes, he noticed that Cross threw a switch. The regular announcer explained that Ted was no longer on the air. He had made his debut without knowing it. Then he became nervous.

Husing put in long days. It was virtually a matter of opening at 9:00 A.M. and closing at 11:30 P.M., handling half-hour and full-hour programs in the morning, followed by luncheon and dinner music, and then remote dance bands at night. He was off and running.

George Hay thought he detected greener radio pastures in Chicago in 1924. He left WMC, Memphis and went to WLS (World's Largest Store), owned by Sears & Roebuck. The Solemn Old Judge abandoned the use of the steamboat whistle since he was no longer broadcasting from the banks of the Mississippi. He chose the more appropriate train whistle sound for the railroad center.

(Toot) Hello, everybody, WLS, Chicawgoooo, the Sears-Roebuck station, broadcasting from our Center Theatre studio. We are presenting Art Kahn and his Columbia Recording Orchestra in "Lucky Kentucky." All aboard for Kentucky on the unlimited train. Let's go, Art. (Toot)

The *WLS Barn Dance* (later called the *National Barn Dance*) had been started shortly before George Hay reported for work, but he became an announcer for the show. Various announcer awards were beginning to appear. In the Fall of 1924, George Hay won the *Radio Digest* Gold Cup announcer contest.

With so much sports activity in the Chicago area, it was inevitable that someone would begin doing play-by-play. In 1924, WMAQ, owned by the Chicago *Daily News*, was interested in carrying the University of Chicago football games. No one on the radio staff seemed to be capable of such an assignment. A newspaper reporter was called upon to do the job. Harold O. "Hal" Totten had moved to Chicago when he was eleven in 1912. Hal played football, baseball, and track in high school and edited the school paper. At Northwestern University in nearby Evanston, he played baseball and served as sports editor of the *Daily Northwestern*.

He was also college correspondent for the Chicago *Daily Journal* and the Associated Press. He worked for the *Journal* on a full-time basis from 1922 to 1924, gaining recognition for his work in the Leopold-Loeb murder case. In August 1924, Totten joined the *Daily News*; and because of his sports background, he was selected for the radio stint. The following year he would be the first announcer to broadcast Chicago Cubs baseball games from Wrigley Field.

Colonel Robert McCormick, publisher of the Chicago *Tribune*, bought WDAP and changed the call letters to WGN (World's Greatest Newspaper). Quinlan Augustus "Quin" Ryan had been a reporter for the *Tribune* for seven years. He was named station manager and chief announcer. His natural enthusiasm on the air drew the comment that he was "weaned on mike juice." Ryan would soon become established as a name sports announcer, reporting such events as Cubs and White Sox baseball, Illinois football (covering the Illinois-Michigan game in which Red Grange scored four touchdowns in the first twelve minutes of play), the Kentucky Derby, and Indianapolis Speedway races. Ryan also read funny papers on the air, first using the name "Uncle Walt" and later "Uncle Quin." WGN was located in some bedrooms at the top of the Drake Hotel. Band remotes were carried from the Drake ballroom, and announcers were often kept busy running down and up three flights of stairs between the studio and the remote broadcast.

Harold Arlin's popularity at KDKA had extended to an international status. Because of the station's short wave outlets, he was known on several continents and was voted the world's most popular announcer.

H. V. Kaltenborn, after being released from his commentary program on WEAF, began searching for another station on which to air his observations. He found it—WAHG, Richmond Hills, Long Island. The station was owned by A. H. Grebe & Company, a manufacturer of radio receiving sets. During the first two weeks in February 1924, the station received thirty thousand letters in support of his talks.

Joe Barnett and WOR performed one of radio's first emergency tasks in January 1924. The dirigible *Shenandoah* broke loose from its mooring one night during a storm. Area radio stations received the SOS and went off the air. Barnett called and offered the use of WOR as a radio guide. When permission was given, the station returned to the air and asked listeners to call WOR should they hear the craft's motors overhead. The phone began ringing, and the *Shenandoah's* position was then broadcast periodically to its crew. The station's engineer was on the roof of Bamberger's Department Store receiving answers in code. At one time it passed directly over the store. About eight hours after the first SOS was sent, the airship was back in its place at Lakehurst. Radio had come through during a public emergency.

Cam Arnoux left Harold Hough at WBAP, Fort Worth and went to a new station, KTHS (Kum to Hot Springs), Hot Springs, Arkansas, as announcer-manager. He put the station on the air the night of December 20 with a remote by the Meyer Davis Orchestra from the new Arlington Hotel ballroom: "Greetings to radioland! Station KTHS in Hot Springs National Park, Arkansas, is now on the air!"

Various announcer-personalities and formal-type announcers were being developed around the country. Walter "Uncle Bob" Wilson was the bedtime story teller at KYW, Chicago. Logan "Steve" Trumbull was the "World Crier" at KYW. Edward Borroff was also a KYW announcer. At KGW, Portland, Richard "Dick" V. Haller ran the *Hoot Owl* program: "Keep growing wiser, order of Hoot Owls, orchestra, grand screech, and cast." L. W. Zimmerman at WTAM, Cleveland had a radio personality that greatly appealed to listeners. Howard J. Milholland was chief announcer at KGO, Oakland. Ty Tyson did the first broadcasts of University of Michigan football games for WWJ, Detroit. Roy F. Thompson joined WFBG, Altoona as an announcer.

Hayden Huddleston began his more than fifty-year career in radio in Roanoke, Virginia. While working for an electric company, he helped build the firm's amateur station which later became WDJB. A church in Roanoke wanted to broadcast its Sunday morning services. After learning the cost of remote telephone lines, the board decided the church couldn't afford the expense. Huddleston had an idea. The station was owned by an electric company, and didn't it have plenty of wire? Of course! A private line was strung from the station to the church building, and services were put on the air each week.

Sigmund Spaeth, who had appeared on various stations in a musical capacity, joined WGBS, New York when it started broadcasting. He was the MC of a celebrity show and put Eddie Cantor on the air for the first time.

44

A few ladies were also active at the microphone. Bertha Brainard continued as a winsome talker for WJZ. Dorothy Gordon was in charge of the first program for children on WEAF. Aleta Smith was an announcer and soprano soloist for WFI, Philadelphia. Marie K. Neff conducted a Women's Club feature on KDKA. She was later transferred by Westinghouse to KFKX, Hastings. A "Miss Jones" was a very popular feminine personality on KSD, St. Louis.

III

A Word From Your Announcer

His speech was a fine sample,
on the whole,
Of rhetoric, which the learn'd
call "rigmarole."
                            —Lord Byron

Several announcer personalities began to capitalize on their immense popularity for financial gain. Leo Fitzpatrick invited a group to Kansas City in 1925 for a big radio show. A huge crowd turned out to see the stars of the airwaves. Fitzpatrick also went on the road for an extended tour of personal appearances and drew thousands. Lambdin Kay of WSB, Atlanta was heard in St. Louis, and he took George Hay's place in Chicago while Hay visited WFAA and the Texas State Fair at Dallas. Harold Hough of WBAP, Fort Worth was heard on WSB.

WJZ announcers were called to a staff meeting in early 1925. They were told that they could stop using initials as an identifier on the air. Real names would be permitted. Norman Brokenshire wanted to establish an individual greeting, something he could use anytime during the broadcast day—morning, afternoon, or night. It had to be informal and courteous. Broke tried to imagine what he would say if he were speaking to a group of personal friends. He discovered that he would voluntarily say, "How do you do." His trademark became, "How do you do, ladies and gentlemen." Soon other announcers began using that, too. Then he adopted, "How do you do, ladies and gentlemen, how DO you do. This is Norman Brokenshire."

WEAF and WJZ continued their competitive battles for audience and recognition. Each station broadcast the presidential inauguration of Calvin Coolidge in Washington March 4, 1925. Graham McNamee was at the remote mike for WEAF, and

46

the lesser known Norman Brokenshire covered the event for WJZ. McNamee was in a glass-enclosed booth with a good, clear view of the platform in front of the Capitol. He had brought a staff to assist him. Since it was the first time to broadcast an inauguration, there was not an established method for getting information regarding a time schedule for the various phases of the proceedings. It was difficult to determine when to go on the air. McNamee stationed messengers at various places in the building with orders to rush information to him such as when the President and Vice-President left the Senate Chamber on their way to the Capitol steps.

Before he went on the air, Mac needed to give an instruction to a staff member. He was the only one at the booth. Thinking it would be safe to leave for a minute or two, he headed for the assistant, who was in another area of the crowd. It was necessary for him to climb a temporary fence which had been put up to maintain a clear aisle for the President to make his way to the platform. When Mac started back to the booth, he was stopped by a determined guard, who made it plain that nobody was allowed to cross there. The announcer explained who he was and that as many as twenty-five million listeners would be waiting to hear him report the ceremonies. Nothing doing. This went on for ten minutes. Mac left in search of a longer way to get back to his destination. Luckily, he found one. When he did finally go on the air, he didn't have sufficient time to read all of the background material he had prepared. It was not his best effort.

It was a completely different story for Norman Brokenshire. The inaugural established him as a bigtime announcer. He was there without any help, no staff to do the leg work. His vantage point was not the best. His microphone was situated on a rail in front of a chair in the first row on the Capitol steps. Broke had gone out to the area the previous day to get the feel of the setting. He learned that the activity was scheduled to begin at 12:00 noon. He planned to go on the air at 11:45. Then word came through that WEAF might go on at 11:00, and he was told to start at 10:45. Rumors circulated that McNamee would go on even earlier. At 9:44:30, the operator yelled for Brokenshire to take it. During the long wait, he talked about everything from hats to history. He told what the weather was like, described the great throng of people, and observed how the plaza in front of the Capitol seemed to be covered with hats. He gave interesting historical facts about the Capitol itself. Once he happened to look across toward the Senate Office Building and saw a man running along the roof. From where Brokenshire stood, it looked as

47

though the man was on the narrow peak of the gable. He couldn't see the flat surface behind. He described how the man looked up there against the sky, thinking he could be killed by taking the wrong step. After building up suspense, the announcer laughed and said, "It's all right. He didn't fall off!" Brokenshire gave his own name rather often and even spelled it a few times.

The Marine band set up and began playing, and this provided some respite from his talk. Mr. Coolidge appeared and the formalities began. Brokenshire contrasted the Vermont twang of the President and the rolling, Ohio hard-R roundness of Chief Justice Taft. Soon it was completed: "This is Norman Brokenshire, who now returns you to the studio in New York."

He broadcast the funeral services of William Jennings Bryan in July 1925. He had covered the final rites for Woodrow Wilson the previous year. Broke didn't like funerals. He still retained the image of his two-year-old sister who had died when he was a youngster.

Although Graham McNamee didn't receive as much acclaim for his inauguration broadcast as did Norman Brokenshire, his overall popularity was extremely high. McNamee won the *Radio Digest* award as the most popular announcer of 1925. He and Phil Carlin teamed up during the fall as a football play-by-play team, describing the action of important collegiate games. They were known as the "WEAF twins." The two alternated as the principal reporter each Saturday, the other serving as the observer. On Saturday October 17, Carlin was at the mike at Yankee Stadium handling the Army-Notre Dame game while McNamee watched for details which only one pair of eyes could not detect. Since both men were capable play-by-play announcers, each was able to select significant points that contributed to the quality of the broadcasts. The man at the mike watched for the type of play and the distance gained or lost. The observer determined the name of the ball carrier and the tackler as well as other details that contributed to better listener understanding of what was happening. On October 24, McNamee did the regular work when the University of Pennsylvania played the University of Chicago. He also broadcast the World Series again that year. The station received fifty thousand pieces of mail as a result of the baseball broadcasts.

Graham McNamee became famous as a play-by-play man because of his enthusiasm and excitement. He developed a preparatory technique to help get himself into this type of mood.

48

Before the beginning of a sports event, he would force himself to get excited over some unrelated situation. He would throw himself into a feeling of elation with thoughts different from those of the upcoming contest. His vigorous personality flowed through the microphone when he went on the air.

The WEAF twins didn't receive all of the glory for football announcing in 1925. Sigmund Spaeth broadcast the Rose Bowl game between Stanford and Notre Dame for WGBS. It was carried by direct wire from California to New York. Spaeth also broadcast the prize-fights from the Polo Grounds that year.

Bill Hay had left KFKX, Hastings for Chicago late in the previous year to work in business for a relative. Drought conditions in Nebraska adversely affected the piano business. His reputation as an announcer was well established because of his wide popularity and the wide coverage of KFKX. After staying out of full-time radio for several months, Hay joined WGN, Chicago, where he met two singers named Freeman Gosden and Charles Correll. The following year they would begin a comedy series using Negro dialect and portraying all the characters themselves. They would be known as *Sam and Henry*. Bill Hay would be their announcer. Bill was in the right place at the right time.

On Christmas Eve 1925, Quin Ryan, WGN's station manager and chief announcer, met Floyd Gibbons in the lobby of the Chicago *Tribune* Building. Gibbons was a rollicking, free-wheeling, around-the-world reporter for the paper. He had been aboard the liner *Laconia* on his way to cover World War I as the *Tribune's* London correspondent when the ship was sunk by a German submarine. It was five weeks before the U.S. entry into the conflict in 1917. Gibbons survived the sinking, but he was wounded while covering the fighting of U.S. Marines in Belleau Woods in France. He lost his left eye. An eye patch became his trademark.

Ryan asked Gibbons to do a Christmas night broadcast based on his many experiences. The reporter knew nothing about radio but agreed to do it. He arrived at the studio two hours early. He was not the same confident Gibbons. The little microphone was frightening. Ryan tried hiding it behind a bouquet of flowers and then behind a telephone. Ryan coached him on radio technique. He tried to make Gibbons feel natural, telling him to smoke. Next, Ryan sat on the other side of the table and told him to pretend he was holding a conversation. That suggestion helped the most. Gibbons didn't have a prepared script, just some notes.

He found it difficult to concentrate. He had visited some strange places around the world and had experienced some unique sensations but nothing had left him as shocked as the little mike. The bright shining metal around the mouthpiece hypnotized him, and he imagined he was seeing many faces of all demeanors in the device's opening.

The broadcast began. Thoughts of what was happening as he spoke had a tendency to cause him to lose track of what he was saying. His throat dried. His heartbeat accelerated. The face became red and hot. The palms of his hands moistened. Trying to shake the instability, Gibbons began forcing a pencil point into his note paper. He knew that when he told of a humorous incident to friends, he could see whether or not they thought it was funny, but on the air he could not measure the response. It bothered him.

In spite of his doubts and fears, Floyd Gibbons' first broadcast was a great success. Letters and telegrams and phone calls affirmed it. His series of talks continued. Listeners requested copies of his scripts. The *Tribune* began printing stories of his experiences and asked whether people would rather read about them or hear him tell them on the air. Four barrels of mail arrived, most in favor of the broadcasts. Nevertheless, in January the newspaper sent him back to Europe, but the radio world would hear from him again.

WGN broadcast what was perhaps the biggest news story in the nation in 1925. John Thomas Scopes, a high school biology teacher at Dayton, Tennessee, taught the doctrine of evolution to his students. This was an infraction of state law. Scopes was brought to trial July 25. The proceedings drew national attention. Crack Chicago attorney Clarence Darrow agreed to defend the teacher. Famous William Jennings Bryan, three times unsuccessful candidate for president, volunteered to assist the prosecution. Newspapers ballyhooed the event as the "Scopes monkey trial." WGN arranged to broadcast the complete trial. Their expense was a thousand dollars a day. The courtroom was arranged in a manner to allow microphones to pick up all speech. Quin Ryan announced. Scopes was convicted and received a token fine. The radio coverage was another milestone in remote broadcasting. Bryan died five days after the conclusion of the trial. His funeral was covered by radio.

WSM, Nashville was started October 5, 1925, by the National Life and Accident Insurance Company. The custom of inviting name guest announcers from other stations to an opening had already been established. George D. Hay was invited to WSM's opening. While in Nashville, Hay was offered the position of radio director. He accepted and left WLS in November. Hay remembered his trek into the Ozarks when he was a newspaper reporter and how the folks enjoyed the musical hoedown he had attended. Also, he had been the announcer on the *WLS Barn Dance* in Chicago, where he learned the popularity of hillbilly-type programming, as it was called during that era. He set out to develop a rural music show for WSM. On November 25, the *WSM Barn Dance* made its appearance. The show would become one of the most popular and long-lasting presentations on the air under its later title, the *Grand Ole Opry*. Hay began using the steamboat whistle sound that had been a part of his Memphis program.

Jack Keefe was also a WSM announcer, having started with the station's inaugural program. He was described as a "cultured, educated, and gifted gentleman." Keefe was a Harvard graduate and a former professor at Vanderbilt. He also held a law degree from Vanderbilt. In addition to his educational achievements, he had performed in vaudeville on the Keith and Orpheum circuits. When George Hay was hired, station management stressed that Keefe's position would not be affected.

H. V. Kaltenborn, sometimes called "the stormy petrel of the air," continued to draw criticism from public officials who were subjects of his broadcast. Station officials were often threatened with various types of recrimination, and this usually resulted in Kaltenborn's departure from the air. In November 1925, he found what he considered to be a permanent radio home. WOR, Newark welcomed his commentaries. Kaltenborn said that WOR gave him freedom of speech. New York Mayor Jimmy Walker's supporters threatened to stop the station from broadcasting New York City events unless Kaltenborn stopped criticizing the mayor. The New Jersey station would not be intimidated.

After Ted Husing was hired by WJZ, he often saw Major Andrew White, who was not actually a full-fledged WJZ staff member but who did the sports broadcasting. Ted mentioned one day that he would like to try announcing sports events. The pioneer broadcaster suggested that Ted "go break his nose." He had talked to some sound engineers, and they believed a widening of the antrums would give Husing more resonance. An antrum is the cavity of a hollow organ, also known as a sinus. It was mostly a matter of a small mallet being struck against his nose. The operation was performed.

His voice did sound better; as a matter of fact, Ted Husing is remembered by those who heard him as having a very smooth and pleasant voice, but there was no immediate sports offer from White. His offer finally came in late November 1925. His persuasion led to a trip to Philadelphia with White on Thanksgiving Day to broadcast the Penn-Cornell game. When they arrived in town, White told Ted to go on to the field to be certain that the equipment was set up early. In the meantime, the senior member was going to visit some relatives. They were to broadcast from the top of a grandstand still under construction. After Ted climbed the scaffold to the temporary booth, a downpour of rain began. At first, a tarpaulin kept the place dry but not for long. The man at the controls reported that all was well technically. Pre-game activity began, but White had not arrived at the stadium. The game was scheduled to be sent to stations in Boston, Pittsburgh, and Schenectady, in addition to New York. The operator signaled for Ted to go on the air. He started talking although he hadn't done any advance preparation because he thought the major would handle such details. Being soaking wet, he commented about the weather. He also talked about almost everything else in view except the teams.

White arrived just in time. The assistant was amazed at the ease and skill the veteran displayed as he described the action on the gridiron. Ted filled in between quarters, each time eager to turn the mike back to White. After the game, White told Ted he had done well and promised to use him the following season.

Ted Husing continued to study and practice. He read aloud at home. The apartment had thin walls. One night a neighbor's angry voice yelled and told him to start practicing on the saxophone, remarking that the instrument wouldn't be as annoying as his talking.

RCA maintained a policy of rotating its WJZ announcers with those of WRC, Washington. Norman Brokenshire had already served his Capital City duty. Next it was Ted Husing's turn. He was given assignments that called for the introduction of various dignitaries, including President Coolidge. Ted already thought he had come a long way.

The voice of Lowell Thomas—adventurer, world traveler, writer, and lecturer—was heard on the air for the first time on March 21, 1925, over KDKA. His topic was "Man's First Flight Around the World." He used no notes. A group of Army flyers had made the flight in 1924. Thomas was their historian and had flown the last leg from the East Coast to the West Coast. The

Pittsburgh station invited him to present an hour talk on the history-making flight.

Harold Arlin, credited with being the world's first full-time announcer, had a decision to make. Westinghouse offered him the opportunity to become a department head at their plant in Mansfield, Ohio. He accepted the offer in December 1925 after five years in radio broadcasting. Arlin had accomplished many "firsts" in the new medium. He was an organizer and vice-president of the Radio Announcers Association. S. L. "Roxy" Rothafel was the group's first president. Arlin had interviewed such notables as Will Rogers, William Jennings Bryan, Marshall Foch, David Lloyd George, Lillian Gish, Babe Ruth, and Herbert Hoover. He had also pioneered baseball and football broadcasting.

Nils Thor "Granny" Granlund was a showman, a Broadway fixture. He handled publicity for the Loew Theatre. He also was an announcer for WHN, New York. The station had direct wires to more than thirty Broadway restaurants, cafes, and ballrooms. "NTG" broadcast from those settings. He was a striking figure, tall and slim, and usually wore perfectly-fitting gray clothes. Granlund seemed equally at ease at the WHN microphone as he did associating with celebrities. Jests and spontaneous humor came easily to him.

WHN was called the "birthplace of song hits." Granlund explained: "The policy of the station is not to educate the masses. People like lyrics they can understand and music that is really tuneful. Let somebody else educate them. What I want to do is to entertain the people and to bring some frivolity into their homes."

Ted Husing greatly admired Nils Thor Granlund, realizing that he was an educated man who talked fluently. Ted felt that Granny could out-talk any five radio announcers, whether he was reciting poetry, issuing insults, or carrying on a phony radio feud with Harry Richman.

John B. Gambling was an Englishman who was a student at the British College of Wireless Telegraphy in 1914. He enlisted in the Royal Navy as a wireless operator, serving aboard several types of ships. The cruises brought him to New York several times. After leaving the British Navy in 1925, he went to work at WOR as a studio engineer for thirty-five dollars a week. On March 8, the announcer for the 6:30 A.M. sitting-up exercises program, which was conducted by physical culturist Bernarr McFadden, didn't show up. Gambling grabbed the mike and ad libbed through the hour period. This resulted in his being assigned to the morning announcer's job. After six months McFadden left the program, and Gambling took over as calisthenics instructor. He rapidly became a morning radio personality with *Gambling's Musical Clock*, which featured the necessary ingredients to keep listeners informed and entertained during the important get-up-and-go-to-work hours.

John S. Young was born in Massachusetts in 1903. His higher education was achieved at Yale, plus a year at Cornell Law School. He was first heard by radio listeners over WBZ, Boston, which he joined in 1925. His variety of programs ranged from the Boston Symphony to football games.

Up in Spokane, Cecil Underwood was the radio sales manager for Stewart-Warner. When KHQ moved from Seattle to Spokane, his company bought an hour program each week to promote the sale of receiving sets. It was Cecil's duty to acquire talent for the show. One night the regular announcer had a sore throat and asked him to read the information on the condition of roads in the area. The station manager complimented him on his voice quality and asked whether he would be interested in doing an announcer's shift. Cecil said that he wanted no part of it. Later he compromised. The manager arranged for him to work at his regular job until noon each day and then take an announcing shift from midday until midnight. On March 15, 1925, Cecil Underwood began what would turn out to be a lifelong career in broadcasting.

Leo Fitzpatrick decided to accept an offer from WJR and transfer his talent to Detroit. Succeeding him in Kansas City at WDAF was Harry Dean Fitzer, who was born in Kansas City in 1898. He was attending the University of Kansas when the U.S. entered World War I. He joined the Navy and was assigned to the Sousa Band at the Great Lakes Naval Training Station. Later he served aboard ship. Fitzer became a reporter for the Kansas City *Star*. When Fitzpatrick left, he was appointed manager of WDAF and radio editor of the paper. He also took over the *Nighthawks* show. Fitzer did the first commercial heard on WDAF. It was for Betty Crocker and was broadcast on September 21, 1925.

Major Edward Bowes was born in San Francisco in 1874. His military rank was obtained as an intelligence officer in World War I. He and a partner were operating the Capitol Theatre in New York when radio broadcasting began in the city. *Roxy's Gang* originated from the stage over WEAF in 1923. When Roxy left the theatre in 1925, Major Bowes assumed the

54

broadcasting chores. His show was called *Major Bowes' Capitol Family.*

As more stations came on the air, announcer activity accelerated. At WHAM, Cleveland, an eighteen-year-old named Bill Stern was doing some football broadcasting. Patrick Henry Barnes had performed in many theatres and had often appeared on radio broadcasts. He joined WHT, Chicago as chief announcer and program director. He would be a program innovator. Joe Barnett was still originating programs with listener appeal at WOR. He created one of the first man-on-the-street shows. Albert L. Alexander also talked to people on the street. He broadcast in New York with a portable transmitter attached to his back. John S. "Uncle John" Daggett was known as the "King of the Hosts" at KHJ, Los Angeles, which was located on the roof of the Los Angeles *Times* Building. Daggett interviewed such stars as Douglas Fairbanks, Mary Pickford, and Mary Garden. His approach to radio was that of no frills, fads, or glib patter— just good, solid entertainment.

Claire Robbins Emery was the "Big Brother" at WEEI, Boston. Vernon "Tex" Rickard was an assistant announcer and popular tenor at WGN, Chicago. Harry Geise did the *Gasoline Alley* program at WQJ, Chicago. Leslie Atlass moved WBBM from Lincoln, Illinois, to Chicago and broadcast from his home on Tuesday and Thursday nights, using a dance band. A man went to his home and offered him a hundred dollars to mention the man's name on the air after each musical number. Atlass accepted. Gene Rouse made the move from WOAW, Omaha to KYW, Chicago in 1925. Clyde R. Randall was an announcer at WSMB, New Orleans (which he pronounced "N'Awlins"). Francis S. Chamberlin, a Yale graduate, joined WMC, Memphis, "Down in Dixie," as an announcer. Letters from listeners commended him for his clearness of enunciation, vocal carrying power, general handling of programs, subtle wit, and happy personality.

John Thorwald, who had been an announcer for WFAA, Dallas, joined WRR of the same city. He possessed a rich, baritone voice. Stephen A. "Steve" Cisler, who would have a broadcasting career in excess of fifty years, had done some announcing while in high school in Omaha and during the summer at KTHS, Hot Springs. He enrolled at the University of Arkansas and went to work for the school's station, KFMQ. The first script he was given to read was entitled "The Castration of Spring Pigs." Chester "Chet" Petersen, another fifty-year prospect, started with WFBM, Indianapolis. He would migrate to Los Angeles. It was a good year for young men who would stay in radio a half century or longer. Rex Howell was in that special category. He had become a ham operator as early as 1920 when he was only thirteen. While a senior in high school in 1925, he worked at KFEL, Denver as an announcer-engineer: "This is RX announcing." .

Hal Totten initiated major league baseball broadcasting in Chicago on June 1, 1925. He handled the game between the Cubs and the Pirates. Station manager Judith Walker arranged for it to be carried on WMAQ.

Harry von Zell had a nickname in high school—"Giggles." Little did he realize at the time that he would parlay that laughter trait and other personal characteristics into radio fame. Harry was born in Indianapolis in 1906. His father was a sports reporter, and the son enjoyed the privilege of going with his father to cover the events. Harry began high school in his hometown but finished in Sioux City, Iowa. Then the family moved to California, and he entered the University of California at Los Angeles. He was active in musical and dramatic clubs. He played a year of football, but an injury terminated that college activity. After he recovered, Harry entered the prizefight ring as a lightweight, winning three bouts, losing one, and getting a draw. Then he took jobs as a bank messenger and a payroll clerk, both being of short duration. Routine business was not for him. He had studied singing but had no illusions about his singing voice. He and some friends went to see a radio rehearsal one day; and for a joke, his companions informed station personnel that Harry was scheduled to sing. He did sing, and his performance led to other radio singing engagements. In 1926, Harry von Zell heard that KMIC, Inglewood was looking for an announcer-singer. He convinced them that he was their man.

Norman Brokenshire went down to Atlantic City in 1926 to serve as the MC and official announcer for the Miss America pageant. The town's local station, WPG, broadcast the event. Shortly thereafter, he made the decision to leave WJZ and do free-lance work. He wanted to produce some talent shows. This venture didn't work out. Brokenshire joined WFBH, New York for $125 per week, an advancement from the $65 he was making when he left WJZ. Soon the WFBH call letters were changed to WPCH (Park Central Hotel). Other announcers on the staff were Lewis Reid, Walter Neff, and Alois Havrilla.

Havrilla was born in Austria-Hungary. He came with his family to the United States when he was four and lived in a Slovakian community in Bridgeport, Connecticut. English was not taught in the elementary school he attended. His singing talents were recognized when he was only seven. He possessed a beautiful alto voice with a range of three octaves. A singing teacher tutored him and began teaching him English. During his adolescent years, he was given solo roles in church musical presentations. Havrilla studied music at New York University and later appeared as a soloist at Carnegie Hall. Because of his voice quality, friends suggested that he become a radio announcer. It was a wise suggestion.

Announcers had become such popular public figures that listeners thought it added to their personal prestige to pretend that they were actually acquainted with one. Graham McNamee was riding in a train's smoker car one night when he overheard two radio fans talking about six- and seven-tube radio sets. Next the conversation turned to announcers. One man asked who had been announcing for WEAF the previous night. The other replied, "McNamee. He's good. An old pal of mine."

His friend wanted to know where he had met the radio personality, and he was told it had been lots of times in lots of places, including dinner with him the night before. Then the inquirer wanted to know about McNamee's looks. "Sort of light-haired. A big guy like Babe Ruth—and some swell dresser."

Nearby, McNamee smiled. He was dark-complexioned and of medium height.

Marion Sayle Taylor grew up in a religious atmosphere. His father was a minister in Louisville. The son worked as a boy organist at the St. Louis World's Fair in 1904. His ambition was to become a surgeon. His musical talent paid his way through William Jewell College at Liberty, Missouri. Next he studied medicine at Pacific University, but a traffic accident left his hand without the coordination necessary to perform surgery. Disappointed, he turned to the study of psychology and sociology and later worked in public health institutions on the West Coast counseling prostitutes. Taylor also appeared on the chautauqua circuit giving lectures on human behavior. He once debated William Jennings Bryan on the subject of fundamentalism. He also served as a high school principal at North Bend, Oregon, and talked on children's problems over a Spokane radio station.

In 1926, Marion Sayle Taylor began a routine that would eventually lead to national radio acclaim. He would enter a town and buy time on the local radio station, presenting talks on human relations and offering to discuss any problems that listeners mailed to him. He would also announce the time and place of a meeting to be held in a local auditorium. Admission was charged. Crowds were usually large. Afternoon meetings were reserved exclusively for the women. After collecting all the traffic would bear, he would move on to another town and repeat the process.

Everett Mitchell was born in Chicago in 1898. He began singing in public at the age of nine. After finishing high school, Everett wasn't financially able to continue his education. He went to work as a bank clerk, and later he became an insurance adjuster. Eventually, he entered concert work, getting engagements with the Redpath Chautauqua, which took him over most of the nation. Arriving back in Chicago after a concert tour, Mitchell decided to try for a singing spot in radio. An audition at KYW resulted in an appearance on a program that evening. In 1926, he went to WENR, where he became chief announcer and farm director. In the latter role, he would soon achieve radio prominence.

Although Martin Provensen was born in Des Moines, his ancestors had lived in Denmark for several hundred years. His father was a bishop in the Lutheran Church. This position led to Martin's receiving his elementary education in Des Moines, England, and Denmark. He came back to Iowa and entered State Teachers College. His major interest was music and drama. After graduation, he headed for New York to take a fling at the theatre. Acting jobs were scarce by 1926. He was in Chicago when someone mentioned that radio needed good voices and enunciation. He stopped by WENR and auditioned. Provensen was hired and soon was handling several of the station's important programs.

Louis Witten had been part owner of WAAQ, Greenwich, Connecticut, when it went on the air in 1924. Later the station was moved to Bayshore. He sold his share of the station in 1926 and went to work as an announcer for WOR, Newark.

Rex Howell, who had started with KFEL, Denver while still in high school, wanted his own station at the age of nineteen. Rex bought some equipment that had been licensed as a portable station. Such licenses carried the stipulation that the station could not operate in a town where there was an existing station. Howell solved the problem by making an installation two blocks beyond the Denver city limits in Edgewater, Colorado.

Curt Peterson was another of the many announcers who entered the field of radio because of their background as singers. He was born in Albert Lea, Minnesota, in 1898. At the age of seven, he was moved to Tacoma, Washington, and later to Eugene, Oregon. In high school, he earned a place on the debating team. At the University of Oregon, he was a baritone soloist in the glee club. During the war, he attended an officer training camp in San Francisco and emerged as a second lieutenant in the infantry. He then trained new recruits at Seattle. After being discharged, Peterson returned to college and got his degree. Then he headed east to New York and studied voice under private tutors. He was given work as a soloist in the University Glee Club and also sang in various church choirs.

Curt Peterson's first radio experience was for an advertising agency. He handled the radio campaign for two political candidates. One day in June 1926, he was walking across 42nd Street. He didn't own a radio, but he had been told that WJZ was located in Aeolian Hall. Curt found himself climbing the stairs to the station's small reception room. His reception was not cordial. He requested permission to see the manager and was abruptly informed that it was necessary to write for an appointment. He complied and received an answer addressed to "Miss" Peterson which said that there no openings for women. Curt promptly called the lady who had written the letter. She took it good-naturedly and connected him with the studio manager. The reception was improving. The official asked how soon he could come to the station. "Ten minutes."

Peterson sang a couple of songs and read a script. He was asked how soon he could start.

"Start what?"

"As an announcer."

"But I don't want to be an announcer. I want to be a singer."

Nevertheless, Curt Peterson became an announcer.

WJZ conducted a poll to get listeners' thinking about hearing women announcers. Five thousand questionnaires were sent out, and returns revealed that male announcers were preferred by a ratio of 100 to 1.

WEAF and WJZ were the key stations for the newly-formed National Broadcasting Company, which made its debut with a star-studded, four-hour broadcast November 15, 1926. WJZ announcers were affiliated with the Blue Network Division, and WEAF staffers were a part of the Red chain. Phil Carlin was appointed an assistant to the vice-president in charge of NBC programs. With the advent of the hookup, many announcers who had been regional favorites would soon be nationwide radio celebrities.

Radio popularity polls of one kind or another were in vogue. A 1927 announcer survey came up with these results:

1. Milton J. Cross, WJZ
2. Lewis Reid, WPCH
3. Norman Brokenshire, WPCH
4. Ralph Wentworth, WEAF
5. Major Andrew White, WJZ
6. Phil Carlin, WEAF
7. Ted Husing, WJZ
8. Kolin Hager, WGY
9. Graham McNamee, WEAF
10. John B. Daniel, WRC.

Bob Hawk's best promoter was his mother. When Bob was only nine, he won an elocution contest in his hometown of Creston, Iowa. Mrs. Hawk believed that her son would achieve great speaking success. She put him through arduous exercises in oratory, poetry, and dramatic readings. By the time he finished high school, he had entered twenty regional and state contests, winning nineteen of them. Hawk enrolled at the Oklahoma Southwestern Institute of Technology, where he decided he wanted to be an English teacher.

He was visiting in Chicago in 1927 when he heard an announcer reading poetry on the air. Instantly, he knew that was for him. Knowing that he was the best dramatic student at his college, Bob Hawk had plenty of confidence. He auditioned for an announcing job on a Monday and was hired. By Friday he was fired. Since there were more than twenty stations in the Chicago area, he was not discouraged. He had a strong determination about the field of radio. He visited other stations. He later said, "It was like a big wheel. You'd get fired from one station and go to the next, get fired, and then move on around." Between announcing jobs, he worked as a soda jerk, mail carrier, piano salesman, and a teller of jokes in a night club owned by Al Capone.

Donald Thomas "Don" McNeill was born in Galena, Illinois, in 1907, but his family moved to Sheboygan, Wisconsin, when he

60

was two. He entered Marquette University in Milwaukee in 1926 as a student in the School of Journalism. Don was humor editor for the school newspaper and editor of the college annual. During his sophomore year in 1927, he got a job as an announcer at WISM for fifteen dollars a week. He was also radio editor for the Milwaukee *Sentinel*, which owned the station.

1927 was a busy year for Graham McNamee. His important activity began the first day of the year with the broadcast of the Rose Bowl football game at Pasadena between Alabama and Stanford. It was NBC's first coast-to-coast broadcast. His assistant, as usual, was Phil Carlin. Carl Haverlin, sales manager for KFI, Los Angeles, had suggested the idea to the network in New York. KFI's remote equipment was used. McNamee described the distant hills, the sunny skies, the roses setting, the pleasant temperature, and other details of atmosphere and background. The 7-7 tie didn't provide him with much scoring excitement, but he made the most of it. Some of his contemporaries contended that he sometimes sacrificed game accuracy for color and excitement. It was said that he wasn't an expert on sports but tried to disguise his lack of knowledge with extra enthusiasm. In a story written for *Radio Guide* entitled "I Cover the Arena," he defended his approach to sports broadcasting. About football reporting, he said:

> The Red team is up against its own goal posts. The Blue team is marching steadily down the field reeling off gain after gain. Third down and two yards to go. The ball snaps back, a few bewildering gestures with it to confuse the Red players and then a plunging mass of tangled arms and legs. The ball is nowhere in sight. Is it a touchdown? Or did they fall just short of that last white stripe?

> Go ahead, tell 'em about it. Out there at the loudspeakers millions of rabid fans are agonizing over the delay. Can't you almost hear their thoughts screaming in your ears, "Come on, what happened?"

> Those are the seconds that are years long for an announcer. You can sense the impatience of the listeners but you can't do anything about it until you see what's happened. Perhaps five or six seconds elapse before you can tell about it. To the announcer it seems like five or six minutes, and to the average listener— according to letters—it seems like five or six hours.

> But I still think honest enthusiasm and the general picture are what the audience wants.... And that's what I intend to give them, because that is the way I feel.

A sports broadcast that Graham McNamee listed among his greatest moments in radio was also one of the most controversial. It was the Dempsey-Tunney "long count" fight at Soldiers Field in Chicago September 22, 1927, in which Dempsey tried to regain the heavyweight championship he had lost to Tunney the previous year. Almost 105,000 people jammed into the stadium for the encounter. There were approximately fifty million listening: "Good evening, ladies and gentlemen of the radio audience. This is Graham McNamee speaking. This is a big night. Three million dollars worth of boxing bugs are gathered around the ring at Soldiers Field, Chicago. Burning down at us are forty-four 1,000-watt lamps over the ring. All is darkness in the muttering mass of crowd beyond the spotlight. The crowd is thickening in the seats. . . ."

McNamee's description of the action was so exciting that twelve people reportedly died while listening. The controversy came in the seventh round: "And now Tunney is DOWN! Tunney is DOWN from a barrage of lefts and rights to the jaw and the head. The count is going on. Tunney is still down. Dempsey is on the other side of the ring now. Eight. . .nine. Tunney is up. And now they are at it again.

Dempsey had not gone to a neutral corner as required when Tunney went down. Therefore, the referee's count did not begin until he complied. The actual count would have been as many as fourteen. Tunney went on to win the fight. McNamee received many letters contending that he said, "Tunney is *out* instead of *up*. A record company was recording the broadcast without the knowledge of McNamee or network officials. The disc later confirmed that he did say *up*. Unfortunately, though, he did not immediately comprehend the delayed count. Phil Carlin explained it when he took over after the end of the round.

In his article McNamee touched briefly on the fight:

Now I'm going to ask you to put yourself in my place for a few moments. We're at the second Tunney-Dempsey fight in Chicago—Soldiers Field—the biggest arena in the country—the biggest crowd that ever saw a fight—men fighting for millions of dollars.

The champ and the challenger are in there fighting away— punching so fast your eye can't follow. Tell that to the radio audience, but tell 'em about every punch, too. Dempsey's down. Tunney's down. The crowd is stark raving mad, but you've got to keep your voice down so the millions of fans on the other side of the microphone can understand you. A tough job? You bet it is!

Another important Graham McNamee broadcast in 1927 was the coverage of Charles Lindbergh's arrival in Washington after his historic solo flight across the Atlantic:

> Ladies and gentlemen of the radio audience, this is Graham McNamee speaking from the Navy yard, Washington, D.C. Just a moment ago the last turns of the propellers of the *Memphis* brought her close in to the dock. The entire white-uniformed crew of the *Memphis* is lined up at attention alongside close to the docks awaiting Lindbergh. Lindbergh is coming down the gangplank! There's the boy. He comes forward, unassuming, quiet, a little droop to his shoulders. He's tired out. Very serious and awfully nice. Walking slowly, his hat in his hand, quietly, dignified, a darn nice boy.

Ted Husing thought he was worth more money than he was getting at WJZ. The manager didn't see it that way. Ted checked out of New York and made his way up to Boston and helped open WBET for the Boston *Evening Transcript*. He wanted to broadcast the Braves baseball games, but the club thought it would hurt attendance. Ted was persistent, and the games were put on the air daily. Boston proved to be too quiet for the loquacious Husing, so he returned to New York and joined WHN. That fall he broadcast the Columbia University football games. The station was owned by the New York *American*, and the paper gave him an enormous amount of publicity. His recognition wasn't limited to his employer's publication. The radio editor of the *Herald Tribune* boosted Ted's ego by writing that he was consistently better than the more famous Graham McNamee and Phillips Carlin.

Under the direction of Major Andrew White, the Columbia Phonograph Broadcasting System made its debut Sunday afternoon, September 18, 1927. The company occupied two rooms in the Paramount Building on Times Square. The facilities of WOR were used as the originating station. White signed the network on the air at 3:00 P.M. and introduced a 23-piece orchestra. Louis Witten was a WOR announcer; consequently, he became Columbia's first chief announcer. Since Andy White had been Ted Husing's early mentor, a deal was made between the two, and Ted joined the new chain on Christmas Day as White's assistant. Both Husing and the fledgling network would eventually greatly benefit from the association.

During his radio career, Norman Brokenshire had consistently increased his consumption of alcoholic beverages. The habit had already caused him some difficulty with station management, but in 1927 it led to his dismissal from WPCH. Broke turned briefly to vaudeville, doing an act that featured a satire on radio. His drinking soon caused his termination from that endeavor. Atlantic City officials invited him to serve as the official announcer of that entertainment enterprise. Temporarily, he enjoyed the status of a celebrity once more. Often he broadcast "direct from the steel pier" over WPG. After the season ended, he got married and left on a honeymoon trip to Europe.

In Los Angeles, officials at KMIC, an affiliate of the new network, heard Harry von Zell on the air at Ingleside. They foresaw greater things for him. Harry was hired as a sports announcer and singer-producer-writer. He would later work at KGB down in San Diego as program director before returning to Los Angeles and radio prominence.

Edmund Birch "Tiny" Ruffner was born in Crawfordsville, Indiana, in 1899, the son of a newspaperman. His family moved to Seattle when he was two. After graduating from high school in 1917, he entered the University of Washington but left to join the Army in 1918. As a heavyweight fighter, he got his nickname "Tiny." Ruffner was six feet, six and three-fourth inches tall. He had curly blonde hair, blue eyes, and a big, broad smile. After leaving the Army, he went to work for Standard Oil Company of California as a junior salesman. A career as a concert tenor was his goal. Much of the money he made went for singing lessons. The oil company started a radio show on KFI in 1924 with Tiny as the leading singer. They presented Victor Herbert and Gilbert and Sullivan operettas. He was also building a reputation on the West Coast as a concert singer.

New York was the next stop for Tiny Ruffner the following year. He desired to make it on the bigtown's concert and opera stages. A West Coast review helped him get a job, but the show folded in Baltimore on Christmas Day 1927. He had known Alois Havrilla when the announcer was working as a singer. Tiny sent him a wire inquiring about the possibility of getting into radio as an announcer. Havrilla's reply informed him that NBC (where Alois was then employed) would hold auditions the following day. Ruffner rushed back to New York and landed a job.

France Laux was an athlete in high school and college in Oklahoma, winning sixteen letters in various sports. France later did high school coaching and operated a minor league baseball club. He was living in Bristow, Oklahoma, about forty-five miles from Tulsa, in 1927. In October, the manager of Tulsa's KVOO made arrangements for the station to receive the action of the World Series by Western Union wire. A local announcer would present a re-creation from the studio. The station's regular sportscaster departed only a few hours before the time for the first game, voluntarily or otherwise. The manager thought of Laux and his knowledge of the game. He called Bristow and learned that France was downtown buying a suit. He then called his sales manager, who commuted from Bristow, and told him to drive down Main Street and look for Laux. Spotting him, the radio man pulled to the curb and asked, "Can you broadcast a ballgame?"

"I don't know," Laux replied, "but I'll try anything once."

"Jump in here. They want you in Tulsa right away."

Speed limit signs were meaningless as they headed for the larger city. As they arrived at the building where KVOO was located, a policeman appeared on the scene. He was ready to take them to the police station for speeding when it was explained that Laux was going to broadcast the World Series. The announcer-to-be was given permission to proceed to the studio on the third floor. "I'll take the driver down to jail," said the officer, "and you can have them call and get him out."

When Laux got upstairs, he knew no one. It was only a couple of minutes until game time. He didn't know how to read the very abbreviated messages handed to him by the Western Union operator: s1c (strike one called), b1l (ball one low), etc. He had to follow the score sheet to get the players' names. Laux didn't have time to get nervous. He struggled through; and after the Series, he remained as KVOO's sportscaster.

Other 1927 activity: Bob Elson went to work at WAMD, Milwaukee. In Washington, Fulton Lewis, jr. (he used a small "j"), was handed an extra assignment by his employer, the Washington *Herald*. He had to read the news bulletins each night on WMAL. In Detroit, Ty Tyson put play-by-play accounts of Tiger baseball on the air for the first time. At WHT, Chicago, announcer Pat Barnes directed, adapted, and acted in the first electrically transcribed program. Harold Fair, who had performed on radio as a musician, became an announcer for KOIL, Omaha. An announcer who would stay a long time went to work for a Washington station. Stanley Bell joined WMAL.

Pioneer announcer Phil Carlin was placed in charge of programming for both the Red and Blue Networks of NBC. *Roxy and His Gang* went on NBC Blue that year with Milton Cross serving as the announcer. Don Lowe announced another program that started on Blue that year. It featured Peter DeRose and his wife Breen.

NBC issued a booklet covering the qualifications for announcers:

> An announcer in the National Broadcasting Company is expected to average well in the following: a good voice, clear enunciation, and pronunciation free of dialect or local peculiarities; ability to read well; sufficient knowledge of foreign languages for the correct pronunciation of names, places, titles, etc.; some knowledge of musical history, composition, extempore speech; selling ability in the reading of commercial continuity; ability to master the technical details in operating the switchboard; a college education.

WSM, Nashville was an NBC affiliate. The Saturday night *WSM Barn Dance* followed a network classical music program that featured Dr. Walter Damrosch. On December 10, 1927, George Hay brought the local show on the air by saying, "For the past hour we have been listening to music taken largely from Grand Opera, but from now on we will present the *Grand Ole Opry.* It became the show's lasting title.

A Philadelphia group bought controlling stock in the Columbia network in 1928, and twenty-six-year-old William Paley took over as president. It was renamed the Columbia Broadcasting System. In the fall of that year, Andy White was scheduled to broadcast a football game in Chicago. During the week before the game, White became ill. Ted Husing appealed to Paley for the opportunity to make the trip. He was given the assignment and quickly became the network's principal sportscaster.

Jimmy Wallington began working at WGY, G.E.'s station in Schenectady in 1928. The company had begun experimentations with television using the scanning-disc system. Wallington was interested in this work as well as their short wave station. Its signal projected to distant points around the world. Admiral Byrd was on his expedition to Little America at the time. Wallington started reading letters from families of expedition members, and they were heard by the group in the icy region. Little did he realize this would be an important stepping stone to a highly successful broadcasting career.

Howard Rice was the son of a horseshoe salesman in St. Joseph, Michigan. The boy was called "Punk" by his playmates. He was interested in show business and learned to play the piano. He could play it while standing on his head. When he entered vaudeville, he was billed as "Don Carney, The Trick Pianist." In December 1925, he joined WMCA, New York as a vocalist. A little later he switched to WOR. One day a toy manufacturer appeared at the station with the desire to sponsor a children's show. Carney quickly devised a routine of telling stories and went on the air with it in September 1928. He later said that he just thought of his mother and everything was fine. Through the years as "Uncle Don," he built a following among the small fry that was extraordinary. Once he was walking down the street after having a drink or two. A little girl fan recognized him and rushed to his arms. He lifted her up and she kissed him. "I love you, Uncle Don," she said. "You taste just like daddy."

George Francis Hicks was born in the state of Washington, but his radio future would have its beginning in Washington, D.C. He attended school in his hometown of Tacoma. As a boy, he spent a great deal of time on Puget Sound, learning such nautical tasks as salmon fishing. George went to the University of Washington for a year and transferred to Puget Sound College for another year. His educational pursuits shared time with such vocational activities as working in logging camps, sawmills, shipyards, and truck driving. Once Hicks was given an audition by a Tacoma radio station. No job resulted, but he was told he had a good speaking voice.

When a feeling of wanderlust struck him, George Hicks wrangled a job from a ship captain and sailed to the East Coast. He left the vessel in New York and went down to the nation's capital to visit relatives. After returning to Tacoma, he again shipped out, this time as a clerk on a freighter to Alaska. His desire to see foreign lands persisted. The consular service appealed to him, so he made another journey to Washington, D.C. There he discovered that it would be necessary to attend consular school at his own expense. His funds were inadequate.

Hicks wrote to every Washington radio station inquiring about an announcer's job. He received no replies. Later he read a newspaper ad stating that WRC was looking for an announcer. He was one of two hundred to apply. He was successful. In September 1928, he received his first announcing assignment. He promptly lost his voice. Fortunately, he was given another chance and made good.

Wallace "Wally" Butterworth was a baritone singer. A friend suggested that he audition at NBC. The network wasn't interested in him as a singer but saw potential as an announcer. Butterworth was put on the staff and soon was opening the Blue Network each morning with *Rise and Shine*. He was described as having "a voice with a smile." Less than a year later, he was sent to NBC in Chicago, a city which was rapidly becoming an important radio focal point.

The National Farm and Home Hour had its beginning during the noon hour on NBC October 2, 1928. It was developed by Frank E. Mullen, NBC Director of Agriculture, as an outgrowth of the farm program he had started at KDKA, Pittsburgh in 1922. Everett Mitchell was the show's MC. His opening blurb was "It's a beautiful day in Chicago!" Mitchell enthusiastically made the declaration regardless of the actual condition of the weather in the Windy City. The expression soon became one of the best known and often-quoted radio lines. The program had the support of the Department of Agriculture and many farm organizations. It was thought of as "the nation's agricultural bulletin board." It was a great factor in increasing the number of receiving sets in rural homes.

Bill Hay moved over to WMAQ in 1928 when Gosden and Correll changed stations with their blackface act. The title of their program had to be changed because WGN claimed the rights to *Sam and Henry*. As the story goes, they heard an elevator operator greet two fellows as "Famous Amos" and "Handy Andy." They decided to go on WMAQ as *Amos 'n' Andy*. Bill Hay continued as their announcer.

Howard Petrie was born in Massachusetts in 1906 and lived in various towns along the coast until he was nine. His family settled in Sommerville in 1915. Howard was interested in a singing career. Between the ages of nine and fourteen, he went to Boston each Sunday and sang in the Cathedral Church of St. Paul choir. In high school, he participated in glee club, debate, and drama. After graduation in 1924, he worked in a Boston bank and studied voice at the New England Conservatory of Music. He also sang bass in the quartet of the old Meeting House Church in Dorchester. During the summer of 1928, a friend who worked at WBZA, Boston commended him on the quality of his voice and suggested that he try radio. An audition led to part time announcing work, and soon Howard Petrie was given a regular position on the staff.

Clinton "Buddy" Twiss was born in St. Paul but grew up in Sand Point, Idaho. He was bitten by the show business bug as a youngster when he worked as a motion picture projectionist. Later he played juvenile leads in a stock company that toured the Middle West. He helped build a radio station in 1928. His broadcasting duties included doing sports broadcasts and playing dramatic parts. Later he would move his voice to a San Jose station, which would be a step closer to an impending network career.

Robert Vahey "Bob" Brown was born in New York city in 1904 of Canadian parents. During the first ten years of his life, he lived in six different towns. His father was a grain broker. His mother had studied for the concert stage. Bob studied civil engineering for two years at the University of Buffalo. Then he worked in that field for two years with the U.S. Engineering Corps. His interest turned to radio, and he auditioned at WGR, Buffalo. There he worked in announcing, continuity, and program directing. He was one of the first announcers to broadcast from an airplane. In 1927, he did a series of shows from a plane for the Army Signal Corps. They were aired on WGR. Brown went to WLW, Cincinnati in 1928, where he was placed in charge of announcers.

Forrest P. Wallace's early radio background was in the field of engineering. He was born in Chicago in 1908. He began experimenting with amateur radio in 1912 while living in California. Wallace became a Pacific Ocean wireless operator and joined the Navy as a radio operator during World War I. In 1921, he entered broadcasting as chief engineer at WHAL, Lansing, Michigan. Later he went to WABM, Saginaw. Next he spent three years at WWJ, Detroit as assistant manager, announcer, and engineer. Wallace joined WMAQ, Chicago in 1928 as an announcer.

William J. Andrews was another broadcaster whose original interest was on the technical side. He was born in Oakland and became interested in radio while still in high school. He accepted a job as a radio expert in the radio department of Montgomery Ward and Company, working as a mail order authority and handling inquiries from all parts of the country asking how radio sets worked or why they didn't work. Then he had some brief experience at an Oakland station as its chief operator, occasionally filling in for announcers. Soon he was doing most of the announcing, which brought his first fan mail. He wrote publicity for an Oakland theatre for awhile in

1928 and joined the National Broadcasting Company in San Francisco as an announcer before the year ended.

Tom Manning began his association with the Cleveland Indians baseball club in 1920 as a megaphone man. He was informed by the team's general manager in 1928 that the games were going to be broadcast and that he was the man who was going to announce them. Manning went on the air over WJAY and talked so loudly that he immediately blew them off the air. Then he settled down and made a career in radio.

Other 1928 activity: Bob Elson switched from WAMD, Milwaukee to KWK, St. Louis. Curt Peterson was made supervisor of NBC announcers in New York. In Baltimore, Arthur Willard moved his *Musical Clock* from WCAO to WFBR. Ray Winters, a future Los Angeles and New York announcer, went from WTAR, Norfolk to KLRA, Little Rock. KTHS, Hot Springs manager Cam Arnoux had a policy of fining announcers 25¢ for each classical music name they mispronounced. When WMAL, Washington joined CBS in 1928, Stanley Bell became the network's presidential announcer, introducing the chief executive each time he appeared on the air. Sen Kaney went to NBC, Chicago as an announcer and assistant program director.

Chicago announcers such as Franklin Wintker who played phonograph records on the air were called "pancake turners," a term given to them by members of the local musicians' union. They wanted only live music played. Wintker was one of the early announcers who incurred the wrath of irate husbands who believed that their wife fell in love with announcers' voices she heard on the radio. One male threatened him with bodily harm. Franklin sent his vocal vibrations out during the early morning *Smile Awhile Time* over WLS.

In North Carolina, a radio announcer's voice frightened away the attacker of a housewife. The invader was struggling with the woman when a booming voice blared over the radio. The intruder quickly fled.

In the spring of 1929, Floyd Gibbons had lunch with M. H. Aylesworth, NBC's president. The meeting resulted in an audition for the veteran newspaper correspondent. The network's entire board of directors listened on another floor as Gibbons spoke at a rapid rate of speed while displaying clean enunciation and dramatic delivery. He articulated 217 words per minute, an average of 3.6 words per second. The turbulent personality was given a Wednesday night program called

Headline Hunters. The content was based on his many personal experiences.

Gibbons was also assigned to the handling of remote broadcasts for NBC. One came on August 5, the arrival of the airship *Graf Zeppelin* at Lakehurst, New Jersey. His rival on CBS for the event was Ted Husing, whose career and life came within a split-second of vanishing during one phase of the broadcast. Husing's network decided to give downtown New York coverage before switching to the actual landing site. Ted was perched on the ledge of the 20th story of the Steinway Hall on West Fifty-Seventh, which housed WABC, the station purchased by CBS in January of 1929. He was waiting to spot the craft. As soon as it was in sight, Ted adjusted his binoculars and subconsciously made a side step and tripped over the microphone cord. As he started to fall, CBS announcer Rush Hughes grabbed his knees with one arm and hung onto the window sash with the other hand. Ted regained his balance and continued to talk in a sitting position. After he signed off there, he hurried downstairs to a waiting car and was rushed toward Lakehurst, where he continued the coverage.

Gibbons was there with a 24-pound portable short wave transmitter strapped to his chest. His words were picked up on the roof of a large hangar and boosted back to NBC headquarters.

On November 2, Floyd Gibbons started an additional series entitled *Adventure in Science*, sponsored by General Electric. The musical portion of the program was by Walter Damrosch and his Orchestra. The one-hour program stayed on the air for almost two years.

Ted Husing was on hand for CBS at Herbert Hoover's inauguration in March 1929. Norman Brokenshire was there for WCAU, Philadelphia, where he had been hired after his return from his overseas honeymoon. With the 1925 inauguration experience under his belt, he was quite confident. This time it wasn't a one-man operation. He was given a staff of assistants. They were posted along the route from the White House to the Capitol. Mail response to the broadcast was so impressive that arrangements were made to transfer Broke from WCAU, which was owned by Paley's brother-in-law, to WABC and CBS in New York. Soon he was handling some of the best shows such as the *La Palina Hour*, which advertised cigars made by a company owned by the Paleys. Younger announcers were told to watch Brokenshire work. He helped to train a young man named David Rosenthan, who elected to use the name David Ross on the air. Ross would be around for a long time.

71

Ted Husing covered the 55th Kentucky Derby for CBS, and Clem McCarthy was on the spot for NBC. The latter's crew was made up of fourteen members. Ted Husing was alone in Louisville. The horse race was close, and each announcer reported a different winner at the finish line. Husing's report proved to be correct. Ted also broadcast the World Series in the fall without an assistant.

Paul Whiteman and his Orchestra went on CBS for Old Gold Cigarettes. After several months, the band headed for Hollywood to make a movie, *The King of Jazz*. Concerts were given in seventeen cities along the way. Ted Husing traveled with the group, serving as the announcer for Old Gold Cigarettes. In the movie capital, filming was delayed, and Ted was forced to return to the East to broadcast the Regatta in Poughkeepsie. Before leaving, it was necessary for him to find an announcer to take his place. Whiteman was displeased because he would be without his established announcer. The famous band leader was pessimistic over the prospects of locating a capable spokesman. Husing started the auditions in a large studio above KTMR, which the band used because of its large size. The station manager asked one of his announcers, Harry von Zell, whether he had auditioned. Harry replied that he hadn't because they had already listened to most of the prominent announcers in the area and he didn't think he had a chance. The boss issued an edict for him to go up and read with the stipulation that if he didn't, he would be fired from KMTR. To pacify the executive, Harry reported to the studio and took his place in line. When his turn came, he read a few lines of the Old Gold commercial and was interrupted by a voice from the control room asking his name. Harry told them and mentioned that he worked downstairs. He was told to read some more. He complied and was given the job. Ted Husing instructed him on two points: please the sponsor and please Mr. Whiteman. Later announcers for Whiteman included Douglas Browning and Alan Kent.

Walter Winchell (originally Winchel) was born in New York in 1897. His father operated a small silk store. Soon the father left, and the mother had the task of raising two sons. Walter began selling newspapers and magazines at the age of eight. George Jessel was a boyhood friend. George's mother sold tickets at the Imperial Theatre. In 1909, she persuaded the manager to give her son and Walter jobs as ushers. The boys, in turn, convinced the manager that they should be singers on the theatre stage. They were joined by another youngster to form the

Imperial Trio. Winchell quit school in the sixth grade. The boys went on the road with Gus Edwards' group, which included a juvenile named Eddie Cantor. Winchell remained in show business until he joined the Navy during World War I. His entire duty was in New York.

After the military conflict, Walter Winchell returned to the vaudeville circuit. Later he began writing a one-page newspaper which reported show business gossip. He would post it on bulletin boards backstage, and soon it became very popular with the entertainers. This led to his eventual fame as a newspaper columnist. He was writing for the New York *Graphic* when he made his first radio appearance on January 18, 1929. The program was called *New York by a Representative New Yorker*. His quick-jabbing, penetrating manner was indeed a departure from the slower, stilted styles that were often heard on the air. Later that year, he went to work for Hearst's New York *Journal* for five-hundred dollars a week. Winchell's radio fame was just around the corner.

Arthur Godfrey made his first appearance on the earth's scene in New York in 1903. His father had an adventuresome nature and found it difficult to settle down to the business of making a living. His mother dreamed of a concert career, often going downstairs at 3:00 A.M. to play the piano. When Arthur was ten, the family economy made it necessary for them to move from Manhattan to Hasbrouck Heights, New Jersey. A couple of years later, he was delivering papers and working in a bakery after school. During the 1918 flu epidemic, employee illness forced him to work full time at the bakery for three weeks. His absence from school resulted in his being removed as captain of the sophomore debate team prior to an important contest. Godfrey left school and wandered around the country doing various kinds of labor. In 1920, he joined the Navy with the hope of being admitted to the Naval Academy. While waiting for a decision, he studied radio. Then he elected to ship out as a third-class radioman aboard a destroyer bound for the Mediterranean. A Hawaiian sailor taught him to play the ukulele; and during the next two years when shore leave was granted in the area, he and other musical shipmates played in joints for free refreshments.

After leaving the Navy in 1924, Godfrey again sought employment and wound up selling cemetery lots door-to-door in Detroit. He saved two thousand dollars in five months. A vaudeville show was for sale. He had thoughts of becoming a show business entrepreneur. Godfrey bought the unit and began traveling west from Chicago. It lost money and the new owner was broke by the time it reached Los Angeles. He went back to Chicago and got a job driving a cab. A passenger in 1927 turned out to be a former Navy friend who was then in the Coast Guard. The sailor told Godfrey that advancement in that branch was rapid, and he enlisted. After completing a Radio Materiel School, he was stationed at a depot near Baltimore.

One Saturday night in 1929, Arthur Godfrey and some friends sat in a speakeasy drinking needled beer (beer with raw alcohol added). The radio was tuned to WFBR and a program called *Saturday Night Function.* The announcer appealed for anyone who could perform to come to the radio station. Off went the fun-seeking contingent. How did Arthur want to be introduced? "Call me Red Godfrey, the Warbling Banjoist." He sang "I'm in Love with You Honey." His bullfrog voice and carefree style led to his getting a regular quarter-hour show on the station, sponsored by the Triangle Pet Shop. His compensation was five dollars per program. His first commercial was for birdseed. Soon his duties included introducing Maryland's governor when he made speeches. A Coast Guard captain recommended that Arthur enter radio on a full time basis. The governor helped him obtain a discharge, and he was launched into full time radio employment at WFBR.

Don Wilson was born in Lincoln, Nebraska, in 1900 but was moved to Denver at the age of two. During his college days, he attended the University of Colorado, where he became a football star. After graduation in 1923, he worked as a salesman but soon quit to join a singing trio. The vocal activity was enjoyable to him, but at first he didn't think there was much of a future in it. Piggly Wiggly stores were an early self-service grocery organization. The company agreed to sponsor the trio on a tour of Western states. The threesome was billed as the "Piggly Wiggly Trio." Beginning in May 1927, they sang on KFRC, San Francisco. The station was owned by Don Lee, who also owned KHJ, Los Angeles. After a year on the San Francisco station, the trio arranged to transfer to KHJ to continue broadcasting for the grocery chain. When the sponsorship ended, one member left the group. The remaining two sang as a duet. Wilson also began doing stints as an announcer. When his singing partner left, Don became a full time announcer.

Don Lee also owned the Cadillac agency in Los Angeles. Wilson was in need of a new automobile, but he was unable to make a deal with the station's parent company. He then went to

Earle C. Anthony's Packard agency and made a trade. When Don Lee saw Wilson driving the new car, he didn't know that his radio employee had failed to deal with his company. He fired Wilson. Since Anthony owned KFI, the 220-pound Wilson thought it would be a logical step to apply there. In 1929, he began announcing at KFI. This would lead to his ultimate success in network announcing.

Frank Singiser was born in Minnesota but moved to Pennsylvania when he was three. His father was a Baptist minister. When Frank was five, his father accepted the pastor's position in an English church in Rangoon, India. The youngster went to school in Rangoon for five years. They came back to the U.S., and Frank graduated from Brown University with an A.B. degree at the age of nineteen. He showed up at the General Electric Company in Schenectady and asked for any kind of job. He was given an announcer's audition at the company's WGY, and a few weeks later he began his career behind the microphone. He also wrote radio dramas and directed programs. In May 1929, Frank Singiser joined NBC in New York.

One day in May 1929, Neel Enslen was an opera singer, and the next day he was an announcer with NBC in New York. He had sung in productions such as *Carmen* and *Princess Flavia.* He had gone to New York in February 1929 for further musical study and to sing in some of the larger churches. He asked for an announcer's audition and won a job without any previous radio experience. He was assigned to the network's evening programs in September of 1929.

Pasqual Gallicchio's father was a musician; and Pasqual, who was born in Chicago in 1902, also worked as a musician, playing in dance orchestras in Chicago restaurants and cafes and at the Crawford Theatre. He took a job as a record librarian at WMAQ in 1929 and a little later began announcing.

Don Thompson entered the world in Rangoon, India, where his father was a sea captain and his mother was a medical missionary in charge of the American hospital. They decided to return to the States to raise their son, settling in California. When the time came for him to enter college in 1920, he enrolled at the University of Redlands. There he enjoyed great athletic success, winning eleven letters. Later he played professional football. In 1928, radio beckoned and he joined the staff of KPO, San Francisco as an announcer and continuity writer. One day just before the famous East-West Shrine football game was scheduled to begin, an announcer failed to show up in the broad-

75

cast booth, and Don was assigned to share the mike with NBC's Graham McNamee. He came through, rising to the occasion well. This experience paved the way for him to become an early top sports announcer in the West.

Alden Russell, with college diploma under his arm, reported to KMBC Kansas City to perform the duties of an announcer, a ukulele player, and handler of various odd jobs that might be assigned by his superiors. One assignment given to Russell had a distasteful aspect. He was told to fill a time period by reading poetry when a group of musicians didn't appear for their scheduled program. Russell insisted that he be introduced with a pseudonym. The other announcer, Hugh Studebaker, quickly gave him the name of Ted Malone. He read the verse so well and listener response was so favorable that he was hooked on rhymes thereafter. It was the beginning of one of radio's best-known and best-loved programs, *Between the Bookends*.

Kelvin Kirkwood Keech was not a person to stick in one place very long. He was born in Hawaii, a natural setting for learning to play the ukulele at an early age. After his growing-up period, Kelvin went to Lancaster, Pennsylvania, to study chemical engineering. World War I interrupted that pursuit, and he landed in France as a military radio engineer. After the war, he and some of his buddies put together a jazz band called the White Lyrics, playing many of Europe's famous entertainment spots. In the old world capital of Constantinople, he found romance, meeting a Russian girl who could not speak English. Although Keech could get along in French, Japanese, Chinese, Portuguese, and his native Hawaiian, he knew no Russian. The language barrier didn't prove to be much of a handicap to courtship. They were married. He took his bride and his ukulele to London and played music over 2LO, a British Broadcasting Company station. The Britishers liked what they heard; in fact, so much that he was given the distinction of teaching the instrument to a member of the Royalty, the Prince of Wales. In 1928, Keech brought his wife to America, where he appeared on several radio programs. The following year he auditioned for an announcer's job at NBC, New York. During his first tryout, he suffered an extreme case of mike fright. A few weeks later, he was given a second opportunity. This time he earned a place on NBC's staff of announcers.

Ralph Livingstone Edwards was a sixteen-year-old junior at Oakland High School in 1929. A skit he wrote was broadcast on KROW. He also managed to land a major role in the cast. The station manager liked what he heard and hired Ralph as a script writer, paying one dollar per script. Also, the youngster was permitted to do part time announcing and acting.

Graham McNamee was the first announcer on Rudy Vallee's NBC program that started in 1929. Mac also took time to broadcast the opening of a new, fourteen-mile tunnel through the Cascade Mountains east of Seattle. In the sports department, he considered his broadcast of the first World Series game that fall as one of the great moments of his radio career. The game featured the surprise comeback start and win for Philadelphia Athletics pitcher Howard Ehmke against the Chicago Cubs.

In Atlanta, sportswriter Bill Munday had begun broadcasting college football games for Georgia Tech and the University of Georgia on WSB the previous year. When Georgia Tech was selected to play California in the Rose Bowl on New Year's Day 1929, WSB's Lambdin Kay convinced NBC officials that Munday should share the broadcast with McNamee. Munday's extreme southern drawl and individual style of reporting made him an immediate national favorite. NBC kept him on the staff and gave him numerous assignments.

Halloween Martin was almost twenty-seven at the time, having been born in 1902 in El Paso, Texas. After graduating from De Paul University in 1922, she joined the Chicago *Herald and Examiner* as an assistant home economist. She also included among her duties the dispensing of advice to readers deprived of love or jilted by a lover. The manager of KYW often called upon girls on the newspaper staff to do some announcing. On January 7, 1929, Halloween Martin was asked to substitute for Prudence Penny. Her college acting background was in her favor, and she projected her sparkling personality through the microphone. The manager decided to use her pleasant voice on an early morning program to be called the *Musical Clock*, featuring phonograph records, the time, temperature, and weather. It was a wise decision.

Announcer Bill Hay made his network debut on August 19, 1929, when the *Amos 'n' Andy* program went on NBC Red for Pepsodent. It was the first daily, quarter-hour program. After reading the toothpaste commercial, Bill would introduce the pair with "Heah they ah."

Bob Elson moved from KWK, St. Louis to WGN, Chicago in March 1929, where he would become a permanent fixture as a sports announcer, using an "alive, rising inflection" type voice.

Another person who also became an estabished Chicago sportscaster made his appearance that year. Pat Flannagan started at WBBM.

Hal O'Halloran joined WLS, Chicago. He would stay a long time. Charlie Stookey began his career as a radio farm reporter on WLS on May 20. He would later transfer his knowledgeable agricultural reports to KMOX, St. Louis.

Ralph Patt became an announcer at WJR, Detroit. J. Lewis Reid moved to WOR, Newark. Cecil Underwood advanced from KHQ, Spokane to NBC, San Francisco on May 1, 1929.

Every announcer at one time or another made a fluff on the air. ("To err is human.") Even articulate Milton J. Cross didn't escape. Once he introduced the "A & G Pypsies."

IV

We Pause For Station Identification

His speech flowed from his
tongue sweeter than honey.
—Homer

Newsman Floyd Gibbons began a series of newscasts on NBC February 24, 1930, sponsored by *Literary Digest* magazine. He was heard at 6:45 P.M., E.S.T., just before *Amos 'n' Andy*. The publication was very interested in the prohibition issue and directed Gibbons to conduct a wet-dry poll during his broadcasts. Running totals were announced each night. During a period of six months, he polled more than a million votes with a majority expressing a preference for legalized alcohol.

A Gibbons imposter traveled across the country piling up huge bills in the name of the newsman. Finally, a reporter in Newark noticed that the man wore a patch over his right eye and remembered that Gibbons had lost his left eye. A judge ended the culprit's opulent living by giving him three months of room and board in jail.

One night during the latter part of the summer of 1930, Floyd Gibbons and a friend, along with two lady companions, selected a Long Island nightspot as a place of entertainment. After leaving the establishment a couple of hours after midnight, they were riding through the neighborhood of the *Literary Digest* president. Floyd thought it would be amusing to let go with various noises of celebration including the singing of the barroom rendition of "Sweet Adeline." Accounts vary as to the response of the executive to their nocturnal visit. The publisher was a teetotaler. One version had him inviting them in for a short stay while another indicated that he pointedly ordered them to go on their way.

Nevertheless, it was quickly suspected that *Literary Digest* was looking for another newscaster. There was a rush to audition anyone and everyone that might fill the bill—speakers, authors, and journalists—but none impressed enough. Bill Paley saw the situation as an opportunity to land the important account for his young CBS. The man who was head of the network's sales department remembered a speaker he had heard once at the Covent Garden Royal Opera House in London. His name was Lowell Thomas. A call was made in August 1930. He told the renowned Thomas he was the only man in the world who could save his job. He invited Thomas down to the city—to Madison and 52nd Street.

Lowell Thomas was born in Ohio in 1892 but grew up in the mining camp area of Cripple Creek, Colorado, where his father was a doctor. It was there that Lowell attended a Sunday School class conducted by a young lady from Waco, Texas. The twelve-year-old boy and a friend walked around a mountain to attend that particular church. Later the teacher would be known to many as Texas ("hello, suckers") Guinan of New York speakeasy fame.

Thomas started his newspaper career in Cripple Creek. His colleges included Northern Indiana University, Denver University, Princeton, and Chicago University. He also taught English literature at Princeton. During World War I, he was a war correspondent, coming up with an exclusive on-the-scene story of the capture of Jerusalem. His association with Lawrence of Arabia and the Arabian Army highlighted his fame as a world journalist.

Thomas, then thirty-eight, arrived at CBS headquarters. Paley didn't tell him much, only to start talking when the buzzer sounded and to continue talking about anything for fifteen minutes. A sponsor group was listening on another floor, but he didn't know that. For a quarter-hour, he talked about some of his world experiences. After the session, he learned that he was being considered as a replacement for Floyd Gibbons. The sponsor was about to abandon the search for another newsman and leave the air. Although Thomas' style was in no way similar to Gibbons', sponsor interest was rekindled; but he wanted to hear the prospect actually broadcasting news. He agreed to listen to Thomas on the air at 6:00 P.M. the following Thursday, which was three days later, and then hear Gibbons at 6:45 for a comparison.

On the day of the on-the-air audition, Lowell Thomas rented the penthouse at the Princeton Club in New York to use as a place to prepare his fifteen-minute newscast. A battery of writers gathered to help. Among them were Ogden Nash, who would later gain fame as a witty poet, and Dale Carnegie, the authority on motivation. There was much general disagreement about the format. The bickering and confusion continued until four in the afternoon. Lowell and another man slipped out for a breather. He bought a couple of afternoon newspapers and proceeded to the CBS studio on the twentieth floor. There he put together some notes. At 6:00 o'clock, he said, "Good evening, everybody," and went on to tell the listening audience about the events of the day. When he finished, Bill Paley made a happy entrance into the studio. They found an also happy sponsor on another floor.

Floyd Gibbons still had a few weeks to go on his contract, until Friday, September 26. He hadn't wanted to lose the program. Gibbons ended the final broadcast by saying that Lowell Thomas was taking over the time slot. He didn't mention anything about Thomas' extensive background, but rather implied that he was a professor. Gibbons would still have two other radio programs—for General Electric on Saturday night and for Libby-Owens-Ford on Sunday night.

Literary Digest decided to put Lowell Thomas on both CBS and NBC simultaneously. At 6:45 P.M., September 29, 1930, announcer Ed Thorgersen introduced him on NBC, and Frank Knight did the announcing chore for CBS. Then his pleasant baritone voice said, "Adolph Hitler, the German Fascist chief, is snorting fire. There are now two Mussolinis in the world. . . ." After six months, the sponsor dropped CBS and stayed on NBC because of the *Amos 'n' Andy* adjacency.

Patrick J. Kelly was born in Australia in 1892 and went to school in Sidney. Then he became a sailor and spent several years on the seven seas. His experiences were varied. He was ship-wrecked three times. He was one of the best boxers in the Royal Naval Reserve. Kelly learned to fly and gained a great enthusiasm for aviation. He passed an examination which earned him a license as a marine engineer. This led to his working a few years in the engine room of ocean liners. During the time, he was studying music and attempting to develop his voice. He left the sea work and completed his musical education in New York. His dramatic voice was recognized by Fortune Galio, who gave him leading roles with the San Carlo Opera Company. In 1929, Pat Kelly was hired as an announcer by NBC in New York. Next he was made supervisor of NBC's twenty-one announcers. Among his duties was the assignment of announcers to programs for which he thought they were best suited. His reply to the comment that his position provided plenty of headaches was, "Shucks, a job wouldn't be any fun if you didn't have some trouble once in awhile."

Many types of businesses were hard hit financially by the Great Depression. The Brooklyn *Daily Eagle* had to make cutbacks. H.V. Kaltenborn was asked to take a large reduction in salary. He decided to leave the paper where he had worked for twenty-eight years and enter radio on a full time basis. He joined WABC and CBS for $100 a week. His duties called for a weekly news commentary and the coverage of important national and international news events.

Walter Lanier "Red" Barber was trying to work his way through the University of Florida at Gainesville, but jobs were scarce. His best opportunity came when he was hired as janitor at the University Club where professors lived. During the closing days of 1929 while school was out for the holidays, Red remained at school in the room provided for him at the club. He was working on a term paper. An agricultural professor who lived there had a forty-five-minute program on the non-commercial campus radio station, WRLT. He had to read three papers on the air during each broadcast, and other profs who usually helped him were out of town for the holidays. He asked Barber to read one of them, but the student declined, stating that he was too busy with his class assignment. Then the professor made Red an offer—he would buy his dinner in return for his assistance on the air. Under the circumstances, that was a good offer. Red accepted. They went to the station, and the student was given the second script to read: "Certain Aspects of Obstetrics." There was no rehearsal, not even a voice level test. He started reading when the teacher pointed.

As soon as he finished his part, he started to leave. The station manager stopped him and asked whether he was the person who had just been on the air. Red replied that he was, and the manager said that his voice registered very well. He added that they needed a part time announcer and offered him the job. Red thanked him but remarked that he couldn't accept because he already was doing all of the work he could handle. That didn't stop the manager. He was new at the station and was trying to get off to a good start. During the weeks that followed, he sent messages by the professor asking Red to reconsider. Finally, the manager wanted to know how much it would take for Red to quit his janitorial job and accept the part time announcing position. Red decided to put an end to this once and for all. He would come up with a figure that would stop the radio executive. He considered his room and board, laundry, pocket money, and incidentals. It came to fifty dollars a month. The manager met the price; and on March 4, 1930, Red Barber started his career in broadcasting. The station had carbon mikes, and about each half-hour the carbon particles would stick together and distort the sound. The control room operator would turn off the mike and hit the back of it with a pocket knife to loosen the particles.

By the fall of that year, the station's regular sportscaster had left, and Red asked to do the college football games. He was given the assignment. For the first game he made no preparation. He didn't even know the players' names and didn't have a game program with which to identify them. The broadcast was a disaster. He was told prior to the fourth game that his play-by-play work was inadequate. Red asked for another chance. This time he watched the team practice, made a spotting chart, and informed himself about the various aspects of the athletic contest. That broadcast brought two hundred favorable telegrams, including one from Florida's governor in Tallahassee.

Because Jimmy Wallington had broadcast from WGY's short wave station at Schenectady to members of the Byrd Expedition in Little America, NBC invited him to New York in March 1930 to meet the group upon their return to the U.S. There was a delay in their arrival, and Wallington had the opportunity to do some network announcing while waiting. It was June when the crew arrived. Jimmy was aboard a seagoing tug which went 350 miles out to sea to meet them. When he called to them, they recognized his voice. He went aboard their vessel and rode to New York Harbor, where he and Graham McNamee handled the remote broadcast. The tall, smooth Wallington was in big time radio to stay.

Harlow Wilcox grew up in a show business family. His father was a cornet player for Ringling Brothers Circus and later became a bandleader. Harlow left his parents during his early teens and performed on the chautauqua platform and on the stage. Next he became a traveling salesman for an electrical equipment firm. After five years, he became sales manager. In 1930, Wilcox entered the field of radio, joining WBBM, Chicago as an announcer.

Kenneth Carpenter lived in Peoria, Illinois, and worked in the advertising and merchandising division of a department store. He was married and had an infant child. His father, a minister, accepted the appointment to a church in Pasadena, California. Kenneth decided to move his family to the West Coast, also. The Depression had hit and finding a job in the new surroundings was very difficult. Since he had worked in a store's advertising department, he applied at an advertising agency. There wasn't an opening, but the executive mentioned that he had a good voice and asked whether he knew anything about radio announcing. After replying that he didn't, the man told Carpenter that KHJ was looking for an announcer. He accompanied the applicant to the station to help arrange an audition. Bob Swam, KHJ's chief announcer, gave Kenneth a piece of copy and directed him to the announce booth. While reading the message, Carpenter got the announcing "bug." The audition was acceptable, but KHJ had already hired someone— an announcer from KFI. The ad man took him to KFI, where Don Wilson was the chief announcer. Their audition copy was filled with classical music terms. Kenneth had taken German in high school and was able to handle the copy satisfactorily. He was told that the station was considering another person, but it was suggested that he hang around. Don Wilson talked with him from time-to-time and let him make an occasional stationbreak. After awhile, he was given a spot on the announcing staff. Carpenter had a musical, rising-inflection type of voice rather than one with low tones brought up from the "bottom of the barrel", as was common among many announcers of that day.

Cesar Saerchinger was born in Germany in 1889 and came to the United States at the age of nine. After World War I, he became a foreign correspondent for the New York *Evening Post*. A five-power naval conference was held in London, and both networks sent newsmen to cover it. The conference lasted longer than originally expected, and the CBS man had to return home. He asked Saerchinger to cover the remainder of the event for CBS. After the assignment was completed, he informed CBS that he could line up various British celebrities for interviews. He was hired, and arrangements were made to use a studio at the British Broadcasting Corporation. Saerchinger organized the first trans-Atlantic broadcasting service.

Bennett Franklin "Ben"Grauer was born in Staten Island, New York, in 1908. When he was six, his family moved to the Morningside Heights section of Manhattan. During his school days, Ben played juvenile roles on the New York stage. The shows included *Betty at Bay, May Time, Floradora, The Blue Bird*, and the Theatre Guild's *Processional*. After finishing high school, he took a part in the motion picture *The Idol Dancer*, which was made in Florida. This led to an extensive personal appearance tour in the Eastern section of the country. Then Ben was starred in the picture *The Town That God Forgot*. He was also attending City College in New York, where he served as dramatic critic for the school paper and editor-in-chief of the literary magazine. During his senior year, he won a prize for extemporaneous speaking in a contest which included two hundred participants.

After college graduation in 1930, Ben Grauer did not choose to pursue a movie career. He was not tall, and he thought he would be stuck with juvenile and villain roles. He wanted to be a hero or nothing. Ben did some radio acting at NBC, and in October he heard that there was an opening on the announcing staff. He hurried into the office of Patrick Kelley, supervisor of NBC announcers, and enthusiastically requested an audition. He was accepted as a staff announcer. Then he competed with ten other announcers for a program to be sponsored by a firm that made bologna. "That's the man!" the sponsor said when he heard Ben. "That's what I sell—baloney." Early in his career, Grauer handled a program which featured Carrie Chapman Catt. During the close, Ben gave out with this spoonerism: "Thank you, Mrs. Catt. We are deepful grately."

Ford Bond began earning money playing the piano at the early age of thirteen in his hometown of Louisville. He had been studying piano since he was five. At seven he had become a tenor singer with a boys choir. After high school graduation, to please his parents, he entered college in Chicago with the intent of becoming a doctor. He soon left. At nineteen, Ford directed various choruses and glee clubs. Then he became a musical representative for a manufacturing company. When he was twenty-two, he went to Alexandria, Louisiana, and directed the community chorus and a church choir. Returning to Louisville, he discovered radio, and radio discovered him. Ford Bond joined WHAS as an announcer. In succession, he became the station's studio director, music director, and program director. In January 1930, Bond was ready to try for a bigger challenge. He made the journey to New York and became an NBC announcer. Soon he was assigned to the famous *Cities Service Concert*.

Howard Claney entered the world in Pittsburgh in 1898. When time for college arrived, he entered Carnegie Institute of Technology, but his interest was in artistic courses such as architecture, sculpture, painting, and drama rather than the engineering subjects. He later studied at the Art Institute of Chicago. One day while in New York, he went with an actor friend to a Broadway booking agent's office. Claney was sitting in an outer office by himself when the booking agent walked through and inquired whether the visitor was there to see him. Howard replied in the affirmative. This meeting led to a part in *A Man of the People.* He later appeared in several other stage productions. He also worked as a member of the NBC dramatic staff. In 1930, Claney auditioned for the announcing staff and was given a job.

Frederick Chase Taylor was a copy writer at WGR, Buffalo in 1930, and Budd Hulick was a staff announcer. One day the scheduled network show didn't come through. There was a quarter-hour to be filled locally. The two employees went on the air with Hulick referring to Taylor as "Colonel Stoopnagle." They ad libbed zany comedy, resulting in a deluge of phone calls to the station. They teamed up as "Stoopnagle and Budd." Soon New York network radio would beckon and they would achieve nationwide radio fame.

Roger T. Krupp's friends in Minnesota often told him that he had a nice voice and that he should try to get into radio. Mostly for laughs, Roger decided to audition. In 1930, when he was twenty-one, he went to WRHM, Minneapolis and was hired immediately. He wouldn't stay in local radio long. Instead, he would be showing up on some of the top network shows.

Ted Bliss (real name Merwin Gouldthrite) was a native of Canada but was brought to the Los Angeles area as a youngster. For several years during the twenties, he participated in drama, performing with various groups including the Pasadena Community Playhouse. In November 1926, Ted accepted a job with a department store in Long Beach, where he advanced from a stock clerk to the position of a buyer. By 1930, he was assistant manager of the basement division of the store. One day he received a call from Forrest Rucker, an announcer at KFOX, Long Beach. (Rucker would later achieve network prominence as "Galen Drake.") Rucker knew that Bliss had previously directed plays for the Long Beach Community Players. The radio man wanted him to arrange for the Community Players to present a series of plays on KFOX. The plan for the drama didn't materialize, but Bliss was asked to join the station as an announcer. The offer was three times as much as he was making at the department store, but he wasn't certain about the stability of the radio industry. Nevertheless, his show business nature prevailed, and Ted Bliss began what would be an interesting broadcasting career.

W. K. Henderson had inherited the Henderson Iron Works, and he was forty-nine when he put KWKH (his initials), Shreveport on the air in 1925. He personally became famous (or "infamous," depending on the listener's point of view) with his nightly biting talks delivered in a folksy manner. He was especially critical of chain stores and the Federal Radio Commission. Here is a 1930 example:

Hello, world. It's 8:00 o'clock. This is old man Henderson talkin' to you. . . . My friend, this station KWKH is supposed to be on 850 kilocycles, and we are bein' interfered with by several other stations, powerful stations—WABC in New York. That's a chain outfit. They drowned us out up in that part of the country, doggone 'em. Then there's that Sears Rareback outfit, WLS in Chicago and WENR. They have plenty of power, and while they may be on their wavelength, they sideswipe us all over the country, doggone 'em. I wanna say this to you, my good friends and listeners. I don't believe that those stations are doing this purposely. The fault is with the Federal Radio engineers. They have put these stations too close together. There should be a separation of more kilocycles. But I'll say this, if I was one of these chain stations, I'll guarantee you they would clear it up mighty quick.

My friends, I want you, everyone one of you, to demand of that branch of government, the Federal Radio Commission, that they have their engineers figure out a channel, 850 kilocycles, that we may use that you may hear us that we will not be interfered with. There's no excuse for this. All the chain stations are using cleared channels, the best wavelengths, and they should be put on one wavelength, giving a place for independent stations. But that's not the idea this day and time. The idea is to chain everything, confound it and plague take it. You wanna write to yore senators, you wanna write to yore congressmen, and you wanna demand that the independent stations have equal rights as to kilocycles and as to power and so forth. . . .

Edward K. "Ted" Jewett was born in Yokohama, Japan, in 1904. His father was in the silk business and also served as the Danish consul. During his six years in the Orient, the boy acquired a good knowledge of the Japanese language. The family came to the U.S. in 1910 and settled in New Jersey. Jewett entered Princeton in 1922. His special interests were elocution and public speaking. He wanted to become an actor or a statesman. After leaving college in 1926, he joined his father in the silk business. Observing the growth of radio, he decided to try to become a part of it. His first attempts were not successful.

Finally, in June 1930, he gained a position on the NBC announcing staff in New York. Ted Jewett was a good mimic; and between programs, he amused other announcers in the announcers' room with his antics.

William L. Abernathy was a Virginian, born in 1894. His education included attendance at a business college. His business experience was a two-year stint in the freight rate department of the Atlantic Coast Line Railway. In the early twenties, he organized a quartet in Detroit. It was the first such group to sing on WWJ. Abernathy went to New York in 1925 and joined the new Shubert production of *The Student Prince*. Other roles followed in top musicals. In September 1930, he joined the NBC announcing staff in Washington.

Death Valley Days, a drama of the old West, started on NBC Blue in 1930. George Hicks was the announcer, extolling the cleansing virtues of 20 Mule Team Borax. *The Ben Bernie Show* also began that year. Announcers for the "Old Maestro" through the years would include Jeff Sparks, Harlow Wilcox, Bob Brown, and Harry von Zell.

Don McNeill received a Bachelor of Philosophy degree in 1930 and went to work at a station in Louisville. There he met singer Van Fleming. The two formed a radio comedy team called "Don & Van, the Two Professors of Coo-Coo College." After losing their sponsor in Louisville, they went to KGO, San Francisco and began a West Coast show for NBC.

Announcer transfers in 1930: Arthur Godfrey made the short move from Baltimore to Washington, joining NBC station WRC. Howard Petrie went from WBZA, Boston to NBC, New York.

Beginnings: A future commissioner of baseball became a radio sports reporter. Ford Frick began a daily program on WOR. Arch McDonald, a 230-pounder who had been born in Hot Springs, Arkansas, in 1901, started announcing at WDOD, Chattanooga, a step that would lead to a career as a major league baseball announcer. Ken Niles became a drama coach at KHJ, Los Angeles. Julian Bently joined WLS, Chicago. He would specialize in news. Ruth Lyons joined the musical staff of WKRC, Cincinnati, her first move toward becoming a talkative feminine air personality in the Queen City.

NBC announcer Alwyn W. Bach won the good diction award in 1930. His speech style was stiff and formal, but it met the articulation requirements of the American Academy.

It was ironic that KFKB, Milford, Kansas, won the golden microphone award of *Radio Digest* in 1930, the year that the FRC refused to renew the station's license because of the nature of Dr. John R. Brinkley's medical talks. His future broadcasting plans would be aimed south of the border down Mexico way.

France Laux had moved from KVOO, Tulsa to KMOX, St. Louis to broadcast sports. He started the pre-game baseball show *Dope From the Dugout* in 1930. For the first couple of weeks, his announcer up in the broadcast booth introduced the program by saying, "And now here's your dope from the dugout, France Laux." Laux requested that the announcer reword the intro.

The Depression caused great economic hardship to many local stations, but the personnel seemed to keep a sense of humor through it all. That was also the era of the "yo-yo" craze. Jay Beard at KBTM, Paragould, Arkansas, knew a young man who was especially adept at the art of yo-yo manipulation. Jay told him they would put him on the air. He was taken to the studio where two microphones were carefully placed to "pick up" all the action. Upon receiving the signal from the control room operator, the guest went through his entire repertoire, not realizing that only recorded music was going out on the air. The next day, after his friends explained the practical joke to him, he was ready to whip somebody at the radio station.

Ranking highest on Arthur Godfrey's list of outside interests was flying. One morning in 1931 after completing his morning radio show, he was driving to the Congressional Airport to practice flying a glider. His car and a truck had a head-on collision. For four months, he lay in a hospital bed covered with bandages and casts. About all he could do was listen to the radio. This greatly changed his outlook on radio broadcasting. "Those days we were all talking to the 'ladies and gentlemen of the radio audience'," he later explained. "I decided there wasn't any such audience. There was just one guy or some girl off somewhere listening by themselves. Hell, if they were together, they'd have something better to do than to listen to the radio." Godfrey began formulating a change of style to take effect when he was physically able to return to the microphone.

Red Barber was given his first play-by-play endurance test when he undertook the broadcasting of the Florida State High School Basketball Tournament on WRLT in early 1931. The games started at 8:00 A.M. and continued throughout the broadcast day. He learned how demanding continuous announcing could be. Red's salary was upped to $75 a month during his second year at the station. Later that year, the chief announcer left for another station. Barber was given the title and raised to $150 monthly. He was twenty-three at the time. The additional earnings enabled him to get married. Friends of his bride often asked her when Red was going to quit playing around with radio and get a real job.

Ralph Edwards finished high school in 1931 and enrolled at the University of California at Berkeley. He began working his way through college by doing many jobs at KTAB, Oakland—actor, announcer, producer, writer, sound effects man, and janitor.

"The house lights are being dimmed. In a moment the great gold curtain will go up." Broadcasts of the Metropolitan Opera began on NBC December 25, 1931. Milton Cross was selected as announcer and host. His cultured voice and knowledge of operatic music and singers assured him a long association with that distinguished production. His most challenging effort as he narrated from Box 44 was the timing of his comments to conclude with the conductor's raising of the baton.

Robert Trout had worked at quite a variety of jobs before he began hanging around WJSV (Willingly Jesus Suffered Victory), Mount Vernon Hills, Virginia, near Alexandria and working as a studio handyman for no pay. As it often happens in the movies, the regular performer didn't show up and the novice had his opportunity. In this case, it was the newscaster who was absent, and the station manager told Trout to read from a newspaper. The microphone appearance earned him a regular place on the staff. On one program, Robert (often called "Bob") used the monicker "Old Nimrod" and dispensed hunting and fishing tips. He also did what he called a "poor man's Will Rogers show."

Harry von Zell's association with singer Bing Crosby on the Paul Whiteman program led to his becoming Bing's first announcer when the "Groaner"began his initial radio show. Harry and Bing had been assigned to the same hotel room during a Northwest swing of the Whiteman band. CBS president William Paley had heard a kid playing a Crosby record on board ship while on his way to Europe. He sent a wireless message back to the network directing them to sign the singer. When he returned to New York, he learned that Crosby still hadn't been signed. Paley asked him to come to New York for a discussion. An agreement was reached, Bing was scheduled to go on nightly at 7:00, which was the time slot opposite *Amos 'n' Andy* on NBC.

When the night of Crosby's debut arrived, he was unable to appear because his voice had disappeared. He blamed the condition on rehearsing in an air-conditioned room, which he had never done before. In a few days, he regained his voice, and Harry von Zell spoke into the mike on September 2, 1931:

Introducing Bing Crosby. Here is the moment you've been waiting for, the delayed appearance of that sensational baritone. Bing Crosby, whose singing has made him a favorite of California through the mediums of the motion pictures, the vaudeville stage, and the radio. It was our announced intention to present Bing Crosby's initial program Monday night, but a severe attack of laryngitis made it impossible for him to appear until tonight. However, his voice is recovered sufficiently to allow him to bring to you now his inimitable song interpretations. So offering Bing Crosby and the popular song of the day, "Just One More Chance."

Bing didn't like to live in New York, and it wasn't long before he decided to move the program to Los Angeles. Harry von Zell would have gladly made the move with him, but his New York commitments prevented it.

One of those commitments was with a new concept of radio news programming. To get the background, it is necessary to refer to WLW, Cincinnati and Fred Smith. In 1928, Smith arranged with *Time* magazine to receive an advance copy of the publication each week from which he wrote ten-minute daily news segments. Later that year, he moved to New York and continued the news feature over WOR. It was called *NewsCasting*, but a newspaper's radio listing didn't capitalize the "C", and it became *Newscasting*, reportedly the first time the term was used.

Fred Smith had broadcast several programs of drama on WLW, and from this he originated the idea of dramatizing news. In September 1929, he produced a five-minute recording which he called *NewsActing*. It was offered to other stations around the country as a syndicated feature. More than a hundred stations bought the program on a once-a-week basis. Out of this grew Smith's concept of a half-hour network program using a similar format and entitled *The March of Time*. Work on a preview program began. Ted Husing was selected as the narrator. Other radio people and stage actors were chosen to emulate the voices of individuals prominent in the news.

91

When the day of the first rehearsal arrived, it was learned that Ted Husing was stranded in a snow storm in Buffalo. This caused a real problem for the production. After some frantic consideration, Harry von Zell was called upon to serve as the "Voice of Time." Westbrook van Voorhis, who later gained fame as the "Voice of Time," was then a member of the cast as the "Voice of Fate." With Fred Smith as the managing editor, the first program went out over CBS on March 6, 1931, sponsored by *Time*. The series ran for thirteen weeks, until June 5, with Ted Husing as the narrator after the first presentation. It resumed in October with Harry von Zell again in the announcer's slot. When Harry left to work for an advertising agency, Westbrook van Voorhis became established in the role. "Time. . .marches on!"

Cesar Saerchinger continued as manager of the CBS London bureau, broadcasting talks by famous personages on Sunday. He explained his theory used in the selection of guests: "The principle I go on is that every man has a message. Some of us communicate that message by singing in our bath." Poet John Masefield was an early subject. In October of 1931, Saerchinger finally landed the prize participant—George Bernard Shaw. He came on the air saying: "Hello, America! Hello, all my friends in America! How are all you dear old boobs who have been telling one another for a month that I have gone dotty about Russia?" Then Shaw proceeded to expound on the merits of that country. The network received many complaints and later granted free time for an American to reply.

Bob Hawk was announcing at WCFL, Chicago in 1931. One day he had some sustaining time to fill. He got together what he called a stack of hot "pancakes" (another reference to the term that was used in the Chicago area to refer to recordings) and played them for an hour. The response was very favorable, and he continued the format, calling the show *Red Hot & Low Down*.

Nelson Case was born in Long Beach, California, the son of an established Los Angeles newspaper editor. Once the senior Case found his son working as an usher in a theatre. This prompted him to give the youngster a job on his paper. On one assignment, Nelson was sent to write a story about a radio station. While there, he was offered a job as a pianist. Immediately, he phoned his father and submitted his resignation from the paper. When it was time for him to go to college, he was sent to William and Mary in Virginia. After graduation, he became an orchestra leader in vaudeville. Later he returned to California on a steamer with a "small but noisy band," as he called it. After that booking was completed, he got a job at a Southern California radio station as an announcer. In 1931, Nelson joined the NBC announcing staff in San Francisco.

Roger Krupp, who joined the NBC, San Francisco announcing staff the following year, later explained the value of working with Nelson Case:

> Nelson taught me now to "pad" my expense account when assigned to a remote, not within walking distance from the NBC studios. Several nights a week, I would go to the Bal Taburin to announce Tom Gerun and his orchestra, or Anson Weeks and his band at the Mark Hopkins, or Ted Fiorito at the St. Francis Hotel. I would always hop a cable car and pay only a nickel or a dime for transportation. I would be reimbursed at the end of the week for about a buck and a half or so. . .exactly what I spent. When Case heard about it, he told me I was an idiot and should keep on riding the cable cars BUT charge NBC for cab fare. This I did. The rest of the staff had been doing it all along, so I just joined the "fraternity," and it was nice to have a little extra in the pay envelope. Salaries were just about enough to exist on. When I traveled to Hollywood each week to announce the *Al Jolson Show* for Chevrolet, I was paid only expenses and not one cent as a talent fee. Announcing big name shows was supposed to be an "honor," and that was pay enough.
>
> Nelson was the original "soft-sell" announcer that I can recall. Most of us could be called "screamers." "Punch the hell out of it," said the producer and the sponsor. I did until I learned better. For many years Nels was the spokesman for Ivory Soap, and when he said, "Ivory Soap. . .99 and nine-tenths per cent pure," you really believed him.

Roger Krupp reportedly was the first announcer to appear in a motion picture as an announcer. The film was *Are You Listening,* made by MGM in 1931-32.

Bert Parks, who was sixteen and still in prep school, got his first radio job at WGST, Atlanta in 1931. He was paid seven dollars per week as an announcer, errand boy, and record custodian. Later he achieved the position of chief announcer, and his pay was increased to fifteen dollars weekly.

Bill Slater, a future network sports announcer and MC, was doing football play-by-play of the University of Minnesota football games on WCCO, Minneapolis in 1931. He was a graduate of the U.S. Military Academy at West Point and had also been a football coach.

John W. Holbrook was born in Boston in 1904 but was educated in Toronto and Quebec, graduating from Bishop's College School in Lennoxville, Quebec, in 1926. He went to work at WBZ, Boston and won recognition while announcing nationwide broadcasts originating in Boston. As a result of this exposure, NBC brought him to New York. Holbrook won the good diction award in 1931 when he was only twenty-seven. Author Hamlin Garland, who was chairman of the Radio Diction Committee of the American Academy of Arts and Letters, stated:

> In making our third award, we have found a decision more difficult for the reason that the general level of announcers has risen. A throng of cultivated young men have demanded recognition. The number of university graduates has multiplied and the managers appear to be increasingly aware of their responsibility to the home circles into which the voices of their staff penetrate.

Garland also said that the Anglo-American standardization of English speech by the microphone and the talking screen could be stopped. "The question which should concern us is whether this standardization is proceeding along the right lines. The radio is even now the chief educative factor in this process. If standards are to be universally adopted, it is important that they should be fine."

Garland was asked by critics to explain why all three winners had been Eastern men. (Milton Cross had been the first winner.) He replied:

> The announcers of the West and Midwest are less schooled in comparative standards. They speak in a local manner. In every case of decided merit we found that announcers had been trained in music and in some foreign language or had studied abroad, that is to say he knows by comparison what constitutes good speech. He is aware of standards.

Four NBC announcers were named in *Musical Who's Who* in 1931: Graham McNamee, John S. Young, Milton Cross, and Alois Havrilla.

NBC's Floyd Gibbons joined International News Service and Universal Service and sailed November 21 to cover the war in Manchuria.

Charles Albert Lyon entered the world scene in Detroit in 1903. His schooling ended after a year at the University of Michigan. Desiring a stage career, he first went to work to earn money for financial support while waiting for his acting opportunity. He served as a seaman on the Great Lakes. Later he signed aboard a ship and went to Germany. After scrubbing decks to earn his way back to this country, he went to Hollywood and spent one winter playing juveniles in "Cameo Comedies." Various stage roles followed, including some runs on Broadway. While between engagements, he called a friend at WTAM, Cleveland, who arranged for an audition. An announcing job was offered; but another acting role became available, and he took it. After playing sixteen weeks in Dayton, Charles Lyon accepted the WTAM job. NBC took over the station and transferred him to Chicago in April 1931.

After his graduation from Wheaton College in Illinois in 1919, Paul Gates served as a minister for ten years. Then he left the pulpit and took a job as a bank representative in Oakland, California. Next he entered the automobile business. A friend mentioned one day the complexity of the reading portion of an NBC audition. This was a challenge to Gates. He wanted to try it. A job with NBC in San Francisco was the result.

William Lundell also served in a church capacity prior to his entry into radio. He was born in Minneapolis in 1900 and organized a concert orchestra consisting of ten children when he was twelve. William played the violin. He even rented a concert hall and presented a program at that early age. Later he received a B.A. degree and a Phi Beta Kappa key from the University of Minnesota. A Bachelor of Theology degree was earned at Harvard. Lundell studied in Paris and traveled through Europe, the Far East, and South America. After returning to this country, he worked for the Boston *Herald* and also preached at a suburban church. His first radio experience was with WBBA, Boston. In 1929, he was credited with being the first announcer to conduct an interview from an airplane. He was the chief announcer for the Massachusetts Bay Tercentenary celebration in 1930. The National Broadcasting Company was impressed with his work on that occasion and brought him to New York May 15, 1931.

Charles O'Connor was bitten by the acting bug early, giving his first recitation at the age of five in his native Cambridge, Massachusetts. After one year at Boston College, he toured the East with a stock company. In January 1931, O'Connor was employed as an announcer at WBZ, Boston, an NBC affiliate. He would soon make the jump to New York and the announcing staff of NBC.

Announcers have historically been somewhat nomadic by nature, always looking for greener pastures at other stations or networks. Some 1931 moves: Alan Kent and Dan Russell switched from WOV, New York to NBC and WEAF and WJZ. Arthur Q. Bryan made the change from WOR down to WCAU, Philadelphia. Carlyle Stevens moved from WLTH, Brooklyn to WABC, New York. Gene Rouse made the transfer from KYW, Chicago to NBC, Chicago. Buddy Twiss advanced from San Jose to NBC, San Francisco. Forrest Wallace went from WMAQ to NBC, Chicago. Foster Brooks, who had been with the announcing and dramatic departments of WHAS, Louisville for seven years, joined the announcing staff of KWK, St. Louis.

A future bigtown sports announcer went into the radio game as a rookie at WCKY, Covington, Kentucky. Russ Hodges was inserted into the station's lineup.

Sigmund Spaeth began his *Tune Detective* show on the Blue Network in 1931. He exposed modern tunes which had been "borrowed" from older pieces of musical work.

Jimmy Wallington was the announcer for Eddie Cantor and his *Chase & Sanborn Hour*, which went on the air over NBC on September 13. Actually, Wallington was more than the announcer. He was also a participant in most of the comedy routines. He would eventually be followed by Harry von Zell.

Broadway columnist Ed Sullivan debuted on CBS with a program of show business gossip along with a dance orchestra.

A comic strip came to life as a radio program on NBC Blue. *Little Orphan Annie* was sponsored by Ovaltine, and announcer Pierre Andre' would gain considerable recognition with his association with the production.

The American Album of Familiar Music made its appearance on NBC Red. Through the years, the announcer list would include Andre' Baruch, Roger Krupp, and Howard Claney. Bayer Aspirin was the sponsor.

Kenneth Niles was the announcer and MC for the 8:00 A.M. *Hallelujah Hour* on KHJ, Los Angeles and the Don Lee Network.

Ira Blue did commentary on *Contract Bridge* over KMTR, Hollywood.

Alois Havrilla was assigned as the announcer on a new program which started in October. It was called *Jack Frost*

Melody Moments. The advertising message was de-emphasized. Havrilla called attention to the sponsor's newspaper ads:

> Because we feel that we are your hosts we are not going to talk shop. You will be more interested in the advertising story of Jack Frost Packaged Sugar as it appears regularly in the newspapers or as your grocer will gladly tell you, than if we told it at length here.

Walter Winchell considered himself to be strictly a newspaperman, but CBS prexy William Paley persuaded him to start a news broadcast over the chain's local New York station, WABC. Gimbels Department Store agreed to sponsor the columnist. His rapid, super-excited style was quickly accepted by the listening audience. Winchell wanted it to sound like a newsboy yelling, "Extra!" Soon the flamboyant president of the American Tobacco Company, George Washington Hill, ordered his advertising department to sign Winchell to do a five-minute news report during the weekly *Lucky Strike Hour* on NBC, which featured orchestra music. His "no-holds-barred" policy resulted in a slander suit against him and the tobacco company.

The nation's radio editors selected top broadcasters in 1931:

Announcers	Sports Announcers
1. Milton Cross	1. Ted Husing
2. David Ross	2. Graham McNamee
3. John S. Young	3. Bill Munday
4. Graham McNamee	4. Ford Frick
5. Bill Hay	5. Clem McCarthy
6. Jimmy Wallington	
7. Alois Havrilla	

Up to that time, immediate identification of football players by the play-by-play man had been a problem. Ted Husing decided to do something about it. He built a spotting board, which included twenty-two lights, each controlled by separate buttons. The member of the broadcast crew who had the responsibility of spotting key men on each play merely had to push the buttons which represented the players' names.

By December 1931, H.V. Kaltenborn had performed 1,583 scheduled news broadcasts without missing any, but the necessity of an operation caused the continuous string to be broken.

In Marquette, Michigan, a fire broke out at a clothing store. An announcer from WBEO rushed to the scene to describe the blaze. The owner of the store was so impressed with his handling of the remote broadcast he bought station time to advertise a fire sale. He recovered most of his losses.

After a parade ended one day in downtown Little Rock, KGHI announcer Manuel Shue took an "educated"horse and its owner to the station's studio located on the sixth floor of a hotel. The state legislature was is session, and the hotel lobby was crowded with politicians. Through the lobby marched the announcer and his two guests, making their way toward the elevator. Ladies attired in long dresses and heading for some social function were shocked at the sight of the four-legged animal in their midst. Neither legislators nor socialites impeded Shue's mission. After the six-floor ride, the trio advanced to the Rose Room studio. The interview with the horse resulted only in taps of foot on the carpeted floor, but the proud owner was able to provide the listening audience with more lucid information. At first, station management considered terminating the employment of the adventurous announcer, but later reconsidered, probably remembering the adage, "You don't have to be crazy to be an announcer, but it helps."

Roanoke announcer Hayden Huddleston's schedule called for him to sign on WDJB one Sunday night and broadcast a remote program of Wurlitzer organ music from a new theatre. Hayden stayed too late at a girl friend's house and wasn't sure he could get to the station on time. He had no car, and he missed the street car. Having insufficient funds for a taxi, he ran seventeen blocks to the station, only to discover he had left the key to the control room at home. Picking up a chair, he knocked a hole in the large plate glass window, crawled through, and brought the organ music on just in time.

During 1930 and 1931, 2,500 spielers hoping to become network announcers paraded before the NBC audition microphone, but only ten were hired: Edward K. Jewett, Ray Winters, Howard Petrie, Ben Grauer, William Lundell, Ezra McIntosh, Allan Kent, David Russell, and Charles O'Connor. In most cases, the only applicants accepted were those who had a good musical education and possessed the ability to speak one or more foreign languages. The first sentence of the tryout script was "The seething sea ceaseth, and thus the seething sea sufficeth us."

The stationbreaks at WABC, New York had an extra function in addition to station identification purposes. The manner in which they were spoken by the announcer informed the director of technical operations whether or not the station was experiencing difficulty. "WABC, New York" meant that everything was fine. "This is WABC in the city of New York" signified trouble.

In January 1932, NBC carried a Floyd Gibbons broadcast from Manchuria during the Japanese-Chinese War. He introduced the general in command of the Japanese forces. The signal was first sent to Tokyo and then relayed to San Francisco and on to the network in New York.

Radio's greatest effort of on-the-spot news coverage up to that time began on March 1, 1932. Just after midnight, CBS, Chicago announcer Harlow Wilcox received a bulletin over WBBM's network monitor wire. He broke into a remote dance band program and announced the story of the Lindbergh baby kidnapping. Both CBS and NBC rushed teams to Hopewell, New Jersey. CBS established a temporary studio in a small room above a store. NBC set up headquarters at a Hopewell restaurant. NBC's George Hicks was assisted by Charles O'Connor, Ed Thorgerson, and Ezra McIntosh. They used mobile transmitting stations mounted on trucks.

CBS president William Paley appealed to their Philadelphia affiliate, WCAU, for the use of their sound truck. Dr. Leon Levy, a former dentist, who was Paley's brother-in-law, owned WCAU. The husband of Paley's sister didn't rush forth immediately with the mobile broadcasting unit. He wanted to deal—something for something. Levy demanded that the arrangement include a WCAU newsman named Boake Carter, a slight, thick-browed man who was an Englishman and who would not become a U.S. citizen until the following year. Carter contended that he had been born in Baku, South Russia, where his father was in the British consular service. Boake had enlisted in the Royal Air Force at the age of fifteen. He had come to the U.S. in 1924 to seek his fortune in oil, but he ended up doing newspaper work in Philadelphia. In 1930, he was working for the Philadelphia *Daily News*. WCAU needed a man to broadcast a rugby match, and Carter was qualified to handle the event. The radio station then engaged him to simulate "live" coverage of an Oxford-Cambridge boat race. He had been a member of a rowing team in

England. During the boat race, he spoke from the radio studio, using newspaper accounts of the real contest and crowd noise effects. It created the image that he was reporting from the bank of the Thames River.

In 1931, Carter began announcing two five-minute newscasts daily for WCAU, broadcasting from the newspaper office. His real first name was Harold, but he changed it to Boake for radio. When Paley requested the use of WCAU's sound truck for the kidnapping coverage, Levy demanded that Carter be permitted to do the reporting. Paley consented. Don Higgins and Herb Glover had been the first to report the event for CBS. Later, Carter and Douglas Gilbert, a reporter for the New York *World Telegram*, took their turn. The CBS coverage was sponsored by Philco. Paley was not impressed by Carter's methods and ordered that he be taken off the air. Listener response supporting Carter forced his return to the broadcasts. (He claimed that he was half Irish, and this was responsible for the superstition that caused him to broadcast with the mike at the left side of his face.) In July 1932, Boake Carter left the newspaper and became a full time newsman for WCAU.

Five-foot, six-and-a-half inch Lester Kroll's first marriage had failed. The court was liberal to his ex-wife in the divorce settlement. At first, she was awarded more than he made each week as a cab driver. Later, the amount was reduced, but he still fell behind in his payments and was sent to jail a couple of times. Kroll investigated what he considered to be the inequities of divorce laws in the United States. As to his education, he claimed to have three university degrees, although he refused to name the schools. Actually, he didn't finish high school. Also, he pretended that he had studied with Freud in Europe. In 1927, Kroll, who would later be known as John J. Anthony, started the Marital Relations Institute in New York City, charging five dollars for each visit. In 1932, it was suggested that he give talks on the subject over the radio. He went to a station and was offered an audition. He started to talk, but no words would come out. The microphone caused a psychological speech block. Next he went to WMRJ, Long Island and was considerably more effective. He spoke on the air for fifteen minutes and was told to keep talking. At the thirty-minute point, he again was given the go-ahead. He continued for an hour. This experience led to a series entitled *Talks by John J. Anthony*—"dedicated to helping the sufferers from an antiquated and outmoded marital relations code."

100

Ronald W. Reagan participated in drama and football at Eureka College in Illinois. After graduation in 1932, he selected the job of a radio announcer as his career goal. He really wanted to be an actor, but he thought radio was a more realistic pursuit. Chicago was a hundred miles from his hometown. His attempt to crash the radio bigtime with no experience soon proved to be futile. A lady assistant at NBC, Chicago recommended that he try smaller markets. After hitchhiking back home, he borrowed the family car and drove to WOC (World of Chiropractic), Davenport, Iowa, a station owned by Colonel B. J. Palmer. Learning from the program director that an announcer had just recently been hired from ninety-four applicants, Reagan turned to leave, remarking that he really wanted to be a sports announcer. The interviewer called him back and placed him in a studio with the instruction to ad lib a make-believe football game. His effort was impressive, and he was hired to broadcast a University of Iowa football game. The compensation was five dollars. His work was effective enough for him to be retained for the three remaining games of the season with a raise to ten dollars per game. After the football job was finished, he was told that WOC might be able to use him again.

Gabriel Heatter grew up on Manhattan's lower east side and went to work for the New York *American* in 1906 at the age of sixteen, the year the paper's owner, William Randolph Hearst, ran for governor. Young Gabriel worked as a boy orator on behalf of Hearst, often being on the receiving end of a barrage of eggs and tomatoes. Once in awhile he was punched in the nose while expounding on the political virtues of his boss. By 1932, Heatter was an established newspaperman. That year he accepted a challenge to debate Norman Thomas on the subject of Socialism. Thomas was a perennial candidate for president for the Socialist party. The ideas which Heatter stressed during the debate impressed an official of WMCA, New York, and he signed Heatter as a radio news commentator at $35 per week.

By 1932, at the age of thirty-two, Harry W. Flannery had achieved an extensive background in journalism, including a degree from Notre Dame. He was editor of the *Hoosier Observer*, a paper which was published in Fort Wayne, Indiana. Flannery began doing a series of news commentaries each week on WOWO as a sideline, but his radio journalistic efforts wouldn't remain a secondary endeavor for long.

Both CBS and NBC gave extensive coverage to the Republican and Democratic Conventions held in Chicago

Stadium in June. NBC used David Lawrence, William Hand, Floyd Gibbons, Wallace Butterworth, Charles Lyon, and Graham McNamee. Gibbons had covered the "Bonus Army" event in Washington after returning from Manchuria. The delegates and politicians at the conventions were not accustomed to being on radio, and it was a chore for the reporters, who had to work diligently to make the proceedings interesting to the listening audience. Interviews and other special features were developed. Lapel mikes were used by the broadcasters. Competition between the two networks was fierce. Both tried to be the first to broadcast new trends in the selection process. Wallace Butterworth went to the airport during the Democratic Convention and met Franklin D. Roosevelt when his plane from Albany landed. NBC officials considered this to be a scoop for their chain.

Radio personnel enjoyed an experiment which was not extended to the convention floor. The Frigidaire Corporation equipped the improvised studios with air conditioning to demonstrate its quietness and to show that the equipment would not affect microphones.

Edwin C. Hill got a late start in radio; but with his effectiveness on the air, he made up for lost time. He was forty-eight and had been a top reporter for twenty-two years when he went on CBS five times weekly in 1932 with talks on current events. He called his program *The Human Side of the News.*

WJSV became a Washington station in October 1932 and joined CBS. The studios were in Alexandria, Virginia, and the business office was across the Potomac River in the nation's capital. Robert Trout was then a news reporter for the station and soon became the announcer who introduced the President each time he appeared on CBS.

Arthur Godfrey was able to return to work in January 1932 after convalescing from his auto accident, but he worked the afternoon shift instead of the morning trick until he felt better. He began putting into effect the ideas he had formulated while lying in the hospital bed listening to the radio. Godfrey began to develop and apply his very informal mike style. This was especially a departure from tradition in the handling of commercials. On one show, copy material on lingerie intended only for newspaper advertisements was given to him. Its revealing terminology about lace undies caused the redhead to blush. He, in turn, criticized the copy; but the next day, the sponsor enjoyed a brisk business with the garments. Godfrey had decided that radio was nothing but door-to-door selling. "They don't care what you say as long as it sells."

When Lyle Van finished prep school in Baltimore, he wanted to get a job and make money as fast as possible. He went to Key West, Florida, and not only failed to make money during the land boom, he lost what he already had. Van was able to get a job as a deputy marshal. His duties were the apprehension of bootleggers. It was necessary for him to make trips to the Federal Penitentiary at Atlanta. In the Georgia city, he met someone in radio, and this acquaintance led to a singing job on WSB. He had previously sung as a soloist in the boys' choir of Old St. Paul's Episcopal Church in Baltimore. Later Lyle opened a retail shop in Atlanta; and when it proved to be unsuccessful, he obtained the position of program director for WGST, Atlanta. A year later, he journeyed to New York for an NBC announcer audition. Lyle Van was placed on the network staff in August 1932.

As a young man, Fred Shawn compiled quite a show business record. He began his career as an entertainer at the age of nineteen while he was a student at Pomona College in Claremont, California, in 1925. His college quartette gained so much recognition, it was given a vaudeville contract in 1927. They traveled until the summer of 1929. At that time, they went to Hollywood and appeared in motion pictures. The group later went to New York and sang in various Broadway productions. After the quartette broke up, Shawn joined the *Ziegfeld Follies*. While performing in Cincinnati, he landed a job with WLW as an announcer and soloist. In December 1932, he went with NBC in Washington.

Radio announcing was a means for Dresser Dahlstead to go to college. A station in Ogden, Utah, gave him a job, which enabled him to work his way through the University of Utah. He began working in radio in San Francisco in 1931 and became a member of the NBC announcing staff there the following year.

Down in Houston, Parks Johnson and Jerry Belcher stood in front of the Rice Hotel and conducted *Sidewalk Interviews* on KTRH radio. Their first questions pertained to the upcoming presidential election between the incumbent Herbert Hoover and Franklin D. Roosevelt. Johnson reasoned that everybody had a story to tell; and he thought if handled the right way, the average man was more interesting than a celebrity. The show would later emerge as a popular network feature called *Vox Pop* (the voice of the people).

103

Although Norman Brokenshire's radio career had fallen on some rough times because of his desire for the contents of the bottle, he made his first of several comebacks in 1932. He was chosen "King of the Announcers" in a New York *Mirror* radio personality poll. Broke was selected to announce the CBS show *Music That Satisfies*, sponsored by Chesterfield. Featured on the program were the Boswell Sisters, Ruth Etting, and Arthur Tracy ("The Street Singer"). On another show, Brokenshire was billed as *Society's Playboy*, which was sponsored by Society Brand Clothes.

Graham McNamee was the first announcer on Ed Wynn's show, *The Fire Chief*, sponsored by Texaco. He would serve as straight man for the zany comedian for three years. Graham also enjoyed one of his greatest baseball thrills that year, the World Series baseball game in which Babe Ruth allegedly called a homerun shot.

Lowell Thomas began a thirteen-year sponsorship association with the Sun Oil Company in 1932.

David Ross started his Sunday afternoon CBS feature *Poet's Gold*. David also won the year's diction award given by the American Academy of Arts and Letters.

Vincent Pelletier was the announcer for the *Carnation Contented Hour* that was first heard on NBC.

Ford Bond drew the assignment for another new musical program that made its entry on the air over NBC, *The Manhattan Merry-Go-Round*. Roger Krupp would eventually succeed Bond.

A science-fiction drama penetrated the airwaves beginning November 7, *Buck Rogers in the Twenty-Fifth Century*. Fred Uttal, Paul Douglas, and Jack Johnstone would serve as the program's announcers during its tenure.

M. Sayle Taylor had broadcast over various small stations around the country since 1926, conducting his human relations lectures. In 1932, he started his feature *The Voice of Experience* on WOR, and nine months later it was picked up by CBS.

The illustrious radio career of funny man Jack Benny began on NBC Blue May 2, 1932. George Hicks, Paul Douglas, and Alois Havrilla would share the announcing duties for a couple of years before Don Wilson would take over as the permanent spieler.

Fred Allen, who would later contrive a phony radio feud with Jack Benny, made his radio premiere with the *Linit Bath*

Club Revue on CBS October 23, 1932. Kenneth Roberts was his first announcer. Next in line would be Jimmy Wallington, Harry von Zell, and Kenny Delmar.

Oriental detective *Charlie Chan* began solving mysteries on the Blue Network with Dorian St. George as the announcer.

Carlton E. Morse's *One Man's Family* was first heard over NBC stations in San Francisco, Seattle, and Los Angeles beginning April 29, and a few weeks later it went to the entire NBC Western chain. The following year it became a full network feature. The announcer lineup through the years included William Andrews, Ken Carpenter, and Frank Barton.

Don McNeill decided he had been a professor at Coo-Coo College in San Francisco long enough, so he headed for New York to seek his radio fortune. Nothing was open for him there. Next he went to Chicago.

New York announcer Kenneth Ellis, known as the "Globetrotter," sold a radio script, "The Trial of Vivienne Ware," to 20th Century for twenty-thousand dollars.

The 1932 I'm-Moving-on-Department: John S. Daggett from KHJ to KGFJ, Los Angeles as program director; Harold Isbell from KGFJ to KNX, Hollywood as chief announcer; Tom Shirley, assistant to movie director Cecil B. DeMille in Hollywood for nine years, to WBBM, Chicago as announcer-actor; Roger Krupp from KFI, Los Angeles to KTAB, Oakland and NBC, San Francisco; Bill Goodwin from KFRC, San Francisco to KHJ, Los Angeles; Bob Brown from WLW, Cincinnati to NBC, Chicago. Rush Hughes from KORE, Eugene to NBC, San Francisco; Ed Laux (France's brother),formerly of KVOO, Tulsa and KRLD, Dallas, to WAAM, Newark as baseball announcer; Jeff Sparks from NBC, New York to WLW; Tom Breneman, formerly at NBC, New York with the name Tom Brennie, appointed studio manager for KFAC, Los Angeles and KFVD, Culver City; Truman Bradley from KMTR, Los Angeles to WBBM, Chicago; Richard "Dick" Wells from WOC, Davenport to WBBM; Bob Hall from KOIL, Council Bluffs to WOR; Jack Douglas (the "Old Nightwatchman") from WJR, Detroit to WLW; Frank Nelson from KFAC, Los Angeles to KMTR.

Other announcer placements: Peter Grant (real name Melvin Maginn) obtained a law degree and joined WLW as an announcer; Bob Prince to WGAR, Cleveland; Jack Brinkley joined the Yankee Network; Douglas Edwards went to work for

WHET, Troy, Alabama; Larry Elliot was employed by WJSV, Washington.

Announcer activities: Nelson Case was given a fifteen-minute song program on KGO, San Francisco. Hal Totten, WMAQ, Bob Elson, WGN, and Pat Flannagan, WBBM covered the baseball spring training camps of the Chicago Cubs and White Sox. Ted Husing had an appendicitis operation. Hal O'Halloran, WLS, Chicago, was inducted into the Ojibway Tribe of Indians in a ceremony at the *National Barn Dance* show at the Eighth Street Theatre and was dubbed "Ba-Zwa-Wa-Ge-Lhig" or "Echoing Skies" (appropriate for a radio announcer). Charles Francis "Socker" Coe, who had been a Navy boxing champion and who had entered radio the year before with a series on NBC about criminal gangs, was praised in an editorial for his announcing of the Sharkey-Schmeling prizefight. Stanley Bell, who had been the CBS presidential announcer at WMAL, elected to stay with the station after it relinquished its CBS affiliation. George T. Case of WCKY, Covington, was voted the most popular announcer among the five Greater Cincinnati area stations. Ted Malone was doing *Between the Bookends* at KMBC, Kansas City. Leo Fitzpatrick, formerly the "Merry Old Chief" and then general manager and part owner of WJR, Detroit, returned to the mike to help broadcast election returns. Pioneer Atlanta announcer Lambdin Kay was one of the two or three oldest-in-experience announcers still on the air. Future network announcer Bill Bivens was the chief announcer at WFBC, Greenville, South Carolina.

Early in Harry von Zell's New York announcing career, he gave a WABC stationbreak every half-hour late at night between dance remote programs. One night a friend came to the studio to play blackjack with him during the inactive 29 1/2-minute periods. Once Harry forgot to close the mike switch after a break, and the listening audience was kept informed of the progress of the card game to the accompaniment of dance music.

WOR decided to stop announcers from using their name on the air. Management thought that it was unimportant for the listeners to know who was speaking. The listeners didn't agree. Because of unfavorable response to the ruling, beginning in September 1932 the mikemen were again permitted to identify themselves.

The new velocity microphone was introduced by RCA that year. It utilized a sensitive ribbon on duralumin instead of a diaphragm. The ribbon, two ten-thousandths of an inch thick, vibrated exactly with the very small variations of the air particles set in motion by sound waves. It was very directional and gave increased fidelity. The mike picked up from both front and back, enabling twice as many artists to position themselves around it. The new type was a great improvement over previous types. The early carbon microphones were unreliable and had poor quality. Even after they were improved, they had high background noise and were susceptible to blasting. With the new velocity microphone, announcers would enjoy better vocal quality.

The broadcasting industry was twelve years old, and radio men had formed some definite ideas about commercial effectiveness. Bill Hay was sales manager for WMAQ, Chicago, in addition to his duties as announcer for *Amos 'n' Andy*. He made a speech to the Milwaukee Advertising Club, giving four rules for success in commercial radio broadcasting: "An advertiser must be fortunate enough to get a good program; wise enough to buy a good station; shrewd enough to get a good hour; and smart enough to get an announcer who doesn't think he is a prima donna entertainer but who is alive to the fact that he must be a salesman."

Norman Brokenshire wrote in *Advertising and Selling*: "To sell a commodity over the air, more than mere reading of words by a man with a pleasant voice is necessary. Those words must come from somewhere deeper than the speaker's larynx. They must be felt as well as spoken."

It was also said during that period: "It is not the power of the voice which brings the hogs to the hog caller, but rather the appeal in his voice."

Poetry corner:

> I introduced the Duchess of Dundee
> Over the facilities of WABC,
> Her organs internal
> Made noises infernal
> And everyone thought it was me.

Journalism was Walter Cronkite's major interest in high school in Houston. After graduating in 1933, the St. Joseph, Missouri, native (born in 1916) entered the University of Texas at Austin, where he worked as a campus correspondent for the Houston *Post* and as a sports announcer for a radio station. At the same time, Cronkite was the state capitol reporter for the

Scripps-Howard Bureau, spending part of the day covering the state legislature. His professors were envious of his knowledge of practical politics while they were teaching only theory.

Arthur Gordon Linkletter's early life was extremely varied. He was born at Moose Jaw, Saskatchewan, in 1912, and his real name was Arthur Gordon Kelley. At the age of one month, he was adopted by the Linkletter Family, who moved him to Los Angeles when he was three. The father became an itinerant evangelist, holding street corner revivals in San Diego, which Arthur attended as a youngster. After high school graduation, he hit the road and traveled the nation hitchhiking and riding on freight trains. His jobs were many: a busboy in Chicago, a stevedore in New Orleans, a meat packer in Minneapolis, and a coupon clerk in New York. While in New York, Linkletter signed aboard a ship bound for Buenos Aires. At the age of nineteen, he enrolled at San Diego State College and worked at various jobs while going to school. In 1933, during his junior year, Art obtained an announcing job at KGB, San Diego. A college friend later said of him, "He was the long playing record of his day. You could get him started with a needle."

Chester "Chet"Huntley was born in Montana in 1911. He lived on a ranch near the Canadian border during his early years. His skill as a debater and his academic standing in high school won him a scholarship to Montana State College in 1929. After three years, another scholarship which resulted from his participation in national oratory contests took him to the Cornish School of Arts in Seattle. While still in college in 1933, he applied for a job at KPCB, Seattle. His timing was good. The station's program director was in the process of being fired. Chet was given the job and soon he was also working as an announcer, writer, and janitor.

An earthquake hit the Long Beach, California, area at 5:50 P.M. on March 10, 1933. KFOX was knocked off the air, receiving considerable damage. Announcer Ted Bliss was on his way to work when the tremor hit. As he approached the station, he saw bricks from the building lying on the street. Ted made his way up the stairs among rubble to the second-floor offices. Chairs, desks, record albums, and other equipment had gone awry. He could find no one at the station. Outside again, he discovered Jack Strock, who had been the announcer on duty when the quake occurred. The town's other station, KGER, was still on the air, and Bliss' main concern was to try to do something to get the station back on the air; thereby, protecting their jobs.

Finally, the chief engineer made his way to the station, and the three pitched in to try to restore some order. In the transmitter room, the engineer began cleaning plaster and dust from the wet batteries. After the station resumed broadcasting, Ted Bliss remained at the mike for fifty-two hours before getting any sleep. An announcer from another station came by and took over while he slept. He was awakened with the message that Elsie Janis, a popular singer and mimic of World War I fame who would later be an NBC announcer, had been listening to him and wanted to meet him.

Down at Georgia Tech in 1933, Charlie Smithgall received his degree and applied at WGST, Atlanta for an announcing job. The previous year, he had handled the school orchestra's dinner hour broadcast over the same station. Charlie was offered the early morning shift with the only compensation being three meals a day from a local restaurant sponsor. Charlie accepted and set out immediately to make himself worth more than just his daily bread. He made a trip to Washington and visited Arthur Godfrey, who had become established as a master morning man. Smithgall returned South and started building up his show, *Morning Sundial*, with "Old Man Smithgalls' son Charlie." He developed an individual style which included a great personal wit. It was an important milestone in the young man's career when he was placed on the station's regular payroll.

NBC, Chicago was originating a not-very-successful morning show called *The Pepper Pot*. Don McNeill was called upon to take over as MC to try to inject some life into it. Since morning time wasn't important to network executives then, Don was given freedom to handle the variety show anyway he desired. While driving down from Milwaukee, he jotted down some ideas, including a new name for the program. On June 23, 1933, he went on the air with *The Breakfast Club*. It was divided into four quarter-hour segments—"first call to breakfast," "second call to breakfast," etc. McNeill's pay was fifty dollars per week. His light, breezy style would propel the show's popularity through the years, and his paycheck would also grow, eventually reaching a figure in the two-hundred-thousand category. The list of announcers on the show during its long run would include Charles Irving, Don Dowd, Bob Brown, Bob McKee, Fred Kasper, Bob Murphy, Franklyn Ferguson, Louis Roen, and Ken Nordine.

After Ronald Reagan finished the footbal season for WOC, Davenport the previous autumn, he was told he would be called when a regular announcing job opened up. Soon after the first of the year in 1933, the call came. An announcer was leaving, and the job would pay one hundred dollars a month. To a young man who hadn't had a full time job since graduating from college the preceding spring, it seemed like a nice sum. He bought a meal ticket at the Palmer School cafeteria for $3.65, which was good for three meals a day, six days a week. In April, WHO, Des Moines, an NBC station and WOC's sister station, called to inquire whether they had a man who could broadcast track. Reagan said that he could, and he was sent to the larger, more prestigious WHO, which was in the process of installing a fifty thousand watt transmitter, power that was not very common at that time. His pay was upped to seventy-five dollars per week, which was three times what he had been making. Believing that the name Ronald didn't sound in character enough for a sportscaster, he chose to be called "Dutch," his boyhood nickname.

Bert Parks reached the ripe age of eighteen after working two years at WGST, Atlanta, and headed for New York and the bigtime. Stretching the truth about his age ("It's the only lie I've ever told in my life," he later declared), he auditioned for CBS and was hired, holding the distinction of being the youngest network announcer in the nation.

Back in July 1919 before commercial broadcasting, President Woodrow Wilson was aboard the liner *George Washington* returning from the Versailles Peace Conference. He used the ship's wireless to talk to his assistant secretary of the Navy in Washington, a man who would become the first prominent governmental leader to use radio as a major device to help accomplish his goal—Franklin Delano Roosevelt. He was elected president in November 1932 and was making an appearance as the president-elect in Miami in February 1933 when a gunman made an abortive attempt on his life. The mayor of Chicago was killed in the shooting. Fred Mizer of WQAM, Miami was on the scene broadcasting Mr. Roosevelt's reception and speech. He immediately gave an eye witness account and later fed a report to CBS.

After his inauguration in March, the President began using radio to communicate with his electorate. WJSV originated his talks for the CBS stations. Following the chief executive's broadcast announcing the bank holiday, WJSV manager Harry Butcher thought that their introduction had been too formal for the speaker's personal style of delivery. He was aware there was a fireplace in the Diplomatic Reception room where Mr.

Roosevelt spoke. Butcher envisioned people listening to their President as if he were right at their own fireside. "Let's call it a fireside chat," he said to an associate. WJSV's presidential announcer, Bob Trout, was the first to use the term.

In addition to his duties as chief announcer at KFI, Los Angeles, Don Wilson was gaining wide (no pun intended) popularity with his broadcasts of sports events. NBC persuaded him to transfer to the East Coast in 1933 to cover sports for the network.

H.V. Kaltenborn was sent by CBS to cover the London Economic Conference in June 1933. He worked with Cesar Saerchinger, the network's European manager. They did a daily man-on-the-street broadcast in Piccadilly Circus to get the British public's ideas about the conference. The interviews had to be done late at night because of the different time zones. Scotland Yard was opposed to the broadcasts, fearing that a person of questionable character might appear on the program. The two American radio men were able to avoid any such incident.

Brace Beemer, who had started in radio at Indianapolis in 1922, was the chief announcer at WXYX, Detroit when the station originated *The Lone Ranger* program January 30, 1933. After it had been on the air less than four months, Beemer began playing the title role. He left the production after a few months, but he would return, serving as the announcer-narrator and eventually playing the hero again. Others performing the duties of announcer-narrator would include during the two-decade run Harold True, Harold Golder, Charles Woods, Bob Hite, and Fred Foy.

Norman Ross' mother was very strict on him when it came to the matter of diction. He was born in Portland, Oregon, in 1896 and attended the Portland Academy, a prep school. He was graduated from Stanford University in 1917 and joined the Army. Later Ross attended law school at Northwestern University for a year. He had been quite an athlete in college, and he went on a trip around the world as a swimmer, winning medals every place where he competed. Ross was the world's champion swimmer for seven years. He participated in the Olympic Games at Antwerp in 1920. After quitting his athletic activity, he entered the newspaper field and became sports editor for the Chicago *Daily Journal*. WIBO placed a rushed phone call to him to broadcast a World Series game. His effort was acceptable enough for him to be retained by the station. In August 1933, Norman Ross joined NBC, Chicago.

An auto accident led George Watson to try for a career in radio. After completing school in St. Paul and spending two years at the University of Minnesota, he worked as a salesman for eight years. His injury prevented his continuing in that work. In 1929, he applied to KSTP, St. Paul for any kind of job. He was added to their staff as an announcer. His duties also included character acting. Watson joined NBC, Chicago in September 1933.

At KFWB, Los Angeles, Al Jarvis had an idea about the playing of phonograph records on the air. He thought the tunes should sound as though they were being played by live bands from a real ballroom. Jarvis came up with the format for *The World's Largest Make-Believe Ballroom*. His approach to song introductions was strictly personal, giving the effect that he was really on the bandstand with the musicians. His commercials were also informal. Martin Block, who had started in radio at XEFD, Tijuana, Mexico, and who was then working at KMPC, Beverly Hills, often listened to Jarvis' live-like record broadcasts. Block would remember.

There were other new shows in 1933.

Ben Grauer was the announcer for *Circus Days*.

Listeners to *Irene Rich Dramas* would hear announcers Ed Herlihy, Frank Goss, and Marvin Miller during its eleven years.

Ma Perkins began a twenty-seven-year run, beginning December 4, 1933. The serial drama would employ announcers Jack Brinkley, Dick Wells, Marvin Miller, and Dan Donaldson. (Both Miller and Donaldson used the name "Charlie Warren" on the program at various times.)

Another daytime drama, *The Romance of Helen Trent*, was first heard that year. Announcers Don Hancock, Pierre Andre', and Fielden Farrington would cover its eleven years.

Tom Mix, taking its title from the popular western movie star, originated in Chicago. The small fry and other listeners would hear Don Gordon, Les Griffith, and Franklyn Ferguson as the announcers.

Jack Armstrong, "the All-American Boy," was also a product of the Windy City. It would be on the air for eighteen years. Announcers David Owen, Tom Shirley, Truman Bradley, Franklyn MacCormack, and Bob McKee would perform the announcing chores.

Kelvin Keech occupied the announcer slot for *Twenty Thousand Years in Sing Sing*.

112

Jergens Lotion began sponsoring Walter Winchell on *The Jergens Journal* in 1933. It was his announcer, Ben Grauer, who suggested that he include in his closing "with lotions of love." The fast-talking New Yorker continued to make every news story sound as though it were of earth-shaking importance.

The WLS *National Barn Dance* expanded from a local show to an NBC program. Jack Holden was the announcer. That year, Joe Kelly came to WLS from KELL, Battle Creek and assumed the role of the show's MC. Also, Holden and Kelly had a local program on which they were billed as the *Two Lunatics of the Air*.

The 1933 announcer trek: Warren Sweeney from WMAL to WJSV, Washington; Boake Carter from newsman at WCAU, Philadelphia to CBS commentator; Rush Hughes from KFRC, San Francisco to NBC, Los Angeles as a news broadcaster; Ralph Edwards from KFSO, San Francisco to KFRC; Jack Costello from KFJN, Grand Forks, North Dakota, to KSTP, St. Paul; Franklin Wintker from KFOR, Lincoln, Nebraska, to WNBR, Memphis; Roger Krupp from KTAB, Oakland and NBC, San Francisco to KFI, Los Angeles; Franklyn MacCormack from WIL, St. Louis to WBBM, Chicago; Tom Shirley from free lance announcer to WBBM; Don Dowd from WLIT, Philadelphia to WLW, Cincinnati; William Randall from Baltimore to CBS, New York; John McIntire from KMPC, Beverly Hills to KRKD, Los Angeles; Harlow Wilcox from WBBM to CBS, New York; Ed Herlihy, a nephew of Fred Allen, from WHDN, Boston to WEET, Boston.

Other announcer placements: Russ Hodges was elevated to sports announcer at WCKY, Covington. Ken Carpenter was appointed chief announcer at KFI, Los Angeles, succeeding Don Wilson. Robert Trout was given the title of chief announcer at WJSV, Washington. Ken Niles was handed the same title at KHJ, Los Angeles. Garnett Marks joined KMOX, St. Louis.

Ted Husing journeyed to the Bahama Islands to introduce the governor to CBS listeners in the first radio relay from that area over a network.

NBC announcers in New York began talking from Radio City in huge Rockefeller Center beginning November 11 when the network occupied space in the central building.

Tom Breneman was injured in a mishap in his office at KFWD, Los Angeles. A falling curtain rod hit him, and he was found unconscious. The blow sent him to the hospital for several days.

113

Jimmy Wallington, who was playing straight man for Eddie Cantor, was awarded the Gold Medal for good diction in 1933.

Harry van Ost. Jr. (who would later be Henry Morgan), announcer for WMCA, New York, was stationed in the city room of the New York *Daily Mirror* each day from 2:00 P.M. until midnight to observe news copy of current happenings. He went on the air during sustaining programs with news flashes.

Fred Waring and his Pennsylvanians were not the only members of the radio show cast to receive applause during their broadcasts at Carnegie Hall. Announcer David Ross was greeted with thunderous applause following his commercial for Old Gold Cigarettes. The first time it happened, he was so surprised he lost his usual composure and looked with open mouth at the audience of three thousand on the other side of the footlights.

Comedian Ed Wynn attempted to establish a third network in September 1933—The Amalgamated Broadcasting System. Norman Brokenshire was the guest announcer during the opening night ceremonies. The new fourteen-station chain folded only a short time later.

It was not good news from the Federal Radio Commission for announcers around the country who played phonograph records on the air. Each disc had to be identified as an electrical transcription.

Because of financial difficulties, W.K. Henderson was forced to sell KWKH, Shreveport in 1933. His down-to-earth, unorthodox speaking personality would no longer jab from the 850 spot on the dial.

The low state of the economy during the early thirties adversely affected many announcers on local stations around the country. Some stations would prorate the available funds among the staff at the end of the week. Some announcers were on half pay. One method that sometimes helped to relieve the financial bind was the trading of radio advertising for merchandise and services. Franklin Wintker later related his experiences of endeavoring to survive during that period. His story no doubt is representative of many others. Franklin was working for KFOR, Lincoln, Nebraska. Often he was not paid a salary, and commissions (if any) were usually late. As a last resort, he sold "trade accounts" in which the value of the advertising was used in trade. There was no exchange of money. An oil company kept him in gasoline. He and his wife had an apartment over a mortuary and reluctantly moved when the contract expired. The

114

same business approach was used to keep them in groceries. The station was sold, and there was no provision for back salaries.

Franklin Wintker and his wife made their way to Memphis, and he went to work for WNBR. Again he had trade account privileges. A downtown hotel housed them for several months; but since the hotel was under contract to an advertising agency, he had to pay the agency a commission on the value of the trade.

Wintker concluded: "Sometimes we were without a dollar in our pockets, and our first child was on the way. We had no welfare then; so no part of our population thought that the nation owed them a living. We made our own way."

President Roosevelt signed a broadcasting code in December 1933 stipulating a minimum wage of twenty dollars a week for announcers, only half as much as specified for technicians.

As a youngster, Jack Paar stuttered badly. This condition prevented his associating to a great extent with other children, so he read books. One contained the story of Demosthenes, the Greek orator, who also stuttered and who cured his speech difficulty by placing pebbles in his mouth and talking on the seashore. Young Jack Paar decided to try a similar treatment. He took buttons from his mother's sewing basket, hung a sign on the door of his room instructing others to stay out, and practiced speaking and reading aloud. Slowly, he made improvement. At the age of fourteen, he was confronted with another problem, tuberculosis. Spending most of the time in bed for eight months, he became well enough to return to school. In fact, he even went out for wrestling.

One day in 1934, when he was sixteen, Jack was walking down the street in his hometown of Jackson, Michigan, on his way to a movie when he approached a radio announcer doing a man-on-the-street program. Jack stopped and stood at the edge of the small group listening. The announcer worked toward him and asked a question about the Michigan penal system. He launched into a commentary on the subject as though he were an expert on penology. The station received several letters asking about the young man whom they had heard on the program. The station, WIBM, Jackson, hired Paar at three dollars a week to work from 9:00 P.M. till midnight. Soon he was offered a full time job at twelve dollars a week. (Apparently, they hadn't heard of the President's code.) The decision was hard to make.

Jack Paar quit school in the tenth grade and entered radio broadcasting. His station, like many others at that time, "borrowed" news from the local newspaper. One edition carried a story about a Russian diplomat named Meti Nelots who was visiting the town to study its industry. Paar read the story on the air with great enthusiasm. The next day the paper ran another story revealing that the Russian story had been a plant to prove where its radio rival was obtaining its news copy. As a matter of fact, the name of the alleged visiting dignitary was "stolen item" spelled backward.

John B. Kennedy was a newspaperman, foreign correspondent (during World War I), magazine writer and editor. He was the managing editor of *Collier's* in 1934 when he was assigned to take charge of *The Collier Hour*, a dramatic radio program the magazine had started on NBC in 1927. It presented stories from the publication. Kennedy thought he had left his editorial position with the magazine only temporarily; but at the age of forty, he had entered radio to stay. As a news commentator, his voice possessed a definite, authoritative trait that caused listeners to attach importance to what he said.

When World War I started, Miss Elsie Janis was a Broadway comedienne, mimic, and singer. She sang to troops during the conflict and became known as the "Sweetheart of the A.E.F." After radio broadcasting began, she was a guest on many programs. On December 19, 1934, Miss Janis was hired by NBC as its first woman announcer. A special program was presented as a welcome by NBC officials. It included an "audition," an I.Q. test, and some supposedly friendly hazing by NBC male announcers.

A young man named Durward Kirby had applied for an announcer's job at WFBM, Indianapolis, but there were no openings. During the State Fair in 1934, he was given the assignment of broadcasting a remote band pickup from the fairgrounds each afternoon from 3:00 to 3:30. Kirby's signal for airtime was a telephone ring—one ring for a thirty-second standby, and then two rings to go on the air. There was also a Saturday night remote to close the activities. Durward was told to report to the station manager back at the studio after the final broadcast. He cancelled a date and anxiously went to the station. The boss discussed the remotes Kirby had done and then asked how he would like to start to work on a regular basis beginning Monday morning. He couldn't believe he was being offered a full time announcer's job. The manager instructed him in running the early morning show—lead-ins to records, how to give the time and weather, and when to insert commercials in the show. The neophyte announcer thought that 6:30 A.M. Monday would never arrive. It did and would be followed by thousands of other broadcast days for Durward Kirby.

Bill Stern had done local football play-by-play for WHAM, Rochester in the mid-twenties. In 1934, he was the assistant stage manager at Radio City Music Hall in New York, but he still yearned for radio. Because of the proximity of NBC to his job, Bill constantly urged network officials to give him an opportunity. Finally, during the autumn season, he was permitted to handle two minutes of a football game that Graham McNamee covered. Bill did well, and this earned him two more assists with McNamee. His progress was so satisfactory he was told he could do the entire Army-Illinois game himself. As the story goes, he was so elated about the opportunity he told relatives to send telegrams to the network praising his handling of the game. Their messages arrived two days *before* the day of the game. Stern was fired before the broadcast—but not forever.

Mary Margaret McBride had been a well-paid magazine feature writer during the late twenties, but the Depression had forced leading publications to rely on their own staffs for material. By 1934, she was badly in need of a job. She received a call from WOR asking her to audition for a women's program. Miss McBride hadn't listened to radio much and had received the call only because an editor she had known was on the station's staff. At the mike, she talked about a recent interview she had done with Scott Fitzgerald, who had been inebriated at the time. Later she was called back for a second audition. This time she talked about her life on a Missouri farm, a barefooted girl doing chores and riding behind her brother on a horse to attend a one-room school. A job offer from WOR came, but it had conditions. She must pretend that she was a grandmother and talk about the lives of her children and grandchildren. Actually, she was thirty-four and single. Her pay was twenty-five dollars per week. Mary Margaret MacBride chose "Martha Deane" as her radio name. She was given a half-hour during the afternoon each day, a period that had a low listenership. She attempted the grandmother sham for a few days, but it wasn't convincing, especially not to herself. She confessed the deception on the air, admitting that she couldn't keep all the names of the pretended grandchildren straight. She declared that she was a reporter who would like to tell listeners about the places she went and the

117

people she met and asked listeners to write if that was what they wanted.

Mary Margaret McBride began conducting her program in her own way, chatting about real things and using her rural Missouri twangy voice. It wasn't long until she had sponsors "standing in line" to get on the program. Her early announcers included Jeff Sparks, Vincent Connelly, and Dick Willard. One day Connelly began giving her a distressed look while she was on the air. She couldn't imagine what was wrong. Finally, she insisted that he tell her. He complied. She was advertising the cakes of her sponsor's competitor.

A sports announcer who would acquire longevity in the Midwest started his radio career in 1934. Jack Brickhouse became sports editor for WMBD, Peoria.

Up in Boston, a successful stockbroker named Frank Gallop won a bet from a friend by auditioning for an announcer's job. He won the audition and accepted a part time job on the air.

It was a busy and varied year for Arthur Godfrey. NBC's WRC-WMAL station combination decided it could operate without his services, and on January 15 he took his early morning *Sundial* show to CBS's WJSV. Godfrey's manner of seemingly talking directly to each individual listener, plus his unorthodox, informal, often ungrammatical style of handling the English language brought him immediate and tremendous success at his new station. Listeners were invited to send for a "license to listen," and they did—140,000 of them wrote for the certificates. Many listeners hung the "authorizations" over their radio. Godfrey possessed a natural, appealing, earthy vocal quality that came through as genuine. They believed him. His voice would be described in various ways: "a south wind blowing over a meadow full of empty bathtubs;" "a shoebox full of bullfrogs." Fred Allen would call him the "Huck Finn of Radio." Godfrey projected confidence, a self-reliance that almost every guy wished he had himself.

To fill the vacant spot left by Godfrey's departure, NBC announced that they were sending an announcer from New York. Godfrey didn't know what to expect in the way of competition from the man from Big Town. His mental wheels began turning. He approached station manager Harry Butcher with the idea of broadcasting all night (a rarity in those days) prior to the debut of his new competitor. Since WJSV usually signed off at midnight, Godfrey had to go to the transmitter site in a swamp near Alexandria, Virginia, to run the show. He had listeners. One girl called continually from New York expressing her affection for his voice. Walter Winchell, while making his rounds of New York night spots, happened to pick up Godfrey and placed a call at 5:00 A.M. Even more important, Winchell gave him a plug in his nationally syndicated newspaper column. Before daylight, the announcer mentioned that he could use some coffee. About eight thousand listeners drove out with sandwiches and Thermos bottles of coffee. Godfrey received thirty-two show business and other business offers, including a $3,200 certified check from a New York night club.

Since Walter Winchell had helped to bring about this new fame, Godfrey went to seek his advice regarding the offers. He found the famous New Yorker lying in bed being shaved by a barber. The former sailor was impressed. Winchell favored the night club proposal, but Godfrey accepted a CBS network contract. His Washington listeners didn't want to lose him completely, so he arranged to feed his *Sundial* show to WJSV from New York from 7:00 to 8:30 each morning. His network show was called *Manhattan Pee-rade* and was heard each Tuesday and Thursday afternoon. In March, he also began doing commercials on network programs sponsored by Chesterfield Cigarettes because the sponsor felt that the "tobacco belt" quality of his voice would appeal to listeners.

But for Godfrey, the New York setting and network exposure didn't continue long—at least, not until a decade later. Both CBS and Chesterfield released him, and he returned to Washington to search for the humility and the common touch which had been responsible for his original recognition.

Jack Benny was sponsored by Jello beginning in the fall of 1934, and he turned to the world of radio sportscasting for an announcer to pitch the enjoyableness of those "six delicious flavors." Portly Don Wilson became his spieler on the Sunday night show. The burly announcer soon extended his role to that of a participant in the skits as well as being a straight man for the comedian from Waukegan. Don's 220 pounds provided funny material for many quips ("I made Don the biggest man in radio.").

When Harry W. Flannery left newspaper work to devote full time to radio news, he wanted to progress in the medium as quickly as possible. He was a hard worker, transferring the same aggressiveness he had applied to the printed page to the airwaves. Flannery left WOWO, Fort Wayne and joined WJJD-WIND, Gary and Chicago. There he tried his voice at sports but was not satisfied with his efforts, doing what he termed "the worst football broadcast ever made." Thereafter, it was strictly news for him.

Red Barber liked Florida, but he wanted to go higher in radio. During his days off, he would take trips to larger cities looking for a better radio job. In Chicago, he took the NBC audition. They were complimentary but nothing was open. He was invited to appear at WLW, Cincinnati for a tryout. Before he left home, he bought a new outfit of clothes to help boister his confidence and to make an impressive appearance. Thirty announcers from various stations reported to chief announcer Chet Thomas in the cathedral studio. Red won the competition and returned to WRUF, Gainesville to give a two-weeks notice. Before the time for reporting to WLW arrived, he received a telegram cancelling the job. Considering this a breach of professional ethics, Barber wrote Thomas an emphatic letter to this effect. On March 4, 1934, he received another telegram from the chief announcer inquiring whether he would broadcast the Cincinnati Reds baseball games for twenty-five dollars a week. They would not be carried on WLW, but on their 5,000-watt sister station, WASI.

The redhead accepted and headed for the bigger time. He asked for a raise even before the season began and was upped to thirty dollars weekly. His inexperience at major league broadcasting led to his interrupting Chicago Cubs manager Charlie Grimm's clubhouse meeting. He was trying to get an interview. Likable "Jolly Cholly" was understanding. During the first game, station management instructed announcer Peter Grant to sit behind Barber in the event the rookie faltered. Grant soon realized that the new man was capable of handling the play-by-play and left before the game was over. After the baseball season ended, Red did the University of Cincinnati football games.

After accompanying Paul Whiteman to New York, Harry von Zell had enjoyed various CBS assignments, including that of MC and commentator on weekly short wave broadcast reports of Admiral Byrd's expedition to the Antarctic. In 1934, Harry joined the radio production staff of the Young and Rubican Advertising Agency. His duties were many—copy writing, program planning, producing, directing, announcing, and performing. He had developed his knack for comedy and made himself available for humorous portions of shows, often serving as a stooge for the show's star, such stalwarts of the laugh as Will Rogers, Fred Allen, Phil Baker, Stoopnagle and Budd, and Ed Wynn.

If the teaching profession had paid a little better in the San Diego area in 1934, radio might have lost a potentially capable program host. Art Linkletter received his A.B. degree with an "A" average from San Diego State College. A teaching job was offered which paid five dollars a month less than his job at KGB, so he remained with the station.

When Old Gold Cigarettes decided to move the show featuring Ted Fiorito's Orchestra and vocalist Dick Powell from New York to San Francisco, announcer David Ross was unable to go with the show. One hundred forty announcers were auditioned for the spot, and KHJ's young chief announcer, Ken Niles, was chosen. His transfer north to KFRC left an opening on CBS' *California Melodies.* Bill Goodwin of KHJ was given the position of announcer.

Ford Frick left WINS, New York early in the year and became secretary of the National Baseball League. He was succeeded at WINS by sportscaster Clem McCarthy. In May, Frick signed to be the announcer for the Chesterfield series on CBS. That autumn, he was elected as National League President, but he still agreed to do some moonlighting by announcing the Columbia-Brown football game for WOR.

There were various polls to measure the popularity of radio programs and personalities. One was conducted among radio editors of 227 leading newspapers. Ted Husing won handily over Graham McNamee as the best sports announcer. David Ross led Jimmy Wallington and Milton J. Cross as the most competent studio announcer. Edwin C. Hill came in ahead of Lowell Thomas and Boake Carter in the news commentator category.

John Mayo joined NBC in New York in 1934. His early background included military duty in Mexico as a member of the National Guard during the Pancho Villa trouble, having joined the field artillery battery while a student at Brown University. During World War I, Mayo served fourteen months overseas with the Air Corps. Then he worked in oil fields in the Southwest. Next, his employment was with a chemical company in New York. While visiting a studio performance of a radio show, he mentioned to one of the actors that he liked the atmosphere. An audition was arranged, and Mayo began doing local announcing before joining the network.

New York NBC announcers in 1934 in addition to those previously discussed were Clyde Kittell and Charles B. Tramont, Jr. Kittell brought a musical background to radio. Tramont was a medical student who was spending a summer away from his

121

studies when he stopped by a radio station in his native Buffalo, New York. Auditions were being held, and Tramont decided to compete with forty-nine other applicants. He was the winner, and his medical pursuit was abandoned.

Other NBC, Chicago announcers were Jean Paul King and Louis Bernard Roen. King was a graduate of the University of Washington and had worked as an actor in a stock company. He started announcing in San Francisco and later transferred to WLW. Roen had a varied career before becoming an announcer: a student for two years at Lawrence College in Wisconsin, a dance band leader, a railroad telegraph operator, and a street car operator. While running a street car in Milwaukee, he met an old friend who was program director at WTMJ. Roen won an audition as an announcer and a singer. Next he announced for CBS for four months. He also was manager of WEBO, Marquette, Michigan, before going to Chicago.

NBC had several more announcers at San Francisco in addition to those already mentioned. Richard Ellers got his start by taking part in radio plays at KGO. David Elton came from KDYL, Salt Lake City. James Kilgore was on a business trip to Hollywood when a friend suggested that he try for an announcer's job at KFI as a lark. He was on the air that same night. Sid Goodwin began announcing in Portland while doing radio news for a paper. Victor Linfoot was born in London and made his way to Canada and jobs singing in motion pictures. Next it was radio in San Francisco. Jennings Pierce toured the Orient with the University of California Glee Club. He was ready to accept a job with the State Agriculture Department when he was invited to audition at KGO. Robert Waldrop worked in the field of copy writing and program production before becoming an announcer. Milton Wood was a law student, a writer of short stories and plays, a violinist, a clarinet and saxophone player, an orchestra leader, a railroad man, an actor, a bank worker, and a termite exterminator before settling for the microphone.

Announcer transitions in 1934: Don Dowd from WLW to NBC, Chicago; Arch McDonald from WDOD, Chattanooga to WJSV, where he would broadcast the games of the Washington Senators. (He was succeeded at WDOD by Frank Lane.) Otis Devine from WFDW, Rome, Georgia, to WDOD; Ray Winters from WMCA, New York to WOV as program director; Ed Hannan from KLRA, Little Rock and Franklin Wintker from WNBR, Memphis to WREC, Memphis; Don Lowe from WRC, Washington, Nelson Case from NBC, San Francisco, and George Ansbro, Jr., who had been a member of staff of guides and pages at Radio City, to NBC, New York; Jack Brinkley, formerly of NBC, from WTIC, Hartford to WINS, New York; Pat Buttram, hillbilly announcer, from WSGM, Birmingham to WLS, Chicago; Del Sharbutt, who had been an announcer for several Southwest stations, to CBS, New York; Hal Moore from WQAM, Miami to CBS, New York; Harlow Wilcox to NBC, Chicago; Roger Krupp, formerly with the Post Broadcasting System in Hawaii and more recently assistant art director for J. Walter Thompson Agency in New York, to WNEW, New York; Garnett Marks from KMOX, St. Louis to KFWB, Hollywood; John McIntire from chief announcer at KMPC, Beverly Hills to free lance status; Ted Bliss from KFOX, Long Beach to free lance; A.L. Alexander resigned from WMCA, New York.

A high school boy in Tulsa named Paul Harvey caught on with KVOO. When he gave the local stationbreak after each network show, he imitated the announcer he had just heard. Someday he would have his own individual announcing style.

Murray Arnold, who had been with WIP, Philadelphia since 1930, was selected as the city's most popular announcer.

House Jameson, a former actor with the Theatre Guild and formerly on the stage in Australia, was chief announcer and dramatic director at WEVD, New York.

Bill Hay took on another duty in addition to announcing for *Amos 'n' Andy* and working as sales manager for WMAZ. He also did the announcing for *The Goldbergs*.

KYW moved from Chicago to Philadelphia during 1934, and Halloween Martin moved her *Musical Clock* show to WBBM. She continued waking Chicagoans in a pleasant manner.

Ty Tyson was busy at WWJ, Detroit. He obtained the first sponsorship for baseball and football games in Michigan. He broadcast the Detroit Tiger baseball games. The club won the American League pennant that year. Then he took part in the World Series coverage for NBC, reporting the St. Louis Cardinals' championship in the seven-game event. Other radio sports activity for Tyson included University of Michigan football games, boxing, and power boat racing.

KMOX, St. Louis announcer Marvin Miller came out of an auto accident with a fractured knee.

Los Angeles announcer Edwin Woolverton was killed in the KHJ studios when he tried to prevent a forty-seven-year-old Montana rancher from stabbing the station receptionist.

Edmund Lytton, chief announcer for KTMR, Los Angeles, died in March 1934.

When Lowell Thomas reported that President Roosevelt went fishing but caught no fish, the chief executive's son Jack jokingly termed the statement "gross libel." In the spirit of the exchange, Thomas retracted his announcement during the next broadcast and said that the President had caught a twenty-ton Moby Dick.

When announcers at WSB, Atlanta reported for duty each day, they had to read correctly before going on the air these two lines:

> She—Are you copper-plating those pipes?
> He—No, I'm aluminuming 'em, mum.

Announcers' voices at WLW, Cincinnati received added amplification beginning May 2, 1934. The station boosted its power from 50,000 to 500,000 watts on an experimental basis.

Four stations, WOR, New York; WGN, Chicago; WLW, Cincinnati; and WXYZ, Detroit, joined together in September 1934 to form the Quality Group. It served as an outlet for *The Lone Ranger* and *Lum 'n' Abner*. The following month, the group's name was changed to the Mutual Broadcasting System.

Another chain was started in 1934. The American Broadcasting System (not to be confused with the later American Broadcasting Company) began operations in October from its headquarters at WMCA, New York. Rules for network announcers were posted:

> Don't smoke in the studio.
> Don't worry.
> Don't change your natural style.
> Don't fail to rehearse your show.
> Don't touch the microphone.
> Don't drink liquor, beer, milk, or soft drinks before going on the air.
> Don't eat ice cream or a heavy meal within an hour of your broadcast.
> Don't go on the air if you don't live up to these don'ts.

Among the new shows to debut in 1934 was *Major Bowes' Original Amateur Hour*. It began on WHN, New York but would move to NBC the following year. Many announcers would find work with the show during its lengthy tenure: Graham

124

McNamee, Phil Carlin, Norman Brokenshire, Jimmy Wallington, Ralph Edwards, Dan Seymour, Tony Marvin, Warren Sweeney, and Don Hancock.

Hollywood Hotel debuted on CBS with Dick Powell as the MC and Ken Niles doing the announcing.

Jimmy Fiddler moved his Hollywood gossip program from West Coast coverage to the full NBC network.

The Kraft Music Hall had premiered the previous year with Don Wilson serving as the announcer. Roger Krupp followed him in 1934. A couple of years later, Ken Carpenter would become a fixture at the show's mike.

Many broadcasters have had difficulty obtaining permission to do live, play-by-play coverage of sports events. In 1934, KGHI, Little Rock was unable to get rights to broadcast the Traveler baseball games of the Southern Association. That was before lighted parks and night games. The station's owner rented a vacant lot beyond the centerfield fence. Sports announcer Waymond Ramsey and color man Leon Sipes climbed a sturdy oak tree, which was about five hundred feet from home plate. Two boards were laid between limbs to serve as a table. A remote line was hooked to a telephone in a nearby house. Before each game, the announcers would buy tickets; but instead of entering the park, they would shinny up the bark. There were also "guests" in the tree-top studio who couldn't raise the price of a Depression-era ticket. Occasionally, during the broadcasts, listeners would hear something like, "Blankety blank! Look at that such-and-such run!" Profane fans were sometimes asked to leave the "studio." Sportscaster Ramsey often became so excited on a crucial play that he was in danger of falling out of the tree. The club didn't know whether to get an injunction or an axe. After a few weeks, legalities were instituted and the broadcasts ceased.

V

Voice Quality and Personality

*The chameleon, who is said to feed upon
nothing but air, has of all animals
the nimblest tongue.*
—Jonathon Swift

Mel Allen (real name Melvin Allen Israel) was born in Johns, Alabama (population 1,404), in 1913. He was the son of a store-keeper. During the summer of 1921, Mel visited relatives in Detroit and got a selling job at Tiger baseball games dispensing soda pop. It was his first association with major league baseball, but it wouldn't be his last. The following year, he lived in Greensboro, North Carolina, a town that had a baseball club in the Piedmont League. Mel served as the team's batboy. In 1932, he received a B.A. degree from the University of Alabama. Then he entered the University's School of Law. During the football season of 1935, Allen handled the public address system, announcing to the crowd which player carried, who tackled, players who came into the game and those who went to the bench, and other details of the contest. This experience led to a sports announcing job with a Birmingham radio station while he was pursuing his degree in law.

Thomas Garrison Morfit, III, (later to be known as Garry Moore) wanted to be a writer. During his senior year in high school in Baltimore (where he had been born in 1915), he joined an amateur theatrical group, the Vagabonds, to write sketches for a musical production. The songs for the presentation were contributed by Zelda Fitzgerald, wife of F. Scott Fitzgerald. Garry's father was a staid lawyer, and he was horrified by his son's stage activity. After finishing high school, Morfit sold merchandise and continued to write, turning out radio scripts. Novelist Fitzgerald liked his writing, and they worked together

126

on some one-act plays, which didn't sell. Fitzgerald helped him get a job as a continuity writer at WBAL, Baltimore. (After his appearance in some radio plays, the station manager told him, "Your scripts are good, but you're a lousy actor."). Soon it was the old story of the regular performer not showing up and the rookie taking his place. When a radio comedian didn't appear, Morfit went on the air instead. Listeners thought his jokes were funny, and the station manager assigned him to the show on a regular basis.

Martin Block started working at WNEW, New York in 1935 for twenty-five dollars a week. When Bruno Hauptmann went on trial in Flemington, New Jersey, for the Lindbergh baby kidnapping, Martin wanted to devise something interesting to put on the air while waiting for trial bulletins. He remembered Al Jarvis' *Make-Believe Ballroom* in Los Angeles. He knew that the West Coast announcer didn't have a copyright on the title and format. WNEW had no phonograph records. On February 3, Block, then thirty-four years old, went to a record shop and purchased a few discs. He then started his own *Make-Believe Ballroom*, pretending to switch from one stage to another. He followed the FCC requirement of announcing the songs as records, but he did it so slyly and cleverly that most listeners didn't notice. The program remained sustaining until May. At that time, he arranged to advertise a reducing pill called Retardo, which sold by mail for one dollar a box. "Now I'm not saying your husband doesn't love you, but when you look in the mirror, are you being fair to him?" The next morning's mail brought six hundred orders. Thereafter, Martin Block wouldn't suffer from a shortage of sponsors.

In 1908, a third son was born to the Murrow Family at Polecat, North Carolina. The boy was named Egbert Roscoe. When he was five, the family left their farm and rode the train to Blanchard, Washington, on Puget Sound, where they eventually settled. At first, the Murrows lived in a tent beside some kinfolks' home. The father became an engineer on a logging company train. (Later during his adult years when someone would ask how he was doing, Egbert would reply, "I'm still on the track and still on the payroll.") Egbert was president of his high school senior class and was a champion debater. By the time he entered Washington State College in 1926, he was having people call him "Ed." He washed dishes in a sorority house the first year but advanced to the position of waiter as a sophomore. Speech was his principal academic interest. The college offered what was credited with being the first course in radio broadcasting. It had put campus station KWSC on the air in 1922. Ed reportedly did a few sportscasts for the station. He also played roles in college plays.

During Ed Murrow's senior year, the stock market crashed. In June 1930, he went to New York and took a job as president of the National Student Federation of America for twenty-five dollars per week. He arranged for economic tours to Europe for college students. Murrow was able to take an overseas trip himself by doing some work aboard ship. Back in the U.S., He made speeches at colleges about education and attempted to raise money for student interests. Radio was also utilized. He and a friend helped CBS obtain speakers for the *University of the Air* program. He made other trips to Europe, where he often filled speaking engagements. In 1932, Murrow became an assistant to the director of the Institute of International Education, helping to arrange for student exchange programs between countries.

In 1935, CBS created a new position, director of talks. The job was first offered to Raymond Gram Swing, an American newspaper correspondent who had some experience as a radio commentator in England. When Swing learned that he would not be on the air himself, he refused the offer. In September, Ed Murrow was given the job. He was in radio, if only behind the scenes.

A young man blew into Grand Junction, Colorado, as master of ceremonies of an endurance-testing, desperation activity of the Depression era, the "walkathon." Bill Baldwin was a native of Pueblo, Colorado. He had a good voice, and serving as a spieler for the tired walkers was not really his ultimate goal. Bill wanted to be a radio announcer. KFXJ, Grand Junction gave him the opportunity. Bill made the most of it, gaining local popularity in preparation for moving on to bigger markets.

One night at about 10:45 in the early summer of 1935, the chief engineer at KTHS, Hot Springs entered the station and went directly to the control room. "Why are we carrying NBC instead of the local dance band remote?" he asked the control board operator.

"We're not carrying NBC."

"Who's that announcer?" inquired the chief.

"Harry Jackson," the operator answered.

Jackson was a local young man who had been attending the University of Illinois at Champaign-Urbana. He had done part time announcing at WILL, Urbana and had asked to do the band remote at KTHS while on summer vacation. He would become an established, longtime network newscaster as Allan Jackson.

Howard Duff was born in Bremerton, Washington, in 1917. He gained experience as an actor at the Repertory Playhouse in Seattle. In 1935, Duff entered radio with KOMO, Seattle.

Webley Edwards was born in Corvallis, Oregon, in 1902. His father was a college professor who became an industrial chemist. The family moved to California, but Webley returned to Corvallis for his senior year in high school. Then he enrolled at Oregon State College. During his four years, he played football, served as associate editor of the school's paper, and worked as a correspondent for Portland and Seattle newspapers. Edwards also helped to run KOAC, the college radio station, during his last two years. After graduation, he stayed one year as an assistant football coach. In 1925, Webley Edwards began his regular radio career with newscasts over KOAC. Later he handled sports for KGW, Portland. In 1928, Edwards went to Honolulu to play semi-pro football. He also did some radio work on the island. Returning to the mainland in 1934, he broadcast football games for KNX, Los Angeles. It was back to Hawaii in 1935 where he became manager of KGMB. That year he originated the program *Hawaii Calls*, which was relayed to the States:

> That's the sound of the waves on Waikiki Beach. This program is coming from Hawaii! And it welcomes you again to Hawaii. This is Webley Edwards right on the beach at Waikiki beneath the famous Moana banyan tree, beside the blue Pacific Ocean. And look at all the people. Where you all from? (Audience response) Just about every state and province, I guess. Well, let's all get comfortable here at Waikiki. Shoes on, shoes off. It doesn't matter. Gather around because we're going to sing some Hawaiian songs here.

Ben Alexander was a native of Goldfield, Nevada, having been born there in 1911. After working as an actor in motion pictures as a child, he attended the University of California and Stanford University. In 1935, Alexander entered radio as an announcer and MC.

Harry Wismer was born in Port Huron, Michigan, in 1914. His college was Michigan State University. Wismer started as a radio sportscaster in 1935 and later became sports director of WJR, Detroit.

Red Barber and Bob Elson handled Mutual's first World Series broadcast in October 1935. The other two networks also covered the games. Barber's additional assignment that fall was the Ohio State football games.

On the first day of the year in 1935, Harry W. Flannery joined KMOX, the CBS station in St. Louis, as news editor and analyst. He began an early morning newscast that soon became very popular.

Ralph Edwards received a B.A. degree in English at the University of California. He wanted to become an English teacher but discovered there was already an abundance of applicants for such positions. Since he had worked in radio while going to college, he took a job with KFRC, San Francisco.

Robert Trout received a promotion in early 1935. He was transferred from Washington to WABC, the Columbia Broadcasting System's key station in New York.

Bill Stern migrated to the Southwest during the year and broadcast some football games. An automobile accident resulted in the loss of a leg.

Norman Brokenshire caught on with the NBC announcing staff in October, but only as a junior staff announcer. This meant he would work in the booth and handle some sustaining shows. Later he was given a commercial show. When the program went on the road, Broke asked to stay in New York and do the commercials from there, regardless of where the show was originating. He was afraid that if he left town, the temptations for drink would be greater. Permission was given by the network, but the sponsor didn't buy the idea, believing that the complete show should be in one place. Brokenshire went to Cincinnati and began drinking before airtime. He collapsed while trying to read the second commercial. Once again Broke was out of a job.

Harlow Wilcox was selected for a new show in 1935. It would be a long and worthwhile association for him. He was the announcer for *Fibber McGee and Molly*, sponsored by Johnson's Wax. Often Wilcox was so closely associated with the product, he was referred to as "Waxey."

Major Bowes Original Amateur Hour had become a great favorite on New York radio over WHN. (The Major had originated the station slogan "This is WHN, Dial Ten-Ten.") In March 1935, NBC made the show a network feature. That year the Major hired a talent scout who would eventually succeed him. Ted Mack (real name William Edward Maguiness) was born in

Greeley, Colorado, in 1905. He began his entertainment career as a bandleader and MC in vaudeville. Mack joined Ben Pollack's Orchestra in 1926 as a saxophone and clarinet player. A fellow member was Glenn Miller. When Ted left the band the following year, clarinet player Benny Goodman joined the group. Next, Mack worked in Los Angeles for a year, serving as a master of ceremonies in vaudeville. Then he put together his own band and toured the country until he became a part of Major Bowes' radio program. Since the local show had been so popular on WHN, it remained after the network version began. Jay C. Flippen, a native of Little Rock, was chosen to be the New York host. He had principally been a minstrel and vaudeville trooper and a stage actor.

Tom Breneman, who had been in radio since 1925, became the MC of *Feminine Forever* on KFRC, San Francisco.

John Gambling, WOR's morning man, was selected as a special announcer for the *Voice of Experience* on CBS.

The daily serial *Bachelor's Children* began in 1935. Don Gordon and Russ Young would be the program's announcer during its eleven-year run. It emanated from Chicago.

Another soap opera also began in Chicago that year, *Backstage Wife*. The announcer lineup would include Harry Clark, Ford Bond, Sandy Becker, and Roger Krupp.

Kelvin Keech was the announcer for a children's show called *Billy and Betty*. Keech also announced for *Popeye the Sailor*.

Cavalcade of America was first heard in 1935. At one stage of its long run, Clayton "Bud" Collier served as the announcer.

The comic strip detective *Dick Tracy* came to life on the air. Don Gardiner, George Gunn, Dan Seymour, and Ed Herlihy would share the announcing chores.

Walter King was the MC of a show called *The Flying Red Horse Tavern*.

Noted Actress Helen Hayes was the hostess of a drama called *The Helen Hayes Theatre*. George Bryan announced.

Louis Witten was the announcer for spectacular showman Bill Rose's *Jumbo*, which he produced on the radio while it was still playing at the Hippodrome Theatre in New York.

The Story of Mary Marlin was switched from WMAQ, Chicago to NBC on January 1. Announcers would include Truman Bradley, Les Griffith, Nelson Case, and John Tillman.

The weekly popular musical barometer *Your Hit Parade* debuted in 1935. Listeners interested in learning song ratings

131

would hear these announcers through the years: Martin Block, Del Sharbutt, Andre' Baruch, Kenny Delmar, and Basil Ruysdael.

Ed Smith announced a serial drama entitled *We Are Four*.

Bob Hope went on the air with his first regular radio show in January 1935. There would be others. His announcers would include Wendell Niles, Art Baker, Larry Keating, Bill Goodwin, and Hy Averback.

MC's Parks Johnson and Jerry Belcher were invited by NBC to bring their interview show from KTRH, Houston to New York. Belcher was later replaced by Wally Butterworth on *Vox Pop*. Future announcers would include Dick Joy and Roger Krupp.

Stan Shaw was a former psychology instructor and an ex-orchestra leader from Kansas City. In 1935, at the age of twenty-seven, he had a radio show on WNEW, New York. It was called *Milkman's Matinee* and was on the air at a strange time in those days, from 2:00 until 7:00 A.M. The year was an important one for him—he obtained his first sponsor. More followed. During each show, he received from 150 to 250 telegrams. Each wire cost the listener twenty cents.

After CBS transferred Robert Trout to New York, he was in charge of the Press-Radio Bureau for the network. The arrangement had been established the previous year. The news wire services made five minutes of material available to the networks each morning and each night. It could not be sponsored; and at the close of each newscast, listeners were told to see their newspaper for further details.

CBS sent H.V. Kaltenborn to Europe in June to broadcast about world events from England, Germany, and Italy.

Also on the news scene, on May 15 United Press and International News Service began offering news service to radio stations. The clack of the teletype was heard for the first time. Many stations in smaller markets could not afford to join. Transradio, a more economical news service, was available to them. News was sent by short wave Morse code, and individual stations had to employ an operator who could take at least twenty words per minute. At KUOA, Fayetteville, Arkansas, the operator had difficulty receiving figures. Announcer-manager Storm Whaley never knew whether ten or ten thousand Ethiopians had been killed in the latest battle with Italy.

Announcers galore were on the move in 1935. Jack Paar got itchy feet in Jackson, Michigan, and went to WIRE,

Indianapolis. Being seventeen, he soon suffered from homesickness and returned to his first station, but not for long. A crack on the air about the triviality of local news items led to his departure.

Johnny O'Hara, who had worked at four Chicago stations— WCFL, WJJD, WIBO, and WBBM—returned to the first, WCFL.

Herbert Morrison, who had formerly talked at WLBD, Waukegan and XER, Villa Acuna, Mexico, landed at WTMJ, Milwaukee.

Russ Hodges departed WCKY (which was then identified as a Cincinnati station) for WIND, Gary, Indiana.

Douglas Edwards, a future network newscaster, moved from WHET, Troy, Alabama to WAGF, Dothan, Alabama.

Charles Godwin went in an easterly direction from WKY, Oklahoma City to WLW, Cincinnati.

Ray Winters crossed the Hudson from WOV, New York to WOR, Newark.

After eight months in the beer city of St. Louis at KMOX, Don Gordon returned to WTMJ at another beer capital, Milwaukee.

Hugh Conover came up from WIS, Columbia, South Carolina, to WJSV, Washington.

Jack Lescoulie abandoned KFAC, Los Angeles for a stock company in New York.

Lou Crosby went west from KVOR, Colorado Springs to KNX, Hollywood.

Art Linkletter took a leave of absence from KGB, San Diego to work as program director for the California Centennial at San Diego and returned to the station later in the year.

Edward J. Herlihy made the big transition from WEEI, Boston to NBC in Radio City.

Garnett Marks switched from WOR to WMCA, New York.

Bob Murphy caught on with WDAY, Fargo, North Dakota.

Harold Isbell changed from the CBS, Chicago announcing staff to the position of assistant production manager.

Henry Morgan served his time at WCAU, Philadelphia and reported to WEBC, Duluth as chief announcer.

Frank Blair went from WCSC, Anderson, South Carolina, to WIS, Columbia as a Transradio newsman.

Lester Griffith made the big leap from WOOD, Grand Rapids to NBC, New York.

Bill Slater also crashed NBC in the big town.

Robert "Bob" McRaney joined WSGN, Birmingham.

Jack L. Cooper of WSBC, Chicago was believed to be the only Negro commercial announcer in the U.S. in 1935.

Jocko Maxwell, a former high school athlete, was a Negro sports announcer at WHOM, Jersey City.

Other 1935 announcer circumstances: Fourteen applicants auditioned for announcing jobs at new station WHIO, Dayton. It took management officials two weeks to hear all of the voices. Tom Slater, Bill's brother, was among those selected. Stan Lomax was a sports announcer at WOR. Connie Desmond, sports announcer at WSPD, Toledo, was named assistant program director. Ken Carpenter was doing sports at KFI, Los Angeles. Truman Bradley left Chicago to serve as an announcer for the Ford exhibit at the exposition in San Diego. Hilmar Baukhage was a commentator for the NBC-WJZ Network. Phil Carlin was the NBC sustaining program manager. Paul Henning was the movie editor at KMBC, Kansas City and also did celebrity interviews at Union Station.

Radio Stars magazine took over the awarding of the diction prize from the American Academy of Arts and Letters. Jimmy Wallington was given the award in 1935. He had also been the winner in 1933. The nationwide "Star of Stars" contest also selected him as the best announcer of 1935.

The advertising agency of Batten, Barton, Durstine, and Osborn had some different ideas about the awarding of diction prizes to announcers. Agency officials felt that a more natural style of announcing should be considered rather than the formal, impersonal delivery that had been the criterion up to that time. They originated a B.B.D.&O. award in 1935. Mr. Durstine described a good announcer as one who had "sincerity, accurate diction, naturalness, persuasiveness, lack of mannerisms and absence of those curious inflections which belong to an unknown language in a world that doesn't exist." CBS announcer Carlyle Stevens was the first recipient. In explaining their decision, they said, "Stevens has definitely not been a member of the stilted school of broadcasting that has come to be resented alike by the public and the sponsors of broadcast programs."

In 1928, Carlyle Stevens took some short stories and plays to WXYZ, Detroit and tried to sell them to be used as radio dramas. The station didn't buy his material, but they recognized his potential as an announcer. Stevens worked at WXYZ until 1931 when the lure of the big town caused him to set out for New York. He caught on with WLTH, Brooklyn and moved on to WABC and CBS later that year.

It was not a "safety first" year for the announcing profession. When Graham McNamee of NBC, New York and Tom Manning of WTAM, Cleveland were chosen to cover the National Soap Box Derby at Akron August 11, it seemed like a comparatively safe assignment. Not so. Both were badly injured when a driver was unable to control his vehicle and crashed into the NBC remote spot. McNamee was knocked to the pavement, striking his head and remaining unconscious for five minutes. Manning received two broken vertebrae in his back, and his legs were badly bruised. Both remained in a hospital for several weeks.

Accident-prone Arthur Godfrey also wound up in the hospital that year. He was thrown from a horse, breaking his collarbone and several ribs. WJSV sports announcer Arch McDonald wanted to introduce Godfrey to Buck Newsom (later known as "Bobo"), the Washington Senators' pitcher. While Godfrey was laid up in the hospital, Newsom was hit on the knee cap by a batted ball and became a patient in the same hospital. McDonald arranged for radio lines to connect the two rooms, and the radio personality and the athlete conversed over the air.

Gary Breckner served as chief announcer at the San Diego Exposition for programs carried by both CBS and NBC. He used a bicycle to travel from one remote point to another. One day he hit a fire hydrant and badly tore both pants legs. Gary hurried to a nearby nudist colony where repairs were made to his britches. After the exhibition closed, Breckner went to work for KNX, Hollywood (wearing new trousers).

Dean Maddox, announcer and program director for KYA, San Francisco, was driving along a street one night when he saw three men beating a policeman. Throwing on the brakes, he jumped from his car and assisted the officer in arresting them. The radio man received a broken right index finger, but the culprits emerged with an assortment of fractured skulls, cuts, bruises, and black eyes.

Heavy announcer Don Wilson lost a little weight that year. Don had an appendectomy.

Newsman Boake Carter received four kidnap notes demanding five thousand dollars. The final note ordered him to alter his usual program closing with a code phrase signifying he would comply with the money request. Carter planted a package of fake currency at the designated spot. Two federal agents waited, but the would-be kidnappers didn't show.

At WOW, Omaha in August, announcer Russell Baker softly introduced a nostalgic program: "And now Aunt Sally is alone in her garden of memories. It is here she dreams the hours away, in peace and quiet. . .away from all noise and confusion." At that moment, the studio door blew open. Two stock trains below whistled and bumped. Pigs squealed and a cow mooed.

Announcer Kenneth Roberts was the spokesman on a CBS show featuring vocal talent in April 1935. He gave the name of a young woman and the title of her song. Without telling the announcer and having him change the script, she and another female singer had changed places on the program. When Roberts unknowingly introduced the wrong singer, she gave him a dirty look and slapped his face, making a loud noise on the air. He rubbed his face and tried to remain calm as the orchestra began playing.

At WLS, Chicago, James Poole turned on an amplifier in a studio in preparation for the noonday livestock report. The equipment shot forth a flash of fire. Close inspection revealed that a mouse had been electrocuted. The broadcast was quickly transferred to another studio.

Ted Malone was program director at KMBC, Kansas City in 1935, and he also broadcast his poetry program *Between the Bookends* over CBS five times weekly. In March, rhymes weren't the only program material he fed to the network. Ted broadcast a dust storm from Salina, Kansas. Some called it the "dirtiest" broadcast ever made.

While re-creating a Chicago Cubs baseball game on WHO, Des Moines, Ronald "Dutch" Reagan experienced an interruption in telegraphic service in the bottom of the ninth with the score tied. According to Reagan's report, the batter hit foul balls for six and a half minutes until service was restored. Then he learned that the batter had popped out.

Visitors were made to feel very welcome at WBT, Charlotte in 1935. In fact, they often acted as though they were at home, roaming through the studios and going into the control room. Once a portly lady visitor sat on a transcription turntable and broke it. Thereafter, the rules were more stringent. No more visitors were permitted in the control room.

A racehorse was named after Chicago announcer Pierre Andre'. One day it came through as a long shot, and the WGN staff cleaned up.

136

Forrest Rucker, announcer at KFOX, Long Beach, won an oratorical championship at the Kiwanis convention of the California and Nevada district.

Western Electric introduced a new non-directional, dynamic microphone in 1935. It was referred to as the "eight-ball" mike. Some radio people also called it a "billiard ball." At WOR an artist inquired about mike placement before singing into it. A technician replied, "You can sit, stand, or lie down if you want to. It will pick you up all the same."

While Dick Joy (who was born in November 1915) was growing up in Putnam, Connecticut, he DX-ed during cold winter nights, searching for distant stations. His success included a 50-watter in far off Montana. During the early thirties, Dick took Mr. Greeley's advice and went west to Los Angeles, where he became a student at the National School of Broadcasting. In 1934, that which he labeled a "cattle call" went out for students to help with a religious broadcast which was piped down to KFOX, Long Beach. He served as the production's sound effects man. An audition landed Joy a spot on the student staff at the University of Southern California in March 1935. He appeared on hundreds of USC programs, some of which were heard on 50,000-watt KNX, "The Voice of Hollywood." In 1936 while still a student at USC, Dick Joy landed his first staff announcing job—at KEHE in Los Angeles. He continued to attend college classes.

The management up at WTIC, Hartford, Connecticut, hired Bob Steele as a young announcer in 1936. If there were any doubts at the time about his stability and his desire to stay on the job, they were without substantial basis. Bob would still be running the morning show on WTIC more than forty years after his original employment.

Tom Casey was on the staff as a page boy at NBC, Chicago in 1936. The young guides were permitted to put on a show during the broadcast of the network's tenth anniversary celebration. The wheels in New York liked Casey's voice. Everett Mitchell, who was in charge of NBC's Chicago announcing staff, gave him some training in broadcasting technique, and Casey was given a regular announcing job.

Vern Carstensen was born in Clinton, Iowa, in 1914. He entered the University of Iowa in 1933. While still a student in 1936, he started his radio career as an announcer at WSUL, Iowa City.

Gabriel Heatter arrived in Trenton, New Jersey, on April 3, 1936, to cover for WOR and Mutual the execution of Bruno Hauptmann, who had been convicted for the Lindbergh baby kidnapping. Heatter had received a tip that the execution would take place at 8:00 P.M. He arranged for an outside signal to be given from the death house. At 7:50 P.M., he entered the hotel room where the broadcast would be made. As a double-check on the outside signal, a Transradio machine was set up in the room. As the time approached, an aide stationed himself at the window to watch for the signal. At 8:00 Heatter went on the air reading a prepared script. The material was consumed in twelve minutes, but he kept talking, retracing the background of the trial. He received both signals at 8:48. Hauptmann had died thirty seconds before. Heatter concluded with: "Bruno Hauptmann is dead. Goodnight." He had spoken fifteen thousand words. His fame as a network commentator was firmly established.

Walter Cronkite decided to switch from newspaper work to full time radio in 1936. He chose Kansas City, which is near his birthplace of St. Joseph, to seek employment. Cronkite entered the new downtown studios of KCMO and talked to program director Henry Pattee. Walter was hired as the station's news and sports director.

It was a crucial year for Ralph Edwards. In March 1936, he switched stations in San Francisco—from KFSO to KFRC. In July, the lure of the nation's largest city prevailed, and he began hitchhiking to New York. (Ralph later said that he came to New York in several cars.) He found it to be a tough radio market. His existence often consisted of dime meals and a park bench for a bed. Edward's persistence paid off. In November, Del Sharbutt left the announcing staff of CBS, and Ralph was hired to take his place. He was assigned to a show called *The Gumps*, based on the comic strip.

Since Art Linkletter possessed centennial celebration experience, he was appointed as radio program director for the Texas Centennial Exposition at Dallas. Art handled forty-five live talent shows weekly, which were broadcast from ten remote pickup points.

Two pioneer announcers swapped visits that year. George Hay, "The Solemn Old Judge," visited Harold Hough, "The Hired Hand," at WBAP during the Texas Centennial, and a few weeks later Hough showed up on the *Grand Ole Opry* in Nashville.

H.V. Kaltenborn racked up a first by broadcasting from a battlefield while action was in progress. The CBS news commentator was in Europe when the Spanish Civil War was in its early stages. He visited the front lines of both sides and talked with the soldiers. Often he was invited to take a rifle and fire at the opposition, but he refused. On the border between France and Spain, a French farm protruded into the area of the battle for the city of Irun. Shells and bullets darted over the neutral French farm. Kaltenborn thought of the idea of originating a broadcast from that spot, dramatizing the sound of gunfire. A French radio engineer was cooperative, locating a telephone line in an empty farmhouse situated in the line of fire. He extended a long cable from the house to a small haystack. The American radio newsman was aware of the historical significance of such a broadcast. When the technical aspects were completed on September 2, 1936, he eventually was able to send a message to CBS in New York stating that he could send an account of raging battle complete with rifle and artillery fire. He was eager to receive a reply. It came, instructing him to stand by because there were too many commercial programs scheduled at that time.

As Kaltenborn waited, he feared that the forces would change positions. Also, the cable broke two times, either from strain or from being hit by ammunition. Both times the French engineer crawled out and spliced the wire. When the network finally sent the message to begin broadcasting, the relay engineer in Bordeaux was away from his equipment enjoying an appetizer. It was 9:00 P.M., U.S. time, when Kaltenborn got on the air. He talked for a quarter hour, elaborating on the action and the equipment and pausing at intervals to let listeners clearly hear the sounds of fire power and explosions. It would be only a few years until such sounds would be a regular feature of American radio.

Robert Trout was virtually a one-man, on-the-air CBS news staff in 1936. He covered both the Republican and Democratic Conventions, using a microwave transmitter installed in a walking cane and a wrist watch mike and carrying a power amplifier in a leather case strapped to his back. Young, twenty-two-year-old Charles Godwin of WJSV served as the CBS presidential announcer in Washington. Godwin had previously worked at WLW, Cincinnati; WKY, Oklahoma City; and WDSU, New Orleans. Trout went on campaign trips with both Franklin D. Roosevelt and Alfred M. Landon. The President was one of Trout's admirers, sometimes playing a waiting game with him to observe how long the newscaster could fluently ad lib before the chief executive began his portion of the event. Once Trout had to talk for almost an hour until Mr. Roosevelt came ashore from a vacation cruise ship.

The NBC presidential convention group was made up of George Hicks, Ben Grauer, Tom Manning, and Graham McNamee. Mutual sent Gabriel Heatter and Quin Ryan.

Raymond Gram Swing brought an extensive journalistic background to radio when he joined Mutual and WOR in 1936. He was forty-seven and had spent a great deal of time in Europe. His second wife, Betty Gram, was a militant-type who campaigned for women's rights. Once she was arrested for picketing near the White House. She agreed to use her husband's last name only after he proposed using her last name as his middle name. Swing was a strong supporter of Roosevelt's New Deal. At first, he was heard only once a week. He was paid forty dollars. Swing appeared to remain calm under the most trying circumstances. Although his voice didn't possess typical radio quality, his stature as a news commentator would soon be recognized.

During the summer, Ted Malone left KMBC, Kansas City and reported to CBS in New York, where he would continue his poetry reading.

Radio listeners were able to hear reports from Berlin on the Olympic games in 1936. Ted Husing and Bill Henry, who was sports editor for the Los Angeles *Times*, handled coverage for CBS. Bill Slater was on the scene for NBC.

A.L. Alexander's *Good Will Court*, which he had started on WMCA in March 1935, went to NBC in 1936. The program provided an opportunity for people to relate their problems to a panel of New York judges who dispensed legal advice to the program's participants. Alexander was the MC and director. Charles Stark, who had worked at WIP, WCAU, and KYW in Philadelphia before joining WMCA in April, was the announcer.

Other new network shows opened up more announcer assignments.

A new series of *Stoopnagle and Budd* shows began on NBC. Harry von Zell drew the announcing appointment.

Big Sister, one of radio's most popular soap operas, debuted. Jim Ameche and Hugh Conover would handle the announcing duties.

Homespun philosopher *David Harum* provided more work for announcer Ford Bond.

Les Griffith was spokesman for the drama *Dan Harding's Wife*.

Famous Jury Trials started as a Mutual feature with Peter Grant, Hugh James, and Roger Krupp comprising the announcer lineup.

Gangbusters came on like gangbusters with Charles Stark, Frank Gallop, H. Gilbert Martin, Don Gardiner, and Ralph Forster working as the announcers during its long run.

Although Kate Smith had been heard on radio for several years, she began a new show on CBS in 1936 with her assistant Ted Collins as host and Andre' Baruch as announcer.

Ken Roberts announced for *The Life of Mary Sothern*.

Milton Cross was MC for *The Magic Key*, and John B. Kennedy appeared as a commentator.

George Ansbro was selected as the announcer for *Mrs. Wiggs of the Cabbage Patch*, which did not enjoy a long run.

The serial drama *Red Davis* became *Pepper Young's Family* that year. It's announcers would be Alan Kent, Martin Block, and Richard Stark.

Announcer Bert Parks would open *Renfrew of the Mounties* by shouting the show's name.

The Shadow had been heard on radio in various formats since 1930, but it went on Mutual with a revised approach in 1936. Sharing announcing duties during its tenure would be Andre' Baruch, Carl Caruso, Sandy Becker, and Ken Roberts.

Uncle Jim's Question Bee was an early quiz show. Jim McWilliams was the first Uncle Jim. He would be followed by Bill Slater.

In 1936, Don McNeill was doing *Tea Time at Morrell's* and the *NBC Jamboree* in addition to his popular *Breakfast Club*.

Don Wilson was broadcasting West Coast sports for $250 a game, and he was still doing the announcing chores for Jack Benny.

Graham McNamee had a contract with Universal Newsreel. It was renewed in 1936.

For the first time in six years, Boake Carter missed a broadcast. While he was suffering from grippe, David Lawrence, a political writer, substituted. Lawrence would be heard again.

Carlton Kadell, who was the regular announcer for the transcribed series *Strange As It Seems*, took over as the announcer for *Amos 'n' Andy* while they were in Hollywood for thirteen weeks.

Alan Prescott was being heard as the *Wife Saver* on NBC Blue.

The CBS crew for the Kentucky Derby consisted of Bryan Field, turf expert for the New York *Times* who described the race, Bob Trout, and Westbrook Van Voorhis.

In Chicago, Bob Hawk transferred his record show *Red, Hot and Lowdown* from WCFL to WJJD.

Ken Carpenter left the KFI staff to free lance on Bing Crosby's *Kraft Music Hall.* He was succeeded as chief announcer at KFI by Tom Hanlon.

Announcers continued to maintain their vagabond image in 1936.

Chet Huntley moved from KHQ, Spokane to KGW, Portland.

John Harrington began his duties as the CBS, Chicago sports announcer. He had previously worked at WGN and WLW.

Hugh Brundage left KRKD, Los Angeles and went to KEHE in the same city.

Herb Morrison left KQV, Pittsburgh for WLS, Chicago, the station on which he would achieve sudden and dynamic recognition.

Dan Seymour changed from the Yankee Network to CBS, New York.

Down in Atlanta, Charlie Smithgall transferred from WGST to WSB and started the *Morning Merry-Go-Round.*

Louis Buck obtained a job at WDOD, Chattanooga. His future success would be with the *Grand Ole Opry* station in Nashville, WSM.

Jack Costello came up to NBC, New York from KSTP, St. Paul. The Minnesota outlet prided itself on furnishing network announcers. In addition to Costello, its alumni had included George Watson, Tom Breen, Pat Murphy, Roger Krupp, and Pierre Andre'.

Douglas Edwards advanced from WAGF, Dothan, Alabama, to WSB. Atlanta.

Arthur Q. Bryan, announcer at WHN, New York, and formerly with WIP, Philadelphia, went to Hollywood to work as a scenario writer for Paramount.

Buddy Twiss was transferred from NBC, San Francisco to NBC, Hollywood.

Likewise, Rush Hughes, who had been doing his *Pictorial of the Air* at NBC, San Francisco, moved the series to Hollywood.

Russ Davis, who had earlier spent fourteen months at KWTO-KGBX, Springfield, Missouri, returned to those stations from XERA, across the Rio Grande River from Del Rio, Texas.

Harry Jackson (later to be known as CBS newsman Allan Jackson) joined the announcing staff of KTHS, Hot Springs as a full time announcer.

Tom Breneman was named manager of KFRC, San Francisco, but he would later return to primarily air work.

Forrest Rucker (later to be known as Galen Drake on the network) went from KFOX, Long Beach to KNX, Los Angeles. Also, he was married that year to Pauline Stafford, who was an aunt of Jo Stafford, the young singer who would rise to national popularity.

Robert "Bob" McRaney was promoted from announcer to program director at WDGN, Birmingham.

Stanley Bell, who had been an announcer at WMAL, Washington since 1927, joined the commercial staff of NBC, Washington.

Other announcer situations: Clem McCarthy was a fight announcer for WMCA, New York. Durward Kirby was an announcer at WLW. Ed Schaughency was on the air at KDKA. Julian Bently was a popular Chicago newscaster on WLS. Jack Holden of WLS was playing the lead on the *Tom Mix* serial. Announcer Tommy Bartlett was at WBBM. Ottis Devine was an announcer on the *Grand Ole Opry* station, WSM. Nelson Case, NBC, New York, after doing an *Esso Reporter* broadcast, was rushed to a hospital because of suffering from appendicitis. Harlow Wilcox also had an emergency appendectomy. Franklyn MacCormack, CBS, Chicago announcer, studied ballistics in the office of a police sergeant after doing his traffic court broadcasts.

In July 1936, NBC announcers Howard Claney and Alois Havrilla sailed on different ships for Europe. Claney's mission was to visit the Olympics and to practice his hobby of landscape painting. Havrilla visited his birthplace in Pressov, Czechoslovakia.

The *Lum 'n' Abner* program had achieved so much network popularity with its fictitious Arkansas town of Pine Ridge that the state legislature passed a law changing the name of Waters, Arkansas, to Pine Ridge. NBC announcer Charles Lyons served as MC of the renaming ceremony on April 26, which was the fifth anniversary of the entry of Arkansas native sons Chet Lauck and Norris Goff into radio.

Hilmar Baukhage worked for the *United States News*, and he was also doing a commentary on the NBC *National Farm and Home Hour* program. He would later become a full-fledged network commentator.

Cesar Saerchinger, the CBS European correspondent in London, and Fred Bate, NBC's London representative, were aboard the *Queen Mary* when it sailed its maiden voyage to New York May 27. Great radio coverage was given to the arrival of the large vessel. NBC utilized the largest reporting crew. Graham McNamee spoke from a Coast Guard cutter which accompanied the ship to its pier. Howard Claney described the arrival while viewing it through field glasses from top of Radio City. Charles O'Connor and Nelson Case reported from other vantage points. For CBS, Saerchinger broadcast from on board. Don Ball also was on duty for CBS. Johnny Johnstine and Ray Winters covered for WOR and Mutual.

Announcers continued to be honored with awards and other types of recognition in 1936. Howard Petrie of NBC was the recipient of the B.B.D.&O. award for good announcing. Jimmy Wallington, who was then Eddie Cantor's ace announcer, came in first in *Radio Guide's* poll. He was followed in order by Don Wilson, Ted Husing, Milton Cross, Graham McNamee, Tiny Ruffner, Don McNeill, David Ross, Harry von Zell, Phil Stewart, Truman Bradley, and John S. Young.

Twenty-five announcers were honored with a dinner given by the New York Advertising Club. Chosen from NBC were Ben Grauer, Ford Bond, Graham McNamee, Milton Cross, Don Wilson, Howard Claney, George Hicks, and Howard Petrie. CBS was represented by David Ross, Paul Douglas, and Robert Trout. Attending for WOR were Arthur Hale, Joseph R. Bolton, Roger Brown, Floyd Ned, John Gambling, and Joe Bier. Others at the dinner were A.L.Alexander and Don Kerr from WMCA, Tommy Cowan from WNYC, Ray Sanders and Brooke Temple from WHN, Kelvin Keech as a free lance announcer, Dick Cook from WINS, and Harry von Zell from the Young & Rubican Agency.

The fifth annual New York *World Telegram* Radio Editors' Poll selected Edwin C. Hill as the best commentator, Ted Husing as the top sports announcer, and Jimmy Wallington as the number one studio announcer.

An analysis of the CBS, New York announcing staff was made to determine the requirements for employment and the origin of its personnel. In the announcer qualifications category, it was stated that the voices of radio represented the voices of America and that an applicant must have small-station experience. Only three of the CBS staff of fifteen were native New Yorkers: David Ross, Kenneth Roberts, and Ted Husing. Two were not born in the United States: Andre' Baruch in Paris and Carlyle Stevens in Canada. Others were Del Sharbutt, Fort Worth; Art Millet, Chicago; William Brenton, Hartford; John Reed King, Wilmington; Hal Moore, Mount Vernon, Indiana; Bert Parks, Atlanta; Frank Gallop, Boston; Bob Trout, Wake County, North Carolina; Paul Douglas, Philadelphia; and Larry Harding, Waukegan, Illinois.

Vitaphone, a Warner Brothers subsidiary, signed twelve announcers for a series of movie short subjects entitled "Our Own United States." The narrators included Milton Cross, David Ross, Jimmy Wallington, Kenneth Roberts, Gabriel Heatter, H.V. Kaltenborn, Howard Claney, Harry von Zell, Paul Douglas, Harlen Reed, John S. Young, and Don Wilson.

Samuel L. "Roxy" Rothafel died in January 1936 at the age of fifty-two. Roxy had envisioned the original plan for Radio City as a world entertainment center featuring the theme of radio. His *Roxy's Gang* was one of the early very popular radio variety shows.

Although Ted Husing was the winner of various announcer awards during that period, many of his contemporaries in the radio business felt that he was extremely egotistical and possessed a "swelled head." The word "arrogant" was sometimes used to describe his personality when he wasn't on the air. "Go on with the parade—Husing's here!" he often said when he arrived at an important event.

During an on-the-spot remote broadcast of a celebration at Great Lakes Naval Training near Chicago, announcer Norman Barry and producer Maury Lowell were describing ceremonies that were in progress prior to the appearance of a rear admiral. Naval gunners standing by to salute the high-ranking officer mistook one of Lowell's arm signals and began firing. As the radio man tried to signal for them to stop, they kept firing salvo after salvo. They barely had enough ammunition left when the admiral arrived.

Gary Breckner was broadcasting a baseball game on KNX when he remarked, "I wish somebody would bring me a drink of water." A little girl listening in Monroma, California, poured a pitcher of water on the radio's loud speaker.

As director of talks at CBS, Edward R. Murrow was not an air man. A spirited holiday occasion led to his first newscast. Bob Trout, who was not an imbiber, was scheduled to do a five-minute Press-Radio news broadcast. As broadcast time drew near, Murrow quickly decided that Trout was not in a stable condition. Non-broadcaster Murrow grabbed the news copy from Trout's hands and positioned himself at the microphone. The regular newsman expected the worst in delivery, but Murrow handled the stories capably. There was only one hitch. Trout gave him the closing signal too early. There was a silence of forty-five seconds at the end.

Up at WKBH, LaCrosse, Wisconsin, the control room announcer and the remote man tried to synchronize their watches as a method of starting a remote broadcast at the right time. Jack Martin was riding the board, waiting to pick up nighttime dance music from the Avalon Ballroom. He called the man on the spot and said he would give it to him at one minute past eight. At the specified time, Martin said, "Now by remote control we take you to the Avalon Ballroom for the sweetest music this side of heaven."

Martin pushed the remote button and heard someone say, "Who the hell sat on my violin case?"

The year had its share of announcer boners:

"All over the country, women are turning to milk."

"Today we celebrate the eleventh wedding of the couple."

"A lot of lady fans are attending the game. Quite a nice crowd otherwise."

"It's a ret, wainy day."

"The meal is ground flesh every day."

"The pipe orphan program is from the Immanuel Church."

"We join the transcription sificilties of the World Transcription System."

Announcers at WHIO, Dayton worked under a demerit system. Bad marks were given for missed stationbreaks, being late for assignments, word fumbling, lazy reading of commercials, and missed announcements. The mikeman having the least demerits at the end of the week received an extra five dollars.

A practical joker or a disgruntled applicant placed a false ad in a San Francisco newspaper, stating that KFSO would hold announcer auditions at a certain time. Five hundred hopefuls showed up. Exhibiting good faith, even for a bogus ad, the station auditioned all applicants.

RCA introduced the Junior Velocity microphone, 74-A. The cost, complete with a thirty-foot shielded flexible cord, was forty dollars.

An FCC decision was very good news for announcers who played records. Instead of identifying each disc as a "recording" as they had been doing, they were required to make the announcement only once each quarter hour.

Bill Stern broadcast some football games for NBC in the fall of 1936. He went to work with the network as a full time sports announcer in April of 1937. His glib, dramatic style would be a vocal trademark for a long time.

Another sports announcer who would achieve bigtime prominence arrived in New York in 1937. Mel Allen made the move after a CBS executive heard him broadcast an Alabama-Tulane football game. The CBS offer of $150 per week caused Mel to abandon his plan to practice law.

Fulton Lewis, jr. (he preferred the small "j"), was born in Washington, D.C., in 1903. During his high school days, he wanted to be a musical composer, writing the words and music for two musical comedies. He continued his composition efforts at the University of Virginia. After leaving college in 1924, Lewis got a job as a reporter with Hearst's Washington *Herald.* He was city editor in 1928 when he moved to Hearst's Universal News Service in Washington as assistant bureau manager. It later became a part of International News Service. Lewis remained on that job for nine years, uncovering several significant scoops. In October 1937, he persuaded WOL, the Mutual outlet in Washington, to take him on as a commentator. The pay was twenty-five dollars a week. A couple of months later, Mutual put him on full network.

John Charles Daly, Jr., was born in Johannesburg, South Africa, in 1914. His father was a mining engineer. The boy had attended only two years of school when his father died of fever. His mother brought him and an older brother to the United States. He was enrolled in Tilton Academy in Tilton, New Hampshire. He stayed until he finished high school in 1930. The following year, John entered Boston College, working as a switchboard operator in a medical building to earn part of his expenses. Lack of finances forced him to leave college without graduating. He later worked as a clerk for a wool firm while performing with the Peabody Players. In 1935, Daly went to Washington and worked as a schedule engineer for the transit company. He returned to Boston and received some radio experience at WLOE. In 1937, John Charles Daly, Jr., joined WJSV, Washington.

Cesar Searchinger resigned as the CBS European director in 1937. Edward R. Murrow accepted the position for eight thousand dollars annually and sailed for London in April. Not even the sharpest network executive could foresee the future significance of that move.

William Lawrence Shirer was born in Chicago in 1904. His father, a lawyer, once served as an assistant U.S. district attorney. William went to school in Chicago and Cedar Rapids, Iowa. He wanted to be a journalist as early as his high school days, but his first setback came when he was not selected as a member of the high school paper staff. After he entered Coe College in Cedar Rapids, he obtained a job as a sports reporter with the Cedar Rapids *Republican*. Shirer graduated in 1925, and with borrowed money headed for Europe, pitching hay on a cattle boat to earn passage. He traveled on the continent during the summer and was ready to head for home when he was offered a job at the copy desk of the Paris edition of the Chicago *Tribune*. Two years later he became an European correspondent for the *Tribune*. Among his assignments was Lindbergh's landing in Paris. Shirer lost an eye in a skiing accident in the Alps. By 1937, he had worked for three years as a correspondent in Berlin for the Universal News Service.

That year Ed Murrow hired him to work as the CBS Central European representative with headquarters in Vienna. Upon acceptance of Murrow's offer, William L. Shirer wrote: "I have a job. I am to work for the Columbia Broadcasting System. That is, *if*. . .I have the job if my voice is right. Who ever heard of an adult with no pretenses to be a singer or any other kind of artist being dependent for a good, interesting job on his *voice*? And mine is terrible." His first duties for CBS consisted largely of arranging for broadcasts by foreign correspondents and introducing speakers. Network executives in New York didn't consider his voice suitable for long broadcasts. The imminent turn of world events would soon alter that concept.

Ronald "Dutch" Reagan of WHO, Des Moines accompanied the Chicago Cubs to Catalina Island near Los Angeles, their spring training site, in 1937. Dutch had been re-creating their games from Western Union reports. Also in the movie capital at the time was a western musical band from WHO that was appearing in a movie. Reagan enlisted the band leader's help in getting some screen tests. The twenty-six year-old sports announcer was signed to a seven-year contract by Warner Brothers for two hundred dollars a week. Before settling in Hollywood, he returned to Des Moines for some farewell radio appearances, including a two-hour stage show of the *Iowa Barn Dance Frolic*. When he reported to the movie studio in May, he was assigned the lead in the film *Sergeant Murphy*.

Walter Cronkite left KCMO, Kansas City in 1937 to open a bureau for United Press in El Paso. He was back in radio come autumn of that year, broadcasting football games for WKY, Oklahoma City. In late November, Cronkite was appointed to the station's news bureau.

California's Golden Gate International Exposition was scheduled for 1939, but preparation was begun early. Since Art Linkletter had experience in the radio phase of expositions, he was named radio director and began his duties in 1937. Art presented a series of radio broadcasts over KYA, San Francisco. A building in Union Square housed a $30,000 model of the proposed site. Linkletter stood outside the building and interviewed people as they came out of the building, getting their impressions of the elaborate exposition model.

In May 1937, Robert Trout was sent to London by CBS to cover the coronation of George IV of England. From London he journeyed across the channel to France to report the controversial wedding of the Duke of Windsor, who had given up the British throne, and U.S. citizen Wallis Simpson of Baltimore.

Chet Huntley was still on the move, but this was his most important transition up to that time. Chet went to KFI, Los Angeles, which was a step nearer to a network career.

Red Barber was in Havana on New Year's Day 1937 to broadcast the Villanova-Auburn football game for Mutual. The contest was played as part of Cuba's National Sports Festival.

Ed Thorgersen, who was then a sports commentator for Fox-Movietone News, did some sports reporting on Lowell Thomas' quarter-hour newscast. He appeared on the program each Monday and Friday during the football season and was on each day during the World Series.

Rex Marshall was born in Pemberton, New Jersey. He began what would be a long broadcasting career when he broke into radio in Boston in 1937. Other stops before entering military service would be Providence and Boston.

Herb Morrison was an announcer at WLS, Chicago in May 1937. He was thirty years old, and he liked dirigibles. The *Hindenburg* was scheduled to arrive from Germany and land at Lakehurst, New Jersey. It had been making the trip regularly for a year, so it was not a potentially newsworthy event. Nevertheless, Morrison persuaded station management to permit him and an engineer, Charlie Nehlsen, to take a disc recorder to Lakehurst to cover the landing. It was to be an experiment in reporting news events by transcription. They left Chicago on a new twenty-one-passenger flagship of American Airlines and flew three hours and fifty-five minutes nonstop to Newark. There they learned that the dirigible would be late and would arrive the next day. They took another American Airlines plane to Lakehurst and waited. The equipment was set up inside a hangar. At 6:00 P.M. on May 6, they began recording before the airship was in sight. The recording was not continuous. When Morrison spotted the Hindenburg, he said:

Now they're coming in to make the landing of the zeppelin. I'm going to step outside. So as I move out, we'll just stand by a second. (pause) Well, here it comes, ladies and gentlemen. We're out now—outside of the hangar,. and what a great sight it is—a thrilling one. It's a marvelous sight coming down out of the sky pointed directly towards us and towards the mast mooring. The mightly beat of the motors just roared. The propellers biting into the air and throwing it back into a gale-like whirlpool. No wonder this great floating palace can travel through the air with such speed with these powerful motors behind it. . . . The ship is gliding majestically toward us like some great feather. . . .

It's practically standing still now. They've dropped ropes out of the nose of the ship. It's starting to rain again. The rain has slacked up a little bit. They have been taken hold of down on the field by a number of men. The back motors of the ship are holding her just enough to keep it from—

The dirigible exploded, knocking the needle from the disc, but Nehlsen put it back quickly. Morrison's style immediately became hysterically dramatic.

It burst into flame! Get this, Charlie! Get this, Charlie! It's afire and it's crashing! It's crashing terrible. Oh, my, get out of my way, please. It's burning, bursting into flames, and it's falling on the mooring pads. And all the folks. This is terrible. This is one of the worst catastrophes in the world. Four or five hundred feet into the sky. It's a terrific crash, ladies and gentlemen. The smoke and the flames now, and the frame is crashing to the ground. Not quite to the mooring mast. All the humanity and all the passengers. (crying) I can't even talk to people whose friends are on there. (faltering) I can't talk, ladies and gentlemen. Honest, it's just laid down masses of smoking and wreckage. And everybody can hardly breathe, talking and screaming. Lady, I'm sorry. Honestly I can hardly breathe. I'm gonna step inside where I cannot see it. Charlie, that's terrible. Listen, folks, I'm gonna have to stop for a minute because I've lost my voice, and this is the worst thing I've ever witnessed.

Morrison resumed recording a few minutes later in a more calm manner.

Ladies and gentlemen, I'm back again. I've sort of recovered from the terrific explosion and the terrific crash that occurred just as it was being pulled down to the mooring mast. The terrible amount of hydrogen gas in it just caught. The tail surface broke into flames first, then there was a terrific explosion and that followed by the burning of the nose and the crashing nose into the ground. And everybody tearing back at break neck speed to get out from underneath it because it was over the people at the time it burst into flame. . . .

Morrison went on to say that there was not a possible chance of anybody being saved. Actually, it turned out that a majority of the passengers were not killed. Sixty-two of the ninety-seven aboard survived.

The recording process continued intermittently until 9:11 P.M. Three full Preston blank discs and a portion of a fourth were used to record forty minutes of talk. Morrison and Nehlsen caught a plane to Newark and left there at 1:00 A.M. for Chicago, arriving at 6:00 o'clock. The program was broadcast on WLS, beginning at 11:45 A.M. The uniquely spontaneous nature of the report prompted NBC to relax for the first time it's ban on the broadcasting of recordings. A portion of the coverage was used by the network that evening.

Although the broadcast was a milestone in dramatic radio news coverage, there was some isolated criticism later of Morrison's style. It was felt by some that tragic as the event was, he shouldn't have succumbed to the highly emotional, sometimes almost incoherent delivery. The thinking of some critics was that a reporter should maintain an impersonal, detached and objective description of any misfortune. Later that year, Morrison left WLS and went to work for WOR, New York.

A.L. Alexander's *Court of Good Will* gained tremendous popularity in a short period of time, but legalities forced an early termination of the program. A New York court ruled that judges and lawyers could not give legal counsel over the air. John J. Anthony never missed an opportunity to promote himself. He made a quick appeal to WMCA to let him take over the program, citing the fact that he directed the Marital Institute and possessed broadcasting experience. He would give the advice himself with no necessity of depending on legal authorities. The station consented, and on John J. Anthony's *The Goodwill Hour* he gained sudden acclaim by dispensing personal advice to troubled people who appeared on the program.

Gabriel Heatter started *We the People* in 1937, which he conducted in addition to his news commentaries. People told strange and unusual stories that had occurred in their lives.

Mary Margaret McBride went on CBS with a quarter-hour daily program, using her real name. She remained on WOR as Martha Deane.

NBC special events announcer George Hicks took a sea trip, sailing with the U.S. Navy Eclipse Expedition to Enderbury Island, a very small uninhabited spot of sand five thousand miles from San Francisco. He covered an eclipse with the National Geographic Society. A radio station was installed on the island for the NBC broadcasts.

The year saw more new programs emerge on the networks, offering more announcer opportunities. Many were "soaps." Roger Krupp announced *Arnold Grimm's Daughter*.

Our Gal Sunday began its twenty-two-year run in 1937. Announcers Art Millet, James Fleming, John A. Wolfe, Bert Parks, Charles Stark, and John Reed King would introduce the serial drama.

> And now, *Our Gal Sunday*, the story of an orphan girl named Sunday, from the little town of Silver Creek, Colorado, who in young womanhood married England's richest, most handsome lord, Lord Henry Brinthrope. The story that asks the question, "Can this girl from a mining town in the West find happiness as the wife of a wealthy and titled Englishman?"

Clayton "Bud" Collier, Ron Rawson, and George Bryan would share the announcing duties during the twenty-two-year life of *The Road of Life.*

Andre' Baruch was the announcer for *Second Husband.*

The durable *Stella Dallas* also began that year. Announcer assignments would go to Ford Bond, Howard Claney, Frank Gallop, Jack Costello, Jimmy Wallington, and Roger Krupp.

Other new programs in 1937 and their anouncer and MC personnel: *Dr. Christian*, Art Gilmore; *Grand Central Station*, Jack Arthur, Tom Shirley, and Ken Roberts; *Houseboat Hannah*, Olan Soule and Gene Baker; *Mr. Keen, Tracer of Lost Persons*, Larry Elliot and James Fleming; *Terry and the Pirates*, Douglas Browning (Announcer Kelvin Keech sang the theme and played the ukulele.)

Don Wilson appeared in an important role in RKO's *Radio City Revels* in 1937. Bill Slater did a sports show for NBC Red dealing largely with collegiate sports. Floyd Gibbons was doing the *Speedshow* program. Graham McNamee was on *The Time of Your Life* and *Royal Crown Revue.* Jack Costello replaced Milton Cross as the announcer on *Vox Pop.* Costello also began announcing *Radio Newsreel.* Ralph Edwards was announcing programs for Major Bowes and Horace Heidt. Tommy Bartlett started *The Misses Goes to Market* on WBBM.

There was an increasing number of announcer changes in 1937. Jack Paar; formerly with WKBN, Youngstown, the Atlantic Screen Service, and WCAE, Pittsburgh; went to WGAR, Cleveland as announcer and program director. Carlyle Stevens transferred from CBS, New York to CBS, Hollywood. Ben Gage, who had once worked as a singer for the Anson Weeks Orchestra, joined NBC, Hollywood to handle remotes from the Ambassador Hotel. Bill Baldwin moved from WOW, Omaha to WGN, Chicago. Roger Krupp joined WBBM, Chicago. Frank B. Goss, who had been working part time, was hired as a full time announcer and publicity director at KFOX, Long Beach.

After spending several weeks in Hollywood, Charles Lyon returned to NBC, Chicago. William T. Crago, who had been with WXYZ, Detroit, WHK, WTAM, WGAR, and wired Radio in Cleveland, joined the announcing staff of NBC, Chicago. Karl Zomar, who had worked for three years at KWTO-KGBX, Springfield, Missouri, moved to KFAB-KOIL, Omaha but returned to the Missouri stations after a few months. Hugh Brundage went from KEHE, Los Angeles to KHJ. Jim Britt, former broadcaster of Notre Dame football games for WIND, Gary, went to WBEN, Buffalo. Jack Wolever, a former actor, joined the announcing staff of KCMO, Kansas City.

Norman Brokenshire was getting some air work again. He was MC for the *American Woman's Serenade* on WOR. He also began a new series called *Journal of Living*. Later he established a morning show on WMAL, Washington and was cutting into Arthur Godfrey's audience. Then Broke had an automobile accident. Afterwards, he returned to his drinking ways.

Aubrey Guy transferred from WHBQ, Memphis to WMC in the same city. Kelvin Keech, who had been on the NBC announcing staff from 1929 to 1935, rejoined the staff. Alois Havrilla left NBC to free lance. Martin Block was named program director of WNEW. Harry (Allan) Jackson left WKZO, Kalamazoo because his doctor recommended that he live in the South. Frank Blair, formerly with WCSC, Charleston and WIS, Columbia, South Carolina, was named program director at WFBC, Greenville, South Carolina. Jay Jackson, who was new to radio, joined WCOL, Columbus. Jack Bailey, former chief announcer at KFSD, San Diego and before that with WHO, Des Moines, joined KEHE, Los Angeles. Jim Bannon, formerly with KMOX, St. Louis and prior to that with WABC, New York, also joined KEHE and changed his name to Tom Forsythe.

Durward Kirby left WLW, Cincinnati and joined NBC, Chicago. Ted Bliss of KHJ, Los Angeles was named director of program operations for the Don Lee Broadcasting System. J. Olen Tice, Jr., formerly of WFBC, Greenville and WAIM, Anderson, South Carolina, joined the announcing staff of WIS, Columbia. Russ Davis, formerly with WFBF, Abilene and KWTO Springfield, went to KCKN, Kansas City. Charles Godwin moved from WJSV to WOR. Rod O'Connor went from KVEC, San Luis Obispo to KLO, Ogden, Utah.

Other announcer circumstances in 1937: Al Helfler was Red Barber's sports assistant in Cincinnati. Al had been in radio in Pittsburgh. Vincent Pelletier was an NBC, Chicago announcer. George Ansbro was an announcer at NBC, New York. Peter Grant was the chief announcer at WLW. Bob Elson was doing a *Man-on-the-Street* show on WGN in addition to Chicago baseball. Dan Seymour was the CBS announcer on *Summer Hotel*. Carlton Kadell was announcing for NBC's *Chase and Sanborn Hour* and for Hal Kemp's Band and Alice Faye on CBS. Jay Sims was a CBS, Chicago announcer. Ira Blue was an NBC sportscaster in San Francisco. Frank Singiser was a news broadcaster at WOR. Mort Lawrence was an announcer at WCAU, Philadelphia.

There were bad flooding conditions in parts of the nation in 1937. Many radio reporters were assigned to cover the high

154

water conditions. WJSV sent Arthur Godfrey by plane to Louisville and Memphis. He did his own piloting.

Other Godfrey activities during the year included working as *Professor Quiz* on CBS and engaging in a baseball broadcasting contest with Arch McDonald in June to try to determine which one was the better sports announcer.

Lowell Thomas took his microphone overseas, broadcasting his regular newscast from an ocean liner during the journey. He reported the coronation in London and also broadcast from Paris and Rome.

Wen Niles, who was announcing for the *Burns and Allen* show, decided that a name change was in order to avoid confusion with his announcer brother Ken Niles. He chose Ronnie Drake, but the change wouldn't last. Later he would again be known as Wen Niles.

Network announcer Jean Paul King took on some extra activity, conducting a class in broadcasting technique at the Provincetown Wharf Theatre.

Truman Bradley, commentator on the Sunday night *Ford Concert* and a newscaster on WBBN, bought a talc firm as a sideline business venture.

John Nesbitt was the narrator on the *Passing Parade*, heard on fourteen Mutual-Don Lee stations. He was signed by MGM to direct and produce a movie short subject with the same title.

WOR decided to give Mary Margaret McBride some extra work. She began broadcasting as a news commentator in addition to her regular program.

Cedric Adams of WCCO, Minneapolis was quite a popular personality in his listening area. He performed a variety of services and received an abundance of favors. He found homes for thousands of animals of many species. Once a listener reported that she had lost the thirty-seven dollars she had saved for income tax payment. More than 57,000 listeners sent Cedric a penny each to pass on to her. On one broadcast he mentioned that his shoe strings were worn. This brought forty-six new pairs. Listeners also gave him news tips. One in particular in 1937 turned out to be very accurate. Adams said that a prominent labor leader would be taken for a ride within two weeks. Ten days later, a union official was found murdered.

KNX, Hollywood boasted of having the youngest news commentators in a major market. Their trio consisted of Richard "Dick" Joy, who had come over from KEHE; Maurie Webster, and Ken Craig—all twenty-one. Webster was the veteran of the group, having started in 1930 at KVI, Tacoma.

KNX didn't boast about a statement made by announcer Bob Moon on a commercial for Barbara Ann Bread: "Ladies be stubborn! Demand the breast in bed."

Popularity polls continued. Results of the first annual poll of radio editors of Hearst newspapers awarded the following honors:

Best Commentator—1. Edwin C. Hill; 2. Boake Carter; 3. H. V. Kaltenborn

Best All-Around Announcer—1. Harry von Zell; 2. Don Wilson; 3. Milton Cross

Best Sports Announcer—1. Ted Husing; 2. Clem McCarthy; 3. Ernie Smith (KYA, San Francisco)

Frank Austin was announcing a wrestling match for KDKL, Salt Lake City. Suddenly, one of the participants charged out of the ring and grabbed Austin, who was sitting in a third-row seat. The grunt-and-groaner then proceeded to apply a headlock on the announcer and drag him into the ring. Later the muscle man apologized, explaining that a crack on the head as he went through the ropes had left him momentarily confused.

Chet Petersen handled concert orchestra remotes from an internationally famous hotel in Los Angeles. Chet rode the street car from the downtown area to the hotel. One day the street car had an accident, and there was a delay. He always tried to check in at least ten minutes before airtime. He operated the remote amplifier in addition to serving as the announcer by giving the introduction. Petersen became anxious about getting there on time—to a point where he was about to wet his pants. When the street car finally arrived at his getting-off place, he still had one block to walk. He knew he would never make it through the broadcast in his condition. It was two minutes until program time when he dashed upstairs to the rest room. Trying to hurry, he caught his shirttail in his pants zipper. Thinking quickly, he wrapped his coat around his waist and walked through the main dining room. He threw the switch, and the equipment warmed up just in time.

A cartoon depicted a sports announcer covering a football game. The caption quoted him saying to a buddy, "I can't allow myself to get excited over a touchdown. I'm trying for the radio diction award."

Bob Cunningham, program director at KOIL, Omaha, wrote an announcer audition for what he described "cocky"

156

applicants:

Some aspirants regard an announcer's audition as a chance for a coup; others with all the apparent symptoms of the ague. However formidable it may appear to be, it is best to enter into it with all the savoir faire at your command; much as a Irishman enters a melee—to be enjoyed, win or lose. A bona fide announcer will do the best he can with words he doesn't know, and will try sincerely, even though he misses.

The comptroller of currency in any radio station hears many things about announcers which are refutable; but a man's status as an announcer is never improved by a listener's vagary, and often a machination, if repeated ad infinitum, will ricochet till it results in the final ultimatum for the announcer.

Confidence, with the paprika of energy added, is one of the surest ways to avoid being impotent in this profession. Here, too, caution must be used, since in the sacerdotalism of announcing, co-workers are prone to emerse an egotistic neophyte in the natatorium of ridicule. To avoid being embroiled in any such imbrogilo, the newcomer should be bade to revere those who have precedence over him, and who regard KOIL as their alma mater and sanctuary.

En route to this estimable estate, via long hours and probably mediocore menus, the embryonic announcer must have inherent strength in his abdomen, viz., in order to cope with such men as Bizet, Paderewski, Benes, Mussolini, Petain, Lenin, Saint-Saens and Roosevelt; with such things as lingerie, eggs, programs, carnivora, news and exigencies.

Even in closing, not to jest, it's time to say this joust has been marked "finis."

Western Electric put the "salt-shaker" microphone on the market in early 1937. It was well suited for studio use and could also be adjusted for remote broadcasts. The salt-shaker could be mounted on desk or floor stands, and it could be adjusted from non-directional to semi-directional.

Radio technology lost an industry giant August 1, 1937. Guglielmo Marconi died in Rome of a heart attack at the age of sixty-three.

Announcer Bill Baldwin obtained an exclusive interview for WOW, Omaha. Bill interviewed His Holiness, the Papal Secretary from the Vatican. The setting was unique for such a broadcast. It was conducted in the men's rest room at the airport. Baldwin was a friend of the founder of Boys Town, the famous Father Flanagan. His Holiness had become air sick and was seeking relief in the rest room. Father Flanagan arranged for Bill, and no one else, to talk to him. The good Father stood guard outside to be sure that nobody went in and flushed a toilet during the interview. A short time later, his interviewee became Pope Pius XII.

David Cunningham "Dave" Garroway, Jr., ad libbed his first cry in 1913 in Schenectady, New York. His father's job as a mechanical engineer led to the family's moving to various cities. In 1927, they went to St. Louis. Dave's interest in astronomy while in high school resulted in his construction of several telescopes. He enrolled at Washington University in St. Louis in 1931, majoring in English. After earning a bachelor's degree in 1935, he worked a few months selling piston rings. Next he studied for a short period of time at the Harvard Business School. Later he and a friend devised a publication of eight hundred mispronounced words entitled *You Don't Say!. . .Or Do You?* Garroway directed his sales effort toward school teachers. The book contained many words he would use in his future career.

Garroway was peddling his publication in New York in 1938 when the National Broadcasting Company gave him a job as a pageboy at the salary of fifteen dollars a week. His aptitude for the work paved the way for his advancement to the position of guide and later to guide trainer. While doing these jobs, he also was attending NBC's school for announcers. In the first audition given in the course, Garroway finished twenty-third in a class of twenty-four.

After completing the announcer training, Dave Garroway was hired by KDKA, Pittsburgh as a special events announcer. His refreshing approaches to covering various events brought him considerable recognition. He entered golf tournaments as a participant and broadcast the matches with a portable transmitter strapped to his back. He ended the coverage of a canoe race by making a gurgling sound. Dave swam along with a water polo team, describing the progress stroke-by-stroke. He tried to report a bowling ball's feeling as it rolled down the alley on its way to making a strike. Other clever vantage points included a broadcast from under a bridge being built, and an account of a piece of steel that was in the process of being riveted during the construction of a new high-rise building while he was under the steel beam.

Dennis James was born in Jersey City in 1917. He graduated from St. Peter's College in his hometown and also from the

Theatre School of Dramatic Arts in Carnegie Hall. In 1938, the fledgling Dumont Television Network was in need of an all-around, versatile announcer. James was then working as a radio actor and announcer. He agreed to join the new medium and handle programs designed for the some three hundred television set owners in the Greater New York area. In this position, he racked up a number of TV firsts: MC of a variety show; host of a sports show; MC of a daytime show; host of a commercial show; narrator of the Easter Parade; on-the-spot live news commentator; actor in a dramatic show; commercial announcer; wrestling announcer; and kinescoped announcer.

Art Baker was born in 1898 in the Bowery section of New York, where his mother ran a settlement house. Young Art wanted to be a minister. While serving in the Army in World War I, he was transferred from the front lines to a less dangerous position and instructed to lead the soldiers in community-type singings. Through these exercises, Baker became aware of his strong voice. After the war, he became an evangelist and toured the nation preaching. After he arrived in California, he took a job as a lecturer at Hollywood's famous Forest Lawn Cemetery. He made more than five thousand talks at gravesides. This further developed the smooth, spiritual expression in his voice.

Art Baker's first radio experience came in 1936 when he was given the assignment of announcing *Tapestries of Life*. Next came the audience participation show called *Reunion of the States*. CBS signed him for *Hollywood in Person*, which ran in 1937 and 1938. He interviewed movie stars. In 1938, he was given *Pull Over, Neighbor*, a show that would later become *People Are Funny*. Also in 1938, Baker started what would be his most popular program, although it was not a network feature. It was *Art Baker's Notebook*, broadcast on KFI.

Walter Cronkite resigned from his position as newscaster-sportscaster at WKY, Oklahoma City to do what was called "exploitation" work for Braniff Airways at Dallas.

During the early days of March 1938, Edward R. Murrow left his headquarters in London and went to Berlin where he met William L. Shirer, who had come from his office in Vienna. After leaving the German capital, Murrow went to Warsaw, Poland, to put together a children's program to be used on the CBS feature *American School of the Air*. Shirer's assignment sent him to Yugoslavia to line up a chorus composed of youngsters from mining families for the program. On Friday, March 11, Shirer arrived back in Vienna and learned that Hitler's troops had

159

entered Austria. He tried to telephone Murrow in Warsaw but was unable to get through. That night he went to the radio station to make a broadcast to New York, but the Nazi regime told him that all broadcasts would have to go through Berlin. Even this proved to be impossible because no lines were available. Shirer returned to his home early in the morning and completed a call to Murrow. "The opposing team has just crossed the goal line," he told his boss.

Murrow suggested that Shirer fly to London and originate a broadcast. He was finally able to get a seat on a plane to London. After arriving in the English city, he went directly to the BBC and made a broadcast. The time was 6:30 P.M. on Saturday. Murrow wanted to get to Vienna. He caught a plane from Warsaw to Berlin but was unable to get one from there. As a last resort, Murrow chartered a twenty-seven seat Lufthansa plane. He was the only passenger. The cost: one thousand dollars, a tremendous sum for a news story.

Hurried arrangements were made for the first *CBS World News Roundup*. Newspapermen, radio people, and engineers were reached in various places on the continent. It was 8:00 o'clock Sunday night, New York time, when Bob Trout in Studio 9 introduced the feature, not knowing for certain whether it would work. First heard was William Shirer in London, where it was 1:00 A.M. Englishwoman Ellen Wilkinson, a member of Parliament, followed him. Next were Edgar Ansel Mowrer from Paris, Pierre Huss from Berlin, and Frank Gervasi from Rome. Ed Murrow concluded the experimental half-hour roundup from Vienna. It was his first significant news report. Both Murrow and Shirer received silver plaques from the Atlantic City Headliners Club. Radio news had just begun to prove that it could get the job done.

But it was only the beginning. Radio reports from overseas continued through the spring and summer. Intensified coverage began September 12 when Hitler made his threatening declaration against Czechoslovakia in a speech to the Nazi Congress. Frequent reporting continued for eighteen days with a step-by-step analysis of the Munich Crisis that led to Germany's occupation of Czechoslovakia.

Although H.V. Kaltenborn had been associated with radio news for sixteen years, it was during this period that he really became established as a commentator. He virtually lived in Studio 9 and occasionally napped on an army cot in an office. His wife assisted by bringing coffee, soup, and sandwiches from a drugstore. In the studio, an electric fan sat on a large speaker cabinet behind him. Kaltenborn made 102 broadcasts during the eighteen days. Some were as brief as two minutes; others were as long as two hours. None had advance preparation. All were ad libbed. He attempted to analyze and interpret bulletins as they were handed to him. At the same time, he had to keep an eye on the control room. Often a signal told him to finish in one minute so they could pick up a report from a foreign capital.

People listened around the clock. They listened everywhere. They liked Kaltenborn's instant summaries. More people were discussing him than any other radio personality. There was a great increase in the sale of portable radios. Most taxicabs were equipped with radios. After the eighteen-day ordeal, Kaltenborn was noticeably fatigued. Nevertheless, when the Archbishop of Canterbury broadcast a prayer for peace, H.V. analyzed it, too.

The other networks immediately began searching for someone that could do the job that Kaltenborn was doing for CBS. During the Munich Crisis, Mutual hired author Quincy Howe to do some news analysis. He had been born in Boston in 1900 and had attended Harvard. His radio speech style was once described as that of a "caustic-tongued Yankee." Also, Mutual increased Raymond Gram Swing's schedule to five times weekly after he returned from Europe in October. For NBC, Cesar Saerchinger began *The Story Behind the Headlines*.

Ed Murrow arrived back in the U.S. aboard the *Queen Mary* for a two-weeks vacation after his demanding activities during the Czech-German Crisis. After the home visit, he returned to his headquarters in London. William L. Shirer was stationed in Vienna. NBC had Fred Bate and Max Jordan in Basel, Switzerland. John Steele covered for MBS in London.

One day in August 1938, Boake Carter was making $150,000 a year as a CBS commentator. Although he was at the peak of his popularity, the next day he wasn't making a cent. The network banned him forever from their chain. His sponsor since February of that year had been General Foods. Prior to that, his longtime sponsor had been Philco. The controversial reporter had stepped on too many toes and had criticized the administration of Franklin D. Roosevelt too often and too harshly. In an interview conducted shortly before his dismissal, Boake Carter said:

> The most serious fight in which I've been involved since I first went on the air has been the slow struggle to defend expression. It has been a long hard fight against continual pressure—a fight which has turned into a rear-guard action since 1933. The

pressure has been mostly political and it is no secret to any commentator or anyone in radio broadcasting that the pressure goes all the way down the line from the White House at one end to the smallest bureaucrat at the other.

Boake Carter would return to the air later, but his same effectiveness would never be regained.

Garry Morfit (Moore) was keeping busy both on and off the air in Baltimore. He was MC of the "Stardust Revue" at the Hippodrome Theatre. A cast of fifty entertainers broke all previous records. Also, Garry made a personal appearance at a local automobile dealer's showroom along with the entire cast of the "High Jinks" show. Later in the year, he left WBAL and went to KWK, St. Louis. There he began as a newscaster and sports commentator. His reputation as a comedian soon caught up with him, and he was given a program on which he was a humorist. A listener called and told him he was "the funniest feller on the air." Garry was finally convinced that he was a talented comedian.

It was new show time again in 1938.

Jim McWilliams and Ed East served in order as the MC of a program called *Ask It Basket*.

The *Battle of the Sexes* would feature as MC's Frank Crummit and Julia Sanderson, Walter O'Keefe, and Jay C. Flippen. Competent Ben Grauer was the announcer.

The Green Hornet had been heard on WXYZ, Detroit since 1936. In 1938, it went on Mutual. During it's sixteen-year run, the announcers included Charles Woods, Mike Wallace, Fielden Farrington, Bob Hite, and Hal Neal.

Kay Kyser's Kollege of Musical Knowledge made it's first lively appearance. Announcer Verne Smith was called the "Dean." The wearing of caps and gowns was required.

Orson Welles brought his *Mercury Theatre on the Air* to CBS in July 1938. On October 30, he scared a portion of the population with his presentation of "War of the Worlds."

Good old *Scattergood Baines* first showed up on the air that year. George Walsh and Roger Krupp would announce.

Tommy Riggs was a ventriloquist. His *Tommy Riggs and Betty Lou* show debuted in 1938. Don Wilson, Bill Goodwin, and Mike Roy did the announcing.

Quiz show *True or False* went on the air. The MC's would be Dr. Harry Hagen, Eddie Dunn, and Bill Slater. Glenn Riggs announced.

162

Silver Theatre began presenting its dramas. Actor Conrad Nagel was the program's host. The announcers through the years were Bill Conte, Dick Joy, and Roger Krupp.

More daytime serials found places in the program schedules. Clayton "Bud" Collier announced for *The Guiding Light.* Ken Roberts did the job for *Joyce Jordan, Girl Interne* (which would be renamed *Joyce Jordan, M.D.* in 1942). During the sixteen-year programming of *Life Can Be Beautiful,* Ralph Edwards, Don Hancock, Ed Herlihy, Ron Rawson, and Bob Dixon would share announcer chores. Sportscaster Mel Allen took time from the playing fields to be the announcer for *This Day Is Ours.* George Ansbro drew the announcing assignment for *Young Widder Brown.*

Some other announcer and program situations in 1938: Dick Joy became the announcer for *Vox Pop.* Carlton Kadell handled the chores for *Big Town.* Art Gilmore announced *Dr. Christian.* Lou Crosby did likewise for *Lum 'n' Abner.* Nelson Case was the one who introduced Johnny on the *Phillip Morris Playhouse*: "Here comes Johnny stepping out of thousands of store windows to greet you." John Conte was the announcer for John Nesbitt's *Passing Parade.* Bob Poole started a morning half-hour show on WNEW, New York called *For City Farmers.* The Fulton Lewis, jr., newscast on Mutual was offered for local participating sponsorship. Sportscaster Clem McCarthy didn't get much work handling the broadcast of the Joe Louis-Max Schmeling fight. Louis won by a knockout in the first round.

Announcers continued to have itchy feet in 1938. Glenn Riggs, who was chief announcer at KDKA, Pittsburgh, journeyed to the big town and participated in announcer audition competition at Radio City, emerging as the winner. Glenn joined the announcing staff at NBC in August. Before leaving Pittsburgh, he was given a gold ring with the initials of his KDKA announcer associates.

Larry Elliot, who had been with WJSV, Washington since 1932, was transferred to the CBS announcing staff in October, Warren Sweeney of the WJSV Announcers Guild presented to him a pipe kit on behalf of the staff. Jimmy McClain, a future "Dr. I.Q.," left WOAI, San Antonio and took the position of studio director at KABC in the same Texas city. Foster Brooks, who had been at WHAS, Louisville for seven years, joined the announcing staff at KWK, St. Louis. Alan Kent left NBC for WNEW, New York. Frank Blair made the jump from WFBC, Greenville, South Carolina to WOL, Washington. Douglas Edwards joined WXYZ, Detroit. Ted Malone took a hiatus from *Between the*

163

Bookends on CBS to accept a job as continuity writer for WOR. Truman Bradley quit as announcer on Ford's *Sunday Evening Hour* to make movies for MGM. Frank B. Goss went from KFOX, Long Beach to KWFB, Hollywood. Al Helfler switched from WLW to WOR. Jay C. Flippen resigned as MC of WHN's *Original Amateur Hour*. Bill Goodwin left agency work and rejoined the CBS staff. Vern Carstensen went from WHBF, Rock Island to NBC, Chicago.

Van Patrick, formerly of KOCA, Kilgore, Texas, joined KRMD, Shreveport. Jerry Doggett, who had worked for a Chicago agency, became a member of the announcing staff of KFRO, Longview, Texas. Bob Lemand returned to KEHE, Los Angeles after a short stint at KYA, San Francisco. Randall Jesse, formerly with KCKN, Kansas City and KWOS, Jefferson City, Missouri, was named manager of KWOC, Poplar Bluff, Missouri. Bill Leyden, a product of Everett Mitchell's NBC announcing school for guides, became an announcer at WCFL, Chicago.

Other announcer news: Russ Hodges was a sportscaster at WIND, Gary. Rosey Roswell was doing baseball for KDKA. Carlton Brickert, who had been the Horlicks Malted Milk announcer for *Lum 'n' Abner* for three years, was on the staff of NBC, Chicago. Earl Godwin, a commentator for WMAL, Washington, was president of the White House Correspondents Association. Al Jarvis was elevated to program director at KTMR, Hollywood. Harry (Allan) Jackson of KTHS, Hot Springs, a future CBS newsman, was placed in charge of local talent for a merchants' trade day broadcast. Ted Bliss was appointed the Southern California radio contact for the upcoming Golden Gate Exposition. Ted was scheduled to report to the headquarters at Treasure Island after January 1. Art Van Horn was an announcer at KFRC, San Francisco. Webley Edwards, KGMB, Honolulu, made a six-weeks tour of the U.S. George D. Hay returned to the *Grank Old Opry* in March after an absence of more than a year because of illness.

Peter Grant was experiencing a problem at WLW because of the sound of his voice. Many people thought it had the qualities of President Roosevelt's voice. Peter declared that he didn't try to sound like FDR. The White House didn't want anyone to purposely mimic the radio style of the chief executive. WLW was told to take him off the air. Grant had been the announcer for Red Skelton when the comedian did a network show in the WLW studios. Red supported the announcer when the controversy

164

arose. "You can't take a man's livelihood away from him just because he sounds like the President," the comedian said. Grant made an alteration in his style and stayed on the air.

Charles Tramont, who had been an NBC, New York announcer since 1929, left radio to begin the practice of medicine in Mt. Vernon, Ohio. Since 1933, Tramont had announced at night only while attending medical school at New York Medical College in the daytime.

In the movies it was the Marx Brothers, but in radio it was the Laux Brothers. They claimed to be the only brother trio working on the air. France was chief announcer and sportscaster at KMOX, St. Louis. Edward was chief announcer at WAAT, Jersey City. Roger was a sports announcer at WCBS, Springfield, Illinois. France was awarded the *Sporting News* trophy as radio's outstanding baseball announcer in 1938.

John Charles Daly of WJSV was selected as the best Washington announcer. WJSV's Warren Sweeney came in a close second. There was a third-place tie between Jim McGrath of WRC-WMAL and Frank Blair of WOL.

NBC announcer Neel Enslen, forty-five, died in his New York apartment. Jets on a gas stove had been opened. Enslen had joined NBC in 1929 after having been a member of the American Opera Company.

Lowell Thomas, David Ross, and Alois Havrilla contributed some of their ideas on speech to some research that was done in 1938. Thomas reported that his father, who was a Colorado surgeon, had him memorize poems in dialect and practice them until he had the correct inflection and until he had eliminated all nasal tones. Thomas also added that he thought a person's speech depended on the individual's physical condition.

David Ross gave suggestions for making the voice flexible. He recommended the mimicking of various animal sounds—the dog's bark, the cat's meow, the cow's moo, the hen's cackle, the rooster's crow, the tiger's snarl, the lion's roar, etc. Ross also included the vocal behavior of children in their various moments of feeling.

Alois Havrilla believed that relaxation was a key factor. He gave examples of exercises such as lying flat, or bouncing a large ball while walking and speaking during practice to take the pupil's mind off "voice production."

WNEW, New York personality Stan Shaw learned that a murderer had eluded New Jersey police and headed for the highways. Stan sounded an alarm between the records "Mexicali

165

Rose" and "The Very Thought of You" on his early morning *Milkman's Matinee* show. Within fifteen minutes, a lunchwagon owner had the culprit cornered.

Nelson Olmstead, an announcer at WBAP, Fort Worth, wished that his listeners would listen a little more closely. Each week he conducted a program called *Thirty Minutes Behind the Walls* from the Texas State Penitentiary at Huntsville. When he appeared at the institution one week to do the program, he found a letter from a former schoolmate: "I heard your program from the Huntsville prison last Wednesday night for the first time. I was never so shocked in all my life. I remember how you were in school, and I just couldn't imagine what you were doing in a place like that. How long have you been there and when did you get in trouble? I'm enclosing some stamps, and if you need anything else, be sure and tell me."

In St. Louis an announcer said, "The next words you hear will be those of the Pope." There was a pause, and then the listeners heard, "Ajax is the beer for me!"

CBS announcers in the Los Angeles area enjoyed new working quarters beginning in the spring of 1938. The network dedicated a new Hollywood center called Columbia Square.

An early "tomato can" mike was donated by KDKA to the U.S. National Museum of the Smithsonian Institution.

With the outbreak of hostilities in Europe in early September 1939, American radio had its first major war to cover. William L. Shirer was in Berlin for CBS. Edward R. Murrow reported from London. H.V. Kaltenborn had flown from the U.S. aboard the *American Clipper* on August 9 for three weeks of coverage of important European news. He originated his broadcasts from the BBC. It was a year of personal recognition for the veteran commentator. For his coverage of the Czech crisis the previous autumn, he was awarded an honorary doctor of law degree by the University of Minnesota. He won first place in the annual poll of the Women's National Radio Committee. Regardless of his plaudits, Kaltenborn didn't always hit the nail on the head. Near the end of August, he was asked whether he thought war would come soon. He replied, "The odds are seven to five in favor of more appeasement." Two days later, Hitler's forces stormed into Poland.

While Kaltenborn was overseas, a standby was ready in New York. CBS put Elmer Davis on the air August 22. In his calm, flat, straight-forward, midwestern Hoosier twang, Davis

166

announced on September 3, "Great Britain went to war against Germany today, twenty-five years and thirty days from the time she entered the war of 1914 against the same enemy. France is expected to follow suit within the next few hours." Elmer Davis was born in Indiana in 1890. He received a Rhodes scholarship to Oxford in 1910. During the many years before he entered radio, he worked as a newspaperman and a novelist.

Ed Murrow had first used "This is London" for the opening of his broadcast September 22, 1938. His former speech teacher at Washington State College listened to every broadcast he made. After the war started, she made recommendations as to how he might make his style more effective. She wrote that his opening was rushed, that it should be more deliberate and meditative in keeping with the historical significance of his mission. He made the change: "This...is London." The additional emphasis became his widely-known and familiar identifier.

After the bombing of London began, Murrow had to get permission from the Ministry of Information to ad lib broadcasts from rooftops. He was required to make six transcriptions so that the censors could listen to them and make their decision. Murrow made records on six successive nights, but somehow or other, the discs were lost in the offices of the Ministry of Information. He was forced to submit another six nights of transcriptions before approval was given. The BBC studio used by American broadcasters had previously been what was referred to as a "waitresses' robing room," another way of saying a "ladies lavatory."

Eric Sevareid entered the world in North Dakota in 1912. His family later moved to Minneapolis, where he went to high school. When he was seventeen, he and a young man who was three years older began a canoe trip from Minneapolis to a point on Hudson Bay, Canada, to prove that it was possible to travel by water through the continent. The Minneapolis *Star* had advanced them a hundred dollars for stories Sevareid would write about their experiences. They used the money for supplies, which they loaded into their canoe. The two young men paddled northward all summer and fall, narrowly escaping tragedy on several occasions. Abandoning their plan was considered but rejected. After finally completing the 2,200-mile journey, Sevareid attempted to evaluate their decision to press on: "I knew instinctively that if I gave up, no matter what the justification, it would become easier forever afterwards to justify compromise with any achievement."

Sevareid's experience paved the way for a job with the Minneapolis *Journal*, first as a copy boy and six weeks later as a fifteen-dollar-a-week reporter. He attended the University of Minnesota at night, majoring in political science and economics. A short time later, he was assigned to the morning shift, which enabled him to go to classes in the afternoon.

During the summer of 1932, Eric Sevareid hitchhiked to California and attempted gold mining in the High Sierras. For him there wasn't much "gold in them thar hills." He came out with eighty cents worth. It was necessary for him to ride freight trains back to Minneapolis. This time he entered college on a full-time basis, becoming active in campus politics and supporting radical movements. While he was going through the liberal stage, his activities included the joining of a left wing student organization, holding rallies against the growth of fascism, helping to do away with compulsory ROTC training at the college, and voting for a pledge that stated, "I will not bear arms for flag or country." Writing articles for the *Star* and working early in the morning in the campus post office helped to pay his expenses. Sevareid received a B.A. degree in political science in 1935 and returned to the *Journal* the following year. An economy move in 1937 caused his termination at the paper.

Eric Sevareid then went to Europe. First, he studied political science at the London School of Economics before going on to Paris and attending the Alliance Francaise. In 1938, he got a job as a reporter for the Paris edition of the New York *Herald Tribune*. He became the city editor the following year. He also worked as night editor for United Press.

Sevareid received a long distance call from London in August 1939. It was from Edward R. Murrow offering him a job to report for CBS. Murrow told him, "I don't know very much about your experience, but I like the way you write and I like your ideas." Murrow also told him that there wouldn't be any pressure to provide scoops or anything sensational. They just wanted the news—honest news; and if there wasn't any news, he could just say so. Sevareid was scared, but he agreed to broadcast a closed circuit talk to executives in New York as an audition. A couple of hours before the scheduled delivery, he learned it would be carried over the entire network. As he read a revised script, his hands shook uncontrollably. The powers in New York felt that his speech style was not suitable. Murrow overcame the objections of his superiors, and Sevareid joined "Murrow's boys," which was a team of experienced newspapermen organized shortly before and soon after the outbreak of World War II.

Sevareid worked out of Paris, accompanying French forces to points in France, Belgium, Holland, and Luxembourg.

Larry Lesueur was born in New York City in 1909. His family had a journalistic background. His grandfather was the publisher of two newspapers in Iowa, and his father had been a foreign correspondent for the New York *Tribune.* Lesueur earned a B.A. degree from New York University in 1931. Before obtaining a job with United Press in New York in 1933, he worked as a floorwalker at Macy's Department Store and as a reporter for *Women's Wear Daily.* In 1939, Larry went to Europe and became a part of the CBS radio news staff, covering the British Army and the Royal Air Force in France during the first year of the war.

Martin Agronsky, who was a foreign correspondent and free lance newspaper reporter, broadcast for NBC in Geneva in December 1939.

Bill Henry was in Europe when the war broke out in September. He had gone in August to preview the 1940 Finnish Olympics Games for CBS and the Los Angeles *Times.* Since he was already there, he was assigned as a radio correspondent for CBS to cover the British Expeditionary Forces in France.

On the lighter side, announcer Frank Gallop walked into the 17th story CBS studio one day in September ten minutes prior to time for him to introduce H.V. Kaltenborn on the program *Kaltenborn Edits the News.* Sitting down at the mike, Gallop made a hand gesture of greeting to the engineer in the adjacent control room. Thinking that Gallop wanted to interrupt the current program for a war bulletin, he cut the *Alibi Club* and turned on Gallop's mike. The announcer, not knowing he was on the air, was clowning with the introduction: "Kaltenborn edits the news!" The commentator was listening in his office. Thinking he was late, he grabbed his notes and dashed for the studio. Then Gallop began saying Kaltenborn's name to the beat of "Old McDonald Had a Farm":

"Aich Ve-ee Kal-ten-born,

E-yi, E-yi-O!"

A few days after the outbreak of hostilities overseas, Arthur Godfrey remarked on his *Sundial* show on WJSV, "We now interrupt a war news broadcast to bring you a spot announcement." Godfrey tried his hand at newspaper journalism during the year, writing a daily column for the Washington *Daily News* called "As I Was Saying. . ."

Myron Leon Wallik (later to be known as Mike Wallace) was born in Brookline, Massachusetts, in 1918. His father had come to this country from Russia at the age of sixteen. An immigration official understood his last name as "Wallace" and that it remained. In Brookline High School, Mike was active in public speaking, dramatics, and the school paper. He also played the violin in the school orchestra and captained the tennis team. He entered the University of Michigan in 1935, where his uncle was a professor. Mike worked at waiting on tables, washing dishes, and working for the National Youth Administration (a Roosevelt-era school program). While in college, he became interested in radio and became an announcer at a local Ann Arbor station. During a summer vacation, he taught radio broadcasting at a music camp. After receiving a B.A. degree in 1939, he caught on as an announcer, continuity writer, and salesman at stations WOOD-WASH, Grand Rapids. (The stations were owned by a furniture store and a laundry.) His pay was twenty dollars per week.

If young Hugh Downs hadn't been sent out to get a jug of fresh milk, he might never have entered the field of broadcasting. Hugh was born in Akron, but his family moved to Lima, Ohio, when he was only two. After graduation from high school in 1938, he entered Bluffton College in Ohio. Hugh returned home following his freshman year, and his father directed him to start looking for a job. After several abortive attempts to land employment with various businesses in town, he considered leaving. It was in May 1939 when he was eighteen when his mother asked him to go to the milk depot downtown to fill the gallon jug since it was more economical than buying it by the quart.

Radio station WLOK was located next to the milk depot. As Downs approached his destination, suddenly he was inspired. After being flatly denied a job with a roofing company earlier in the day, he thought perhaps radio might be for him. He didn't believe it would actually be work. Instead of going first to the milk place, he entered the radio station, carrying the empty jug, and requested an announcer's audition. A young lady told him that the manager would be on the air with the news for eight more minutes. Hugh used that time to get the milk. When he returned to the station, the manager remarked that he thought the young man was selling milk. In the studio, Hugh sat before an RCA 77-B microphone and attempted to read a couple of spot announcements and a page of teletype news copy. It wasn't good, but the manager thought he detected something favorable. Hugh

170

was offered a part time job three hours daily beginning the following Monday. The pay would be $7.50 per week, and he was promised that he might work into a full time announcer's job. He rushed home to report the employment news. Mr. Downs was not impressed, telling Hugh to spend the rest of the week looking for a job, and should he not find one, to report to the radio station. Hugh Downs didn't find another job.

Ernest J. "Tennessee Ernie" Ford was born at Bristol (actually at Fordtown), Tennessee in 1919 and grew up on a farm. He began singing early in life. The county sheriff sometimes asked his mother and him to sing gospel songs to prisoners in the county jail. In 1939, Ernie began announcing at WOPI, Bristol. That fall, he enrolled at the Cincinnati Conservatory of Music with thoughts of becoming a professional concert baritone singer.

Bill Cullen was born in Pittsburgh in 1920. His father operated a garage. At the age of eighteen months, Bill was striken with polio, which left him with a limp. While recuperating in a hospital for nine months after a second automobile accident as a teenager, he decided he wanted to be a doctor. After high school graduation, Bill entered the University of Pittsburgh as a pre-med student. Later, he had to leave school because of a lack of finances. Next he went to work in his father's garage as a mechanic and tow-truck driver. As a diversion on the job, he amused the other workers by imitating radio announcers. This activity encouraged Cullen to audition at WWSW, a 250-watter in Pittsburgh. He was given the opportunity to gain experience, working six hours nightly for no pay. After a couple of months, he was put on the payroll. He had proved what he thought: "that radio was one place that a ham like me, I'm a ham, could limp and still get a job."

J. Fix (later to be known on the networks as Jay Stewart) was a native of Indiana. During his early school years at Summitville, he had a newspaper route, worked as a counselor in a summer band camp, was employed as a soda jerk, and helped to manufacture ice cream (receiving extra benefits by eating his fill). By the age of nine, he had begun playing the saxophone. At fourteen, he started emceeing floor shows. Fix completed grade school and high school at a rapid pace and entered DePauw University before his sixteenth birthday. Later, he transferred to Butler University in Indianapolis, working his way by playing in and leading dance bands. After graduation in 1939, J. Fix was hired as an announcer on WBAW, Terre Haute.

Raymond W. Goulding (later to be half of the "Bob and Ray" duo) was born in Lowell, Massachusetts. Following high school graduation in 1939, he was hired as an announcer at WLLH, Lowell at fifteen dollars a week. His older brother Paul also worked there. Soon WEEI, Boston beckoned, and Ray moved to the metropolitan station.

Garry Morfit (Moore) got an opportunity to do some network radio in 1939. In April, he appeared as the guest MC on Ransom Sherman's *Club Matinee* in Chicago. Then his station, KWK, St. Louis, gave him permission to be away on Fridays and Saturdays so that he could handle the show for Sherman on those days.

In addition to his news broadcasts from Studio 9 at CBS, Robert Trout described the opening of the 1939 New York World's Fair.

After Fulton Lewis, jr., became a radio broadcaster, he found that he didn't receive the same privileges while covering the Senate and House of Representatives that he had enjoyed as a newspaperman. Lewis led a successful fight to gain radio recognition in the press galleries of both houses of Congress and at White House press conferences.

More new shows debuted in 1939, opening up more announcer opportunities. *Against the Storm*, a more serious serial drama, would provide work for Nelson Case, Richard Stark, and Ralph Edwards during its three-year run. The list of *Aldrich Family* announcers would include Don Wilson, Dwight Weist, Dan Seymour, Ralph Paul, George Byran, and Harry von Zell. *Screen Guild Theatre* employed announcers John Conte and Mike Roy. Bill Stern conducted *The Colgate Sports Newsreel. Dr. I.Q., the Mental Banker* came into existence. Former WOAI, San Antonio announcer-singer Lew Valentine was the first Dr. I.Q. Announcer Allan C. Anthony made the taste of the candy bars sound appealing.

Roger Krupp announced the detective show *Ellery Queen*. Durward Kirby handled the announcing for *Li'l Abner. The Milton Berle Show* went on radio for the first time. Frank Gallop was the announcer. *Mr. District Attorney* used announcers Ed Herlihy and Fred Uttal. Hugh James handled *The Parker Family* program. Rush Hughes and Ben Grauer would serve as successful hosts for *Pot o' Gold*, an early giveaway show. *When a Girl Marries* began its nineteen-year run, using announcers Frank Gallop, Charles Stark, Dick Stark, Dennis King, Hugh James, George Ansbro, Don Gardiner, and Wendell Niles. Graham McNamee, Bill Stern, and H.R. Baukhage were featured on a show called *Four Star*.

Announcer assignments to existing shows included Truman Bradley to *The Burns and Allen Show*, Bill Goodwin to *Al Pearce and His Gang*, and Dick Joy to *Silver Theatre*. Once Joy and the show's host, Conrad Nagel, were together in the lobby of CBS' Columbia Square where they met some ladies. Forgetting that he had put his toupee in his briefcase, Nagel tipped his homberg. Blushing, he whispered, "Please, Dick, remind me—next time."

Boake Carter was attempting to get his commentaries back on the air. He arranged to airmail discs to twenty-five stations.

Charles Victor, who had worked as Charles V. Lutz beginning in 1935 at WAIU, Columbus and later at WHK, Cleveland and WKRC, Cincinnati, was doing a street show for WGN in front of the Chicago Theatre called *Chicago at Night*.

Lowell Thomas broadcast the first television news program for NBC in 1939.

Lambdin Kay announced the premiere of the movie *Gone With the Wind* in Atlanta over WSB in 1939.

Other announcer situations: Jimmy Wallington was the commercial announcer for *Texaco Star Theatre*. Dan Seymour announced for *Aunt Jenny*. Jack Lescoulie did the *Grouch Club*. Bill Goodwin worked *The Bob Hope Show*. Norman Brokenshire substituted eight days for Fred Uttal, the regular announcer for *Big Sister*.

The broadcasting of major league baseball began in the Greater New York area in 1939. Red Barber left Cincinnati to do the play-by-play of the Brooklyn Dodger games on WOR and WHN. Al Helfler was hired as his assistant. Barber won the *Sporting News* baseball award that year. He also had the distinction of doing the first telecast of a major league game, the August 26 contest between the Dodgers and the Reds. Barber wore a gas station attendant's cap while doing the Socony-Vacuum commercial. For General Mills, he poured Wheaties into a dish.

There were six hundred applicants for the job of broadcasting the games of the Giants and Yankees. Arch McDonald of Washington didn't apply, but the 230-pound sports reporter was given the job. McDonald had one particular idiosyncrasy. He didn't like for someone to touch him with peach fuzz. He had a real horror of it. In fact, he once broke the jaw of a practical joker who rubbed him with it. The sportscaster chosen as his helper in New York was a name that would be around Yankee Stadium for a long time—Mel Allen.

Sports announcer Russ Hodges moved from WIND, Gary to WBT, Charlotte. During the autumn, Hodges broadcast the Pittsburgh professional football games on KDKA.

Other mikemen were on the move. NBC news commentator Hilmar Baukhage was transferred from WRC-WMAL, Washington to Radio City, New York. Chet Huntley moved from KFI, Los Angeles to KNX. Warren Sweeney left WJSV, Washington for the CBS staff in New York. Tony Marvin went from WNYC to the World's Fair radio staff. Bert Parks left CBS, New York for a singing-announcing assignment on the *Eddie Cantor Show*. Carlton Kadell went from Hollywood to Chicago for a role in the serial *The Romance of Helen Trent*. Roger Krupp moved west from WBBM, Chicago to KMTR, Hollywood. Douglas Browning, formerly with WLW, joined NBC, New York. Allan Jackson, who had been announcing for WLW, Cincinnati and WHAS, Louisville, joined the Texas State Network.

Rod O'Connor, formerly with WTCN, Minneapolis; KVEC, San Luis Obispo; KID, Idaho Falls; KLO, Ogden; and KUTA, Salt Lake City, was added to the staff of KSL, Salt Lake City. Jimmy McClain of KABC, San Antonio joined the Texas State Network to announce a new show, *Texas Hall of Fame*. He was formerly with WFAA, Dallas and the Texas Centennial Exposition. Bob Lemand went from KEHE (changed that year to KECA) to KNX.

Roy A. Rowan launched his broadcasting career in 1939 at WKZO, Kalamazoo. Subsequent announcing jobs before landing in Hollywood would include WGY, Schenectady; WGR-WKBW, Buffalo; and WGN, Chicago.

Other announcer situations: Connie Desmond was at WSPD, Toledo. Jack Brinkley was on the NBC, Chicago staff. Bob Elson of WGN and Red Barber and Al Helfler, both of WOR, broadcast the All Star baseball game for MBS. John S. Young, having earned his doctorate, was appointed director of broadcasting at the New York World's Fair. Quin Ryan returned to WGN after a long illness. Hugh Brundage of KHJ, Los Angeles was given a feature role in the movie *Mr. Smith Goes to Washington*. John Conte was cast in the role of an announcer in the motion picture *Invitation to Happiness*.

WLW's Peter Grant, who did *Front Page Parade* for Mutual, was reported to be reading 2,600 words per fifteen minutes. That was some 400 more than was usually read in that length of time.

Bill Baldwin, announcer for *Yawn Patrol* on KFSO, San Francisco, mentioned one morning that he was from the Midwest and had never seen raw gold. A listener in the Sonora area gold country sent him a tiny nugget. "When I heard your show, I went out and panned until I struck a color for you," wrote the listener. Bill took a hiatus from radio later that year and became publicity director for the Roller Derby in San Francisco.

Dick Joy sought greater sky coverage than his job at CBS could give him. As an amateur astronomer, Dick built a hand telescope, which he mounted on the roof of his home in Burbank.

WOW news editor Foster May received a call one cold night in January telling him that four desperadoes had escaped from the Omaha jail and were believed to be in an area to the southwest about twenty-three miles away. May took WOW's mobile news unit, a station wagon with a short wave transmitter, and headed for the site. By the time he arrived, a large number of officers were on the scene, using a farmhouse as headquarters. While the search was in progress, the newsman got cold. Seeing a small shed with a light in it, he went inside to warm up. Lying on a couch was another man whom May thought was a member of the posse. They chatted until May got warm. He stepped outside and suddenly became suspicious. He went back in and started asking straight questions. Then the man declared, "O.K., Foster. I'm your man. I'm all shot up."

May rushed outside, grabbed a mike, and told the engineer to put him on the air. He interviewed the escapee before police took him away.

During the year, network newsmen broadcast from Pan American Airways' *Atlantic Clipper* on its flight from New York to Portugal. George Hicks was aboard for NBC, and Bob Trout represented CBS. When the plane arrived in Portugal, Trout was arrested because he didn't have a Portuguese visa, saying that he didn't have time to get one before the plane left New York. The matter was soon straightened out.

Radio popularity continued to be measured in 1939. The New York *Telegram* Editor's poll selected Bill Stern as the best sportscaster, Lowell Thomas as the top news commentator, and Don Wilson the number one announcer. The *Radio Guide* poll named commentators Lowell Thomas and Dorothy Thompson and announcer Don Wilson.

NBC announcer Jack Costello was honored by his hometown of Sauk Center, Minnesota (which had been made famous in the early twenties by its noted son, Sinclair Lewis, in his novel *Main*

175

Street). Costello's protrait and biographical record were placed in a special section of the public library. After the future announcer had left the University of Minnesota, he became a newspaper reporter in St. Paul. He joined KSTP, St. Paul in 1933. Costello had been at Radio City since 1936.

John B. Gambling had a virtually captive audience for his show on WOR during that era, especially on icy mornings. John made "no school" announcements. For realism he rang an old-fashioned bell, which had been presented to him by the New Jersey State Education Commissioner. More than six hundred schools used his service. For this feature and all his other program material, Gambling was making $25,000 per year.

Andre' Baruch wrote an editorial for the January 15, 1939, issue of *Broadcasting*, discussing announcing styles:

> More and more the trend is to "humanize." This is a departure from the custom a few years ago, when the announcer was a staid, pompous individual who read his script with a supercilious air— as though he were a king's messenger. Eventually we were allowed to get away from "stiff" announcing and be ourselves, for a change. . . .
>
> There was a time when members of the announcing staff had two tones of voice—the artificial manner they assumed on broadcasts and the tone they used in ordinary conversations. . . . The difference sometimes was so vast that you couldn't recognize a radio announcer's voice if you heard him speak naturally. Today, the difference is small. Announcers are naturally more choosy of their rhetorical p's and q's when they are facing the microphone, but at least they are themselves. They don't put on airs. . . .
>
> While many announcers have become successful as specialists, it is also a good idea to be so versatile that you can fill any type of job at a moment's notice. The veterans are quite accustomed to quick changes. . . .

Swashbuckling news reporter Floyd Gibbons died in 1939.

Another new microphone came on the market. It was Western Electric's cardioid mike.

VI

We Interrupt This Program

Speech is civilization itself. The word,
even the most contradictory word, preserves
contact—it is silence which isolates.
—Thomas Mann

As war activities intensified in Europe during 1940, the first full year of World War II, American radio networks built up their foreign correspondent staffs on the continent. Many reporters were newspaper people who had been there already. Others were individuals engaged in business or educational pursuits in the area. Most of them stopped their previous activity and adapted quickly to the broadcasting medium. CBS had jumped off to a head start in quality overseas coverage, but the other networks soon recognized the significance of foreign pickups because of listener interest.

As the Germans battled to conquer more territory, Eric Sevareid, whose headquarters were in Paris, was kept extremely busy. Although a radio correspondent in Europe might have to work more than ninety-six hours a week, Sevareid said that he wouldn't change jobs with anyone. At first, his CBS associate in Paris was Thomas Grandin. He was replaced by Edmund Taylor, who had been a member of the *Chicago Tribune* Paris bureau since 1928. From the time France went to war with Germany, Sevareid had traveled with the French Army and Air Force in France, Belgium, Holland, and Luxembourg, broadcasting the news. He had been inside a fort in the Maginot Line during Christmas Eve the preceding year, reporting on the soldiers' Christmas service. During the latter part of April 1940, he had to rush his wife to a clinic, where she gave birth to twins. This parental responsibility added to demands on his time and

177

energy. Sevareid made the decision to send his wife and youngsters to the United States.

The fall of France and its capital was imminent. On June 10, Eric Sevareid learned that the French radio station was to be dismantled that night and moved away. He received a promise that they would wait until after his midnight broadcast. He finished his report, and the moving out of the station began. Thereafter, he drove south to Tours and Bordeaux, taking with him all the money that CBS had in Paris, an extra can of gasoline, and a bicycle tied to the top of his car. He later joined Edward R. Murrow in London. In October of 1940, Sevareid returned to the U.S. and was assigned to the CBS News Bureau in Washington.

William L. Shirer was still the CBS representative in Berlin when 1940 began. With him was Edward E. Hartrick, Jr., who had been working for the New York *Herald Tribune* in Paris. Shirer interviewed several German Army and Navy officers. He often had difficulty finding his way through blacked-out streets of Berlin. Also, a personal concern was the question of citizenship of his daughter who had been born in Vienna during the German takeover. His wife had been an Austrian newspaper woman. There was a shortage of food in Germany. There was food rationing in accordance with the number of calories required for a person to do his work. Fortunately, Shirer and other foreign correspondents were classified as hard laborers, which meant they received double rations. In addition to this allowance, Shirer got a box of food every third week from friends in Denmark. It contained bacon, eggs, and butter.

When the German offensive drive to the west began, Shirer was one of the foreign correspondents authorized to accompany the German Army. He accomplished a news beat on the signing of the French surrender in a clearing in the forest at Compiegne, France, June 22. Most correspondents thought that the news would be announced by Hitler from Berlin. Shirer took a chance and stayed at the French location. NBC's William C. Keirker was also there. Shirer reported from outside the window of a train car, the same car that had been used for the German surrender to France in 1918. Shirer announced:

Hitler steps up into the car, followed by Göring and the others. We watch them entering the drawing room in Marshall Foch's car. . . . Hitler enters first and takes the place occupied by Foch the morning the first armistice was signed. The Germans salute. The French salute. The atmosphere is what Europeans call "correct," but you get the picture when I say that we see no handshakes—not on occasions like this. Hitler and the other German leaders rise from their seats as the French enter the drawing room. Hitler, we see, gives the Nazi salute, the arm raised. The German officers give a military salute. The French do the same. . . .

Shirer assumed that his broadcast was being recorded in Berlin for later release. Actually, someone failed to throw the switch, and the report was sent directly to America. CBS officials in New York had no further confirmation on the accuracy of the report that an armistice had been signed between France and Germany and were hesitant to accept its authenticity. After German censorship became more strict, William L. Shirer came back to the United States in December 1940. Harry W. Flannery, who had been working for KMOX, the CBS station in St. Louis, took his place. Before Flannery left the U.S., the Nazis investigated him prior to granting an entrance visa. They thought that Flannery's overseas inexperience would make him more "open-minded" about their objectives.

Cecil Brown was hired by CBS in January 1940 to cover for them in Rome. He had gone to Europe in 1937 and was employed by the International News Service.

During the early part of the year, CBS's Larry Lesueur was with the British Royal Air Force at the headquarters in France. After the fall of France, he was transferred back to London.

Ed Murrow continued to broadcast the Nazi bombings of London and to comment on the people's courage and their determination not to be conquered. The bombings did not put Murrow in a hospital but in February a bout with influenza did. During a broadcast in September, he reported that a direct hit had been made on the CBS office building. The structure was condemned for further use. He began using his apartment as an office. Erland Echlin assisted Murrow in London. Echlin had been covering Europe as a journalist for ten years. At the time he was hired by CBS, he was directing twenty correspondents for *Newsweek* out of London.

NBC began making up for lost time in coverage of the hostilities. Fred Bate was in London. He had been the network's European representative since 1932 and had resided in Europe since 1912. Bate was injured during a bombing attack in December when the NBC offices were knocked out. His injury was not serious.

Max Jordan was the NBC Central European representative. He was stationed in Switzerland. Jordan had been born in Italy in 1895. He later came to America and became a naturalized citizen. He went into newspaper work in Berlin in 1910.

William C. Keirker covered Berlin for NBC. He was a twenty-five-year-old New Yorker and had been studying at the Berlin Institute of Technology since 1938. He had no previous reporting experience. Keirker was hired by the network in February and continued his study between broadcasts.

Paul Archinard was NBC's man in Paris. He had been born in that city in 1899 but had gone to the U.S. at the age of five. He returned to France in 1918 as a member of the U.S. Army. Archinard held a business position in Paris from 1920 to 1926. He went to work for NBC in 1934.

Martin Agronsky, writer, foreign correspondent, and free lance reporter, was added to NBC's staff of foreign correspondents in May. He was stationed in Belgrade. Agronsky had first broadcast for NBC in December 1939 in Geneva.

Mutual, the newest of the three networks, was also organizing a competent European staff. John Steele was in charge of the London and European Bureau. He had begun his career as a newspaperman on the New York *Herald* in 1890. He became head of the Chicago *Tribune* London Bureau in 1924. Soon after Mutual was organized, Steele was appointed as their European representative. He was injured in a raid on September but was able to continue broadcasting soon after.

Arthur Mann also worked for Mutual in the London office. He had a background which included a great deal of newspaper experience, much of it on foreign assignments. Mann was a correspondent in London for the St. Louis *Post Dispatch* and the New York *Times* when he joined Mutual in September 1939.

Victor Lusinchi was the MBS Paris correspondent. He had first gone to work in Paris in 1934 for the British Exchange Telegraph. After the surrender of France to Germany, Lusinchi returned to the U.S.

Waverly Root covered MBS in Paris. He had been an European correspondent since 1927. His first story that year after arriving in Paris as reporter for the Chicago *Tribune* was the landing of Charles Lindbergh at the end of his historic trans-Atlantic flight. Root became the Paris correspondent for *Time* in 1938. He joined Mutual in January 1939.

Sigrid Schutz held two news positions in Berlin. She was chief of the Berlin bureau for the Chicago *Tribune* and she represented Mutual in the German capital. Miss Schutz had been in Germany during World War I and had joined the *Tribune*

180

after the armistice. She added the radio duties in September 1938.

Network commentators on the home front fulfilled the role of analyzing and interpreting world events. Boake Carter, after an absence of two years from a network news program, was hired by MBS. The controversial Carter never received again the listener recognition he had achieved in the thirties.

Cedric Foster, a former news analyst on WTHT, Boston, also went on Mutual. He claimed to be the first daily daytime coast-to-coast commentator. Foster was heard from 2:00 to 2:15 P.M.

H.V. Kaltenborn and the Columbia Broadcasting System finally came to a parting of the ways. CBS management didn't like controversy. Kaltenborn's strongly expressed opinions often created disagreement. It was believed that Paley and company were relieved when he moved his commentary to NBC in May 1940.

Elmer Davis was gaining broadcast journalism eminence with his incisive reporting. Davis claimed to suffer from mike fright, saying, "I haven't yet lost the fear that someday I will go insane at the mike and begin spouting treason, blasphemy, and (worse) libel."

After ten years on the air, Lowell Thomas enjoyed great popularity. His salary reflected his listener appeal to the tune of $200,000 annually. Twenty thousand of that amount went to two news writers.

John W. Vandercook was born in London of American parents in 1900. His father was the European manager of a press association and later was cofounder of United Press. John attended several private schools in the United States and spent a year at Yale. He had a few small acting roles on Broadway. Next he took a fling at newspaper work, but that didn't last either. Then Vandercook became a world traveler and explorer, sporting the appropriate beard. he visited more than seventy countries and wrote a series of books based on his adventurous experiences. One day in 1940, Vandercook was visiting an NBC official in New York. News of an Allied deal for bases in the Caribbean had just been released. The network man asked him whether he knew much about the West Indies. He replied that they were one of his specialties. Vandercook was put on the air that night on NBC's *News of the World* at 7:15, and there he stayed (still with beard). His virile voice and personal knowledge of the places soon led to his becoming a high-salaried radio newsman. Contrary to the thinking of some commentators,

Vandercook expressed the thought that he was amazed by the freedom of radio, saying that no one interfered with anything he wanted to say.

In Kansas City, John Cameron Swayze, a well-known local newspaperman who had been heard on radio, joined the news department of KMBC in August of 1940.

Garry Morfit decided it was time to change his name after he took over *Club Matinee* in 1940. A contest for a new monicker was conducted on the air, and a Pittsburgh woman selected "Garry Moore." She won a hundred dollars and a trip to Chicago.

John J. Anthony and his *Goodwill Hour*, which had been a WMCA feature, went on NBC in 1940. The show captured the leading rating for advice-type programs.

Milton Cross was a very popular announcer by 1940, but revenue wasn't exactly flowing his way in abundance. His basic studio salary was eighty dollars a week as a WJZ staff announcer. He was paid one hundred weekly for *Information Please*; but since he did it on network time, he was docked for three-quarters of an hour of his basic pay, which amounted to about two dollars. Cross was also paid for the program *Metropolitan Opera Auditions*. His failure to earn big money commensurate with his reputation was blamed on his unctuous style, which many thought was not suitable for commercial products.

Ralph Edwards had been playing a parlor game with his friends which he called "Forfeits." He developed the idea into a radio quiz show named *Truth or Consequences*. The program went on NBC in 1940 and soon became a listener favorite. Edward's wife described the program as "crazy." Ralph agreed with her. He was the MC, and the announcers through the years would be Clayton "Bud" Collier, Mel Allen, Jay Stewart, Milton Cross, Ed Herlihy, Harlow Wilcox, and Ken Carpenter.

A quiz show started in 1940 that put a new expression into the language. The program was called *Take It or Leave It*. Should a contestant answer the first four questions correctly, he or she was given the opportunity to try for the big prize—sixty-four dollars. The fifth question was referred to as "the sixty-four-dollar question." The expression was picked up by the American people and any tough decision thereafter was called "the sixty-four-dollar question." (Later TV would inflate the sum to $64,000.) Bob Hawk was the first MC, but a financial disagreement with the sponsor opened the way for Phil Baker to take over. He was the spokesman most listeners associated with the show. MC's during the latter years would include Garry Moore, Jack Paar, and Eddie Cantor. The announcers would be David Ross, Ken Niles, and Jay Stewart.

Whom would you have selected in 1940 to moderate a quiz show with a panel of five intellectually brilliant youngsters? Would you have picked a bald, thirty-nine-year-old man with a third-grade education, who had gone into show business at the age of eight, who had once been half of a radio comedy-singing act billed as "The Two Lunatics of the Air," and who currently was the MC of the Saturday night *National Barn Dance* in Chicago? Well, that type of individual was chosen as the quizmaster for the *Quiz Kids*. Joe Kelly was short, plump, and jolly. He possessed a sparkling personality. He and Jack Holden had worked in radio in Battle Creek for twelve dollars a week and all the milk they could drink, provided by their dairy sponsor. Fort Pearson and Roger Krupp would serve in turn as announcer for *Quiz Kids*.

Lowell Thomas' regular newscast was carried on television also. It was the first sponsored program to be seen daily on TV over a period of months.

Mary Margaret McBride transferred her folksy style from WOR to CBS in October. Her "Martha Deane" label stayed behind at WOR and was assumed by another woman. Miss McBride used her real name on the quarter-hour daily network feature.

More new programs kept coming.

Amanda of Honeymoon Hill began a six-year run that would employ announcers Frank Gallop, Hugh Conover and Howard Claney.

A joke-telling show called *Can You Top This?* used Ward Wilson as the host and Charles Stark as the announcer.

The exciting youngsters' serial *Captain Midnight* had started on WGN, Chicago the previous year and was picked up by Mutual in 1940. Announcers Pierre Andre', Don Gordon, and Tom Moore would bring it on by stretching the title with a prolonged inflection.

The Chamber Music Society of Lower Basin Street had Milton Cross as the host and later Gene Hamilton filled the slot.

The quiz show *Double or Nothing* began a twelve-year daily tenure with the MC's during that time being Walter Compton, John Reed King, Todd Russell, and Walter O'Keefe. Fred Cole did the announcing.

Announcer Lou Crosby took listeners to *Gene Autry's Melody Ranch*.

Ben Alexander emceed *Little Ol' Hollywood*.

The Light of the World would dramatize Bible stories for a decade. Stuart Metz and Ted Campbell announced.

Announcers Durward Kirby, Henry Morgan, Nelson Case, and Richard Stark each traveled portions of the twelve-year trip of the *Lone Journey*.

Portia Faces Life and as announcers she saw George Putnam and Ron Rawson.

Announcer Clayton "Bud" Collier donned the attire of *Superman* when it went on Mutual in 1940. Jackson Beck was the announcer who handled the hyperactive opening.

The Texaco Star Theatre had various formats at different times. One version featured a half-hour of variety entertainment from Hollywood with Ken Murray as the MC and Jimmy Wallington as the announcer, and a half-hour of drama from New York with Larry Elliot announcing.

A comedy quiz called *Play Broadcast* gave a year of employment to MC Bill Anson, announcer Guy Savage, and Marvin Miller, who did comedy voices.

Marvin Miller also had other work which included the announcer's chores on *Wings of Destiny*.

Tommy Bartlett was doing well on WBBM, Chicago. His handling of *Meet the Misses* and *The Misses Goes to Market* was bringing in $22,000 a year. Tom Moore, who was new to WBBM, substituted for Bartlett when the regular MC was on vacation.

Out in Los Angeles, Ben Alexander, a future *Dragnet* performer, was announcing the *Chase and Sanborn Show*. Bill Henry was doing the quarter-hour *By the Way* on CBS' Pacific Coast stations. Truman Bradley was assigned to the *Woodbury Hollywood Playhouse*, replacing Lou Crosby. Harlow Wilcox was announcing the *Don Ameche Show*. Wendell Niles was assigned to the *Al Pearce and His Gang* show.

Don Hancock, who had been announcing for *Stepmother* in Chicago, went to New York to announce for *The Goldbergs*, replacing Carlton Kadell. Ted Malone was conducting *Pilgrimage of Poetry*. WOR's Tom Slater was the MC of *This Is Fort Dix*. Arthur Godfrey went on Mutual at 9:00 each morning in addition to his established show. Rush Hughes joined *Johnny Presents* in New York.

184

Art Carney, a mimic with no previous announcing experience, won the job as regular announcer for *Pot o' Gold.* Del Sharbutt was signed to announce Campbell Soup's programs, which included Martha Wenster, Lanny Ross, and the new *Campbell Playhouse.*

Allan C. Anthony, who was chief announcer at KWK, St. Louis, commuted by air each week to the site of the *Dr. I.Q.* program to work as the show's announcer. Anthony estimated that he traveled 75,000 miles in six months.

In Cincinnati, Ruth Lyons was conducting the *Women's Hour* on WKRC. She was also the station's program director.

Dave Garroway, who had been at KDKA for two and a half years, went to WMAQ, Chicago. The city would be the scene of his future success.

Mike Wallace also made a significant move, going from Grand Rapids to WXYZ, Detroit. This move gave him the opportunity to work as announcer, narrator, and actor on some network shows, including *The Lone Ranger* and *The Green Hornet.*

Hugh Downs made the big move from WLOK, Lima' to WWJ, Detroit. He also was a part time student at Wayne University. Ernie Ford left the Cincinnati Conservatory of Music and returned to radio announcing, this time at WATC, Atlanta. Jay Fix (Stewart) made the precipitous leap from WBAW, Terre Haute to WLW, Cincinnati. Dennis James moved from WATT, Jersey City to WNEW, New York. Van Patrick switched from sportscasting at WDSU, New Orleans to WHBF, Rock Island, Illinois. Douglas Edwards, formerly with WXYZ, Detroit, joined WSB, Atlanta as a newscaster. Mort Lawrence, a Philadelphia free lancer, joined WFIL of that city and then moved on to WIP. Charlie Smithgall transferred his *Morning Parade* from WSB to WATL, Atlanta. Jerry Doggett, a future play-by-play man for the post-war Liberty Network, went to KELD, Ed Dorado, Arkansas. Mark Goodson, a recent University of California graduate and a future television producer, joined the announcing staff of KFRC, San Francisco. Alois Havrilla, who had been free lancing for three years, joined WOR.

Other 1940 announcer situations: Cy Harrice was at WLS, Chicago. Don Gordon was at WBBM-CBS, Chicago. The presidential announcers were John Charles Daly, CBS; Carlton Smith, NBC; and Walter Compton, MBS. Lorne Greene, U.S. television's future Ben Cartwright on *Bonanza,* was the chief news announcer of the Canadian Broadcasting Corporation. Greene was known as "The Voice of Doom." Bill Hay suffered a heart attack, and Ernest Chappell substituted on the *Amos 'n' Andy* program during his absence.

On the sports broadcasting scene, Mel Allen took over as the principal announcer of Giant and Yankee home baseball games. He was assisted by Jack Slocum. Arch McDonald returned to WJSV to again handle the games of the Washington Senators. Jim Britt, sports director of the Yankee and Colonial Networks, broadcast the games of the Boston Bees and Red Sox. Jack Brickhouse, who had been sports director for six years at WMBD, Peoria, joined the WGN, Chicago sports staff. On Mutual's World Series coverage, Mel Allen of WABC, Bob Elson of WGN, and Red Barber of WOR shared the announcing duties. Elson also won the *Sporting News* baseball trophy that year. Harry Wismer was sports director at WJR.

Down in Arkansas, the University's Razorback football games were broadcast by a medical doctor. Dale Alford had handled the games while he was a medical student. After serving his internship out-of-state, he returned and accepted a position on a hospital staff. He resumed Saturday football broadcasting. One trip took him to New York's Polo Grounds for the Arkansas-Fordham game. His color man for the occasion was NBC's George Hicks.

Pioneer announcer Leo Rosenberg, who had announced the results of radio's first coverage of a presidential election for KDKA in 1920, was a special guest on the first televised presidential election returns report. Rosenberg appeared November 5 on NBC's W2XBS. He was then a vice president for the Lord & Thomas Advertising Agency. The television camera showed an Associated Press teletype printing bulletins. Announcer Ray Forrest read the latest figures and interviewed network radio commentators.

Another radio pioneer received an assignment. Major J. Andrew White was signed by Twentieth Century Fox to assist in writing the script for a motion picture feature entitled "Calvacade of Radio."

Martin Block, who was still conducting the very popular *Make-Believe Ballroom* on WNEW, and performer George M. Cohan were the co-MC's of "Swing Carnival" at the World's Fair. The production was staged for the benefit of America's defense program.

186

Popularity polls kept coming. *Motion Picture Daily* polled seven hundred editors and columnists, and the results placed announcers in this order: Don Wilson, Milton Cross, Ken Carpenter, Harry von Zell, Bob Trout, Ben Grauer, and Andre' Baruch. In the commentator category: H.V. Kaltenborn, Lowell Thomas, Elmer Davis, Raymond Gram Swing, and Paul Sullivan. Don Wilson also copped the *Radio Guide* honor again.

October 16, 1940, was registration day for the newly enacted military draft. Many male announcers were away from the mike that day. At some radio stations, secretaries, bookkeepers, and other female employees had to do the announcing.

Ken Roberts' friends often asked him to explain how a radio broadcast was conducted. Explanations finally became tiresome. To solve the problem, Roberts made 16 mm movies of the entire production of *The Goldbergs*, *Life Begins*, and *Joyce Jordan, Girl Interne*. He willingly showed the films when someone asked the question.

Fulton Lewis, jr., made comments from the Capitol radio gallery prior to FDR's message to Congress. He remarked that all cabinet members except the Postmaster General were wearing striped pants. Later, a senator told Lewis that his office had detected a "grievous error" in the broadcast. "How would you know about Labor Secretary Frances Perkins?" the senator inquired.

Joe Ford, an announcer at WSGN, Birmingham, was handling a remote from a theatre where a magician was appearing. During an interview with the performer in his dressing room, Ford noticed a wildcat in a cage over in a corner. The magician explained that he had just returned with it from the Florida Everglades. At that moment, the animal broke loose. Ford quickly announced, "We now return you to our studios!" Then he and the magic man rushed from the room, leaving the door open. The wildcat was loose for thirty minutes before police and firemen using tear gas and a lasso captured it.

During 1940, the Associated Press became the last news service to make its product available to radio stations.

Charles Collingwood was born in Three Rivers, Michigan, in 1917. His father was a forestry expert, and the family moved often. Charles started to kindergarten in Ithaca, New York and attended grade schools in New York State, Michigan, and Bethesda, Maryland. In 1934, he finished high school in Washington, D.C. where he was president of the student council

187

and a member of the National Honor Society. Collingwood won a scholarship to Deep Springs School near Death Valley, California. It was a ranch school with twenty students, taught by five professors under the Oxford tutorial system. During his three-year stay, he branded cattle, rode herd in the mountains, blasted a cattle shed out of rock, was responsible for milking five cows, and was in complete charge of all small animals. Collingwood enrolled at Cornell in 1937 and studied pre-law. During summer vacations, he traveled extensively in the United States and southern Canada. After graduation in 1939, he was awarded a Rhodes scholarship.

While a student at Oxford, Collingwood also worked for the United Press in London. When his journalistic activities increased because of the war, he was notified by the Rhodes Committee that he must choose between college and work. In May 1940, he wrote his parents, ".... The world that comes out of this war is not going to be a world conducted by pale scholars, gorged with useless information, you can be sure of that." The following month, he began working full time for the United Press in London. Charles Collingwood was hired by Ed Murrow in March 1941. First, he broadcast from London, but other assignments would follow.

During 1941, Elmer Davis went to London to originate his broadcasts for a few weeks. The Hoosier was shocked by Murrow's automobile driving when they took a tour of the countryside. Davis later commented, "I had heard of the horrors of war, but I didn't know they included Ed Murrow's driving."

Murrow had been broadcasting twice every twenty-four hours since the beginning of the war. Those who worked with him noticed he was tiring. He had lost thirty pounds. He was a chain smoker. Another telltale sign of fatigue was the angle he held a cigarette in his mouth. He would start an evening with it jutting straight out from his jaw. Later it would begin to droop. Finally, the cigarette would hang almost straight down from the corner of his mouth.

CBS thought it was time to bring Murrow back home for a rest. In October, Robert Trout was sent aboard the *Clipper* to replace him temporarily as the CBS European news chief. Trout covered the London blitz and did a program entitled *Trans-Atlantic Call*, which featured conversations with English people. It was carried in England by the BBC and sent by short wave to the United States.

188

Murrow arrived in the U.S. November 24, 1941. Shortly, CBS president Bill Paley presented a dinner at the Waldorf-Astoria in his honor. The affair was attended by more than one thousand guests, including high government officials, prominent educators, newspaper and magazine editors, and leading industrialists and businessmen. The network broadcast the event, which featured a talk by the guest:

> We have been trying to report a new kind of war, a war that is twisting and tearing the social, political, and economic fabric of the world. We have attempted to give you the hard news of communiques and official statements as well as the climate in which the news has flourished, the humor, the criticism, the controversy and discussion which serves as a background for the more dramatic news action of the war. . . .

Eric Sevareid was assigned to the CBS News Bureau in Washington. He also covered stories from Mexico and Brazil. William L. Shirer was also in the United States during the year. He received a special award from the Headliners Club for general excellence in radio reporting. He went on a lecture tour and served as technical advisor on a war film in Hollywood.

Larry Lesueur was assigned to cover Russia in the autumn of 1941. Before reporting to Moscow, he developed a working knowledge of four hundred Russian words. During his stay, he traveled a great deal in the country, crisscrossing it several times observing fighting fronts and Red Army encampments, as well as factories, schools, hospitals, and collective farms.

Harry W. Flannery, the CBS Berlin correspondent, returned home in September 1941. His assistant, Howard K. Smith, remained to report from Hitler's land.

Cecil Brown, the CBS correspondent in Rome, was kicked out of the country ("denied further use of Italian broadcasting facilities") by the Fascist government because of a "continued hostile attitude." Later in the year, while serving as the CBS Far Eastern correspondent and after having beeen aboard the English battleship *HMS Repulse* when it was sunk, Brown sent a cable to his wife in the United States: "Health reasonably satisfactory. In October the Air Force crashed me. In November, an Army truck plunged over a hill with me. In December, the Navy tried to sink me. Since no additional branches of the force remain, don't worry about the indestructible Mr. Brown."

John Charles Daly was the CBS special events reporter in the U.S. When Robert Trout went to London to relieve Ed

Murrow, Daly was named reporter for the evening news program *The World Today.* He also covered the Army in training camps as they conducted war games. This material was used for the program *Spirit of '41.*

Helen Hiett, NBC European correspondent, used some feminine ingenuity to get a story, which resulted in her becoming the first woman to win the Headliners Club award. During her duty in Spain, Miss Hiett made friends with a group of chorus girls. She joined their troupe on the way to entertain British troops stationed in Rock of Gibraltar fortifications. The area was bombed for three days while she was there. When she identified herself to authorities as a reporter, she was released to return to Madrid to make a broadcast about the bombing.

Alex Dreier, a former correspondent for United Press, joined the NBC news staff in Berlin in 1941. It was the beginning of a long and illustrious radio news career for Dreier.

NBC news commentator John B. Kennedy joined WNEW, New York as a news analyst, heard Monday. through Friday from 7:30-7:45 P.M. Veteran announcer Norman Brokenshire also joined WNEW as a newscaster. He was on the air Monday through Saturday from 5:00-5:15 P.M.

H.V. Kaltenborn addressed the Texas State Legislature in June, speaking on the topic "We Look at War." It was the first time a radio commentator had spoken to the group.

On the morning of Sunday, December 7, 1941, Honolulu listeners heard over KGMB the steady but infuriated voice of Webley Edwards:

> Ladies and Gentlemen, we ask you to be calm and listen carefully. This island, Oahu, is under attack by enemy planes. The Rising Sun has been seen on the wings of these planes, and we believe them to be Japanese. We will keep you advised. Stay under cover, keep off the streets, do not use the telephone; telephone facilities are needed for other very important matters. All automobiles get off the highways immediately. We are not asking you to do these things, we are telling you.
>
> Some of you people think this is a maneuver. This is no maneuver. This is the real McCoy!
>
> Keep calm, and do as you are told to do. Thank you.

At 2:26 P.M. Eastern time, WOR interrupted a Dodger-Giant football game to read a flash of the Japanese attack on Pearl Harbor. Two minutes later, the bulletin was on NBC's Red and Blue Networks. CBS included the announcement on the 2:30

190

stationbreak and then followed with a hastily revised regular newscast. American radio was quickly in the business of reporting its first war involving its own country.

Several radio announcers were called to active military duty during 1941. Regretfully, it is not possible at this late date to determine who all of them were. Also, in giving the particular branch of service, the Army Air Corps designation will be used when referring to someone who entered the flying unit of the Army. The terms "Army Air Corps" and "Air Force" were often used interchangeably, but the Air Force wasn't established as a separate branch from the Army until after World War II.

Here are a few recognizable names who entered in 1941. Army: Robert Q. Lewis, WTRY, Troy; Howard Duff, a former announcer who was then a radio actor on NBC's *Dear John*; Jay Fix (Stewart), WLW, Cincinnati. Fix returned to WLW in November after a medical discharge.

Army Air Corps; Rex Marshall.

Arthur Godfrey seemed to be busier than ever. He was heard on WABC, New York (fed from Washington) six days a week from 5:35 to 6:45 A.M. He was also heard on WJSV from 6:45 to 9:00 A.M. Arthur made a couple of fifteen-minute transcriptions for Carnation Milk each week, which were sent to thirty-eight radio stations. In his spare time he made records for Decca. Gray Court Junior College for women at Ridgefield, Connecticut, discouraged students from listening to news broadcasts before class each morning because it was thought they had an adverse effect on morale. College authorities included daily listening to Arthur Godfrey as part of the curriculum. His cheerful, homey philosophy proved to be an aid to good morale.

Earle W. Graser, the radio actor who played the title role of *The Lone Ranger*, was killed in a car accident in 1941. Brace Beemer, who had been the show's narrator, took over the leading role.

Gabriel Heatter expanded his time on the air in 1941 with a show called *We the People*.

Most "soaps" were already established by 1941, but one called *Bright Horizon* found a time slot on the CBS schedule. It had a lady announcer, Marjorie Anderson.

The Selective Service Act was the impetus for a new show entitled *Dear Mom*. Tom Moore was the announcer during its one-year run.

A show that would enjoy ten years of great success was first heard in 1941—*Duffy's Tavern*. Announcers who would pass through the tavern were Jimmy Wallington, Marvin Miller, Jack Bailey, Perry Ward, Alan Reed (sometimes known as Teddy Bergman), and Rod O'Connor.

The First Piano Quartet was announced by Gene Hamilton.

The Great Gildersleeve was one of the best-liked situation comedies ever presented on radio. The announcer list included Jim Bannon, Ken Carpenter, John Wald, Jay Stewart, and John Hiestand.

Don Dowd served as the announcer for *In Care of Aggie Horn*.

The door in *Inner Sanctum* first started squeaking in 1941. Announcers Ed Herlihy, Dwight Weist, and Allan C. Anthony would endure the scary sequences.

Quality announcers Frank Gallop and Truman Bradley announced the quality presentation *The Prudential Family Hour*.

The light detective show *The Thin Man* used Ron Rawson and Ed Herlihy as announcers.

A serious, helpful program called *This Is Life* was announced by Marvin Miller.

Paul Douglas, announcer on the *Fred Waring Show*, started a daily sports program called *Dial Douglas*.

Other announcer assignments in 1941: Truman Bradley became the spokesman for *Tony Martin From Hollywood*. Basil Ruysdael was the announcer for *Your Hit Parade*. Frank Goss was selected for *Hollywood Showcase*. Bill Goodwin, who was announcing for *Blondie*, also took on the *Burns & Allen Show*. Tony Marvin handled the chores for *Major Bowes' Original Amateur Hour*. Graham McNamee was the MC of the *Treasury Hour*. Jack Costello was heard on the *Fitch Bandwagon*. Jim Bannon replaced Ben Alexander as narrator for *Everyman's Theatre*. Harry von Zell kept occupied handling four shows: *The Eddie Cantor Show*, *The Dinah Shore Show*, *We the People*, and *The Aldrich Family*. Andre' Baruch was heard by listeners of *Second Husband* and *Your Hit Parade*. Ford Bond did the job for *David Harum*, *The Cities Service Concert*, and *Easy Aces*.

Mike Wallace moved from WXYZ, Detroit to Chicago in 1941. He got a job at $150 a week on the soap opera *Road of Life*. In Pittsburgh, Bill Cullen moved from WWSW to the historical KDKA. Mary Margaret McBride left CBS in September and started a daily forty-five-minute program on NBC and WEAF. Ernie Ford transferred his announcing efforts from Atlanta to Knoxville. Bill Baldwin switched from KDYL, Salt Lake City to

KFWB, Hollywood, conducting, in addition to other shows, the daily one-hour feature *Mac the Mechanic*. Frank Goss moved from KWFB to KNX. Herbert Morrison went to WCAE, Pittsburgh. Karl Zomar, a future network poetry reader, returned to KWTO, Springfield, Missouri, from WMC, Memphis.

Sportscaster Russ Hodges changed from WBT, Charlotte to WOL, Washington. Olin Tice, formerly of WIS and WCOS, Columbia, South Carolina, and WDNC, Durham joined WBT. Jerry Doggett jumped from KELD, El Dorado, Arkansas, to WRR, Dallas. Morgan Beatty, a former newspaperman, was broadcasting news at WRC-WMAL, Washington. Ott Devine was listed as the "dean of announcers" at WSM, Nashville.

Radio announcing was sometimes a good starting place for budding actors. Tony Randall was born in Tulsa in 1920. He began his career at KVOO. In July 1941, Randall acquired a job as an announcer at WTAG, Worcester, Massachusetts. In August, he obtained a leave of absence from WTAG to appear in the play *Candida* at Marblehead, Massachusetts.

Richard Carlson worked as a summer relief announcer at WELI, New Haven, Connecticut, and joined the staff as a regular announcer in August.

Mark Goodson, announcer at KFRC, San Francisco, took a summer journey across the country to New York to try to sell several radio shows he had written. Eventually, listeners and viewers would often hear, "A Mark Goodson and Bill Todman Production."

It was a banner year for NBC sportscaster Bill Stern. He was named as director of network sports. Bill was also hired by Columbia Pictures for twelve short features entitled "World of Sports."

Red Barber was still riding high with the Brooklyn Dodger baseball broadcasts and other sports activities. Red was earning $15,000 annually for the play-by-play work and another $15,000 for a daily sports show and sports commentary for Pathe' News. Brooklyn listeners had become accustomed to his southern accent, and they had confidence in what he said. His mail averaged five hundred letters a week. One man wrote: "My wife was a semi-invalid. Yesterday she began to sink, but she heard the last out. She died happy."

Al Helfler assisted Barber with the Dodger games and did a daily sports roundup on WOR.

Mel Allen continued to broadcast the Giant and Yankee games.

Harry Caray, a future major league baseball broadcaster, moved from WCLS, Joliet to WKZO, Kalamazoo. Later in the year, Caray was named director of programs at WKZO's studios in Grand Rapids.

Washington sportscaster Arch McDonald was named chief air raid warden for Montgomery County Maryland. Fortunately, he never experienced any real duties.

Doing sports for WSB, Atlanta was Ernie Harwell.

Van Patrick, tipping the scales at 231 pounds, was still the sports announcer at WHBF, Rock Island.

Durward Kirby, NBC announcer on the staff of WENR, Chicago, was the recipient of the first H.P. Davis Announcer Award that was given on a national basis. The award was created in 1933 by the widow of the Westinghouse pioneer, who had encouraged early radio development. Until 1941, the honor had been limited to announcers on Westinghouse stations. Kirby received three hundred dollars and a gold medal.

Polls designed to rate announcers continued to thrive. The *Motion Picture Daily* survey of radio editors and writers in 1941 showed these results in order of popularity:

Announcers—Don Wilson, Harry von Zell, Milton Cross, Ken Carpenter, and Bob Trout.

Commentators—Raymond Gram Swing, Lowell Thomas, H.V. Kaltenborn, Elmer Davis, Gabriel Heatter, and Wythe Williams.

Sports Announcers—Bill Stern, Ted Husing, Red Barber, Stan Lomax, and Bob Trout.

The *Movie & Radio Guide* annual listeners poll came up with these rankings:

Announcers—Don Wilson, Milton Cross, Ken Carpenter, Bob Brown, Harry von Zell, Harlow Wilcox, Ralph Edwards, David Ross, and Ben Grauer.

Commentators—Lowell Thomas, H.V. Kaltenborn, Walter Winchell, Raymond Gram Swing, Paul Sullivan, Edwin C. Hill, Boake Carter, Gabriel Heatter, and Fulton Lewis, jr.

Sports Announcers—Bill Stern, Bob Elson, Ted Husing, Fort Pearson, Graham McNamee, Red Barber, Sam Balter, Clem McCarthy, Bob Trout, and Hal Totten.

At WTMJ, Milwaukee, an advertiser new to radio was looking over the script for the first show. Seeing the letters ANN beside various segments of the copy, he yelled, "Hey, what's the idea of having a woman read all this?"

Nelson Case enjoyed skiing, but he broke a leg in a ski accident in February. Nevertheless, Nelson continued to announce for *Kate Hopkins*, and Matt Crowley took over his *Ask-It-Basket*.

The NBC Barbershop Quartet competed in the annual quartet contest in New York's Central Park. The foursome was composed of announcers George Hicks, Ben Grauer, Harry von Zell, and Mark Hawley. There is no available evidence that they copped any singing honors.

On April 24, 1942, Graham McNamee announced *Elsa Maxwell's Party Line*. It was his last broadcast. Mac checked into St. Luke's Hospital with a streptococcus infection. He died there in May, two months before his fifty-third birthday, from embolism of the brain (the sudden obstruction of a blood vessel). Among the pallbearers at his funeral were Phil Carlin, Blue Network vice president in charge of programs and a former McNamee announcer associate; Tommy Cowan, WNYC, New York; Milton Cross, Blue Network announcer; and Tom Manning, sportscaster at WTAM, Cleveland.

Shortly before his death, McNamee had listed his eleven greatest moments in sports broadcasting:

1927—The Dempsey-Tunney long-count fight

1929—The World Series comeback of Philadelphia Athletics' pitcher Howard Ehmke

1929—Albie Booth's playing in the Army-Yale football game

1930—Billy Arnold's escape from death at the Indianapolis Speedway

1930—Earle Sand's third Kentucky Derby victory

1932—Babe Ruth's "called" home run in the World Series

1932—Eleanor Holm's unofficial 100-yard backstroke world swimming record

1934—Bill Tilden's tennis victory over Ellsworth Vines

1934—Glenn Cunningham's record-breaking mile at Princeton

1936—His erroneous announcement that Navy had won the Poughkeepsie regatta

1939—Ralph Guldahl's victory in the Masters' Golf Tournament

Perhaps an editorial in the Cleveland *Plain Dealer* best explained Graham McNamee's contribution to early radio broadcasting:

Mr. Radio Is Dead

THE HEARTY GREETING—"How do you do, ladies and gentlemen of the radio audience; this is Graham McNamee speaking"—has been heard for the last time. The owner of the best-known voice in America during the short-pants era of broadcasting is dead, and news of his passing will bring to millions of Americans a moment of nostalgia for the days when radio was taking its first breathless look at the American scene and reporting what it saw in a tone of open-mouthed excitement.

In those days, Graham McNamee was Mr. Radio himself. No event of national importance was complete unless it was described over the air by Graham. He gave most Americans their first intimate glimpse of national political conventions, of presidential inaugurations, of world series and big-time football games and of world's champion prize fights. It did not matter that McNamee knew little more of the technicalities of what he reported than those who listened to him. His job was not to interpret but to transmit ebullition from the ring side and the bleachers to the fireside and the corner store. He made "He's down, he's up, no he's down!" a national phrase. He described a 70-yard run or a three-bagger with the single word, "Whee!"

That was before the days of the expert, when the radio public began to demand to know what was happening on the five-yard line instead of the grandstand's emotions. After the expert arrived, Graham McNamee became just another announcer.

We are glad radio and the radio audience have put on long pants and gained something of adult sophistication, but we wouldn't want to have missed the Graham McNamee period of radio any more than we would want to have skipped over our own childhood.

Another radio pioneer died in 1942. Cornelius D. "Uncle Neal" Tomy's voice was stilled December 14. Beginning in April 1922, Tomy broadcast *The Red Apple Club* over WCX, Detroit. The show featured many stars and personalities of that time. The station was absorbed by WJR in 1929, and Tomy's popularity continued because of his handling of children's programs.

Also added to the broadcaster obituary list was M. Sayle Taylor, who was known on the air as *The Voice of Experience*. The dispenser of counsel to a large and loyal listening audience died at the age of fifty-three.

It was an inclusive year for Cecil Brown, CBS foreign correspondent in the Far East. In January, Brown was banned from the air by British authorities in Singapore for sending out news which "was bad for public morale." Brown insisted on using observed facts rather than official handouts. He left Singapore and stayed in the Dutch Indies temporarily before going to Australia. Brown was named winner of the Overseas Press Club Radio Award for outstanding coverage "contributing to the understanding of foreign policy by the American people." In April, he returned home for the first time in five years to receive the George Peabody Award for "the best reporting of the news." The previous year, Cecil Brown had broadcast an eyewitness report of the sinking of the British warships *Prince of Wales* and *Repulse* by Japanese torpedoes. The broadcast was made from Singapore a few hours after he was rescued from the water where the *Repulse* had gone down.

Cecil Brown was a native of Brighton, Pennsylvania, having been born there in 1909. He attended Western Reserve and Ohio State University, graduating from the latter school in 1929. Then he worked in journalism and joined INS as a foreign correspondent in 1937. When the war broke out, he became a CBS correspondent. In June of 1942, he took over the 7:55 P.M. newscast of Elmer Davis after Davis accepted an important government position—chief of the Office of War Information.

After an extensive lecture tour in the U.S., Ed Murrow returned to London in April, and Bob Trout came home. Eric Sevareid was appointed chief of the CBS Washington News Bureau. Larry Lesueur came back from Russia in December and started a weekly series of broadcasts called *An American in Russia*. Harry W. Flannery was serving as the CBS news analyst for the West Coast, broadcasting from Hollywood. Charles Collingwood was covering the action in North Africa. Quincy Howe switched from WQXR to the CBS news feature *The World Today*. Douglas Edwards came up from WSB, Atlanta to join the CBS news staff. Ned Calmer, who had been a news editor at CBS since 1940, began doing news broadcasts. Calmer's previous journalism experience included working as a reporter for the Paris *Herald* in 1927.

NBC's Martin Agronsky left Singapore and reported to General MacArthur's headquarters at the same time that Cecil

Brown made the move. Agronsky received *in absentia* an award in journalism from Rutgers University, his alma mater.

When the United States declared war against Germany, Alex Dreier, NBC's correspondent in Berlin, was one of the last newsmen to leave the city. Early in 1942, he came back to New York and started a series of news analyses on the network. But in October he went to London to replace NBC's Robert St. John. Fred Bate, chief of NBC's London Bureau, came back to New York in February. Richard C. Harkness, previously a reporter for the Philadelphia *Inquirer* and United Press, joined the NBC news staff.

In January 1942, the Blue Network was separated from NBC and became a chain in its own right. Blue was quickly establishing a competent news staff. George Hicks was appointed head of the London office. Raymond Gram Swing came over from Mutual to do a quarter-hour of commentary four times weekly at 10:00 P.M. Earl Godwin, who had been heard on NBC, was scheduled daily at 8:00 P.M. Also, Don Gardiner was transferred from WRC, Washington to Blue in New York.

Venerable H.V. Kaltenborn was busy with organization in 1942. There was a testimonial dinner on the twentieth anniversary of his first broadcast. He founded the Twenty Year Club of Radio Pioneers. He also put together the Association of Radio News Analysts and became its first president.

Many announcers left radio studios for military posts in 1942. Andre' Baruch received a commission as a first lieutenant in the Army. When the Americans hit the North African beaches in November, Baruch was on a ship off Casablanca. After hostilities subsided and there wasn't much to do ashore, he and a former engineering professor decided to build a radio station. They obtained General Patton's permission and proceeded to collect radio parts from various sources. After the rig was put on the air, Baruch read stories from newspapers and played music from their very small library. Later, they began receiving transcriptions of network radio shows and plenty of recorded music.

Others who went into military service in 1942:
ARMY

Hugh Downs, WWJ, Detroit; Bert Parks, network radio, private; Truman Bradley, announcer for the *Red Skelton Show*, entered in February and was back at the mike in October handling the *Screen Guild Players* and working as a newscaster on the West Coast; Ray Goulding, WEEI, Boston, captain; Ben

Gage, *Bob Hope Show*, private; Herb Morrison, WCAE, Pittsburgh, first lieutenant; Peter Grant, chief announcer, WLW, Cincinnati; Lew Valentine, MC for *Dr. I.Q.*; Murray Arnold, WIP, Philadelphia; Bill Spargrove, Blue Network.

NAVY

Dave Garroway, WMAQ, Chicago, ensign; Jean Paul King, network announcer; Bob Elson, WGN, Chicago.

MARINES

Ernie Harwell, WSB, Atlanta.

ARMY AIR CORPS

Tom Casey, NBC Blue, Chicago; Mel Ruick, *Lux Radio Theatre*, captain; Ernie Ford, Knoxville radio; Bob Lemand, *The Second Mrs. Burton*; George Bryan, CBS, second lieutenant; Ed Laux, WAAT, Jersey City, first lieutenant, Myron J. Bennett, KWK, St. Louis, first lieutenant; Ray Winters, WHN, New York.

NAVAL AIR CORPS

Nelson Case, *Phillip Morris Playhouse* and *Crime Doctor*; Frank Blair, MBS and WOL, Washington.

COAST GUARD

Hugh Brundage, *Junior Miss*, apprentice seaman.

U.S. POWER SQUADRON

Frank Singiser, WOR, New York.

The first announcer fatality was Lieutenant Robert H. Frear, Army Air Corps. He was killed in a plane crash in Florida. Lt. Frear formerly was chief announcer at WIBX, Utica.

Steve Allen was born in New York in 1921. Because his mother was in show business, Steve lived in several places as a youngster. He was attending high school in Chicago in the thirties when a case of asthma influenced their moving to Phoenix for his senior year. He accepted a journalism scholarship to Drake University at Des Moines because no other student wanted it. Steve took a radio course during his freshman year and did some work at radio station KSO. Since the scholarship was good for only one year, he went back to Phoenix and enrolled at Arizona State Teachers College at Tempe in the fall of 1942. He quit college in October and took a part time announcing job at KOV, Phoenix.

When Art Linkletter started trying to obtain a copy of his birth certificate, he learned that he was adopted and was not a citizen of the United States, having been born in Moose Jaw, Saskatchewan, Canada, and brought to the U.S. when he was two years old. He thought he was a native of Lowell, Massachusetts. Upon making his discovery, Linkletter applied for naturalization papers. This led to his being indicted by a federal grand jury on charges of falsely claiming citizenship by participating in activities reserved for citizens only. This included his voting in the 1940 elections. The charge was later dropped because he convinced authorities that there was no intent to act illegally.

As a student at Southern Methodist University in Dallas, Jimmy McClain majored in English and public speaking and made the varsity debating team. Next he took part in drama with the Dallas Little Theatre. Announcing jobs with WFAA and other Texas stations followed. In 1940, McClain became director of radio for a Chicago advertising agency. When Lew Valentine reported for Army duty, Jimmy McClain was selected to become *Dr. I.Q.*

Garry Moore moved himself and his crewcut from Chicago to New York in 1942. ("I only have one haircut a year," Moore said. "Every Thanksgiving our butcher cuts me and the turkey for the same price.") NBC gave him a new weekday early morning show. It was the network's attempt to compete with CBS' Arthur Godfrey and Blue's Don McNeill and his *Breakfast Club*. Moore was assigned to an office with H.V. Kaltenborn. The new program was called *The Show Without a Name*. Remembering that he had paid a listener to give him the name of Garry Moore, he conducted a contest to name the show. He offered a five-hundred-dollar war bond. *Anything Goes* emerged the winner. Howard Petrie was given the assignment of serving as Moore's announcer and straight man.

A new audience participation show, *People Are Funny*, originated from Hollywood. At the beginning, both Art Baker and Art Linkletter worked as co-hosts. After six shows, Linkletter left and returned to his announcing duties in San Francisco. He would be back later.

Because of health reasons, Bill Hay was forced to relinquish his position as announcer for *Amos 'n' Andy* in 1942. He was replaced by Del Sharbutt. Harlow Wilcox would do the work at a future date.

Paul Douglas was concentrating more on his movie career; nevertheless, he was appointed the official Hollywood announcer for the weekly War Production Board's short wave program *Command Performance*.

Bob Hawk started a new service-oriented quiz show called *Thanks to the Yanks*.

Ed Sullivan began doing a Monday evening program entitled *Ed Sullivan Entertains*.

The Army Hour was another show inspired by the wartime status. Ed Herlihy was the announcer.

The Abbott and Costello Show brought the pair's vaudeville and movie hilarity to radio. Ken Niles survived as their announcer.

Howard Petrie announced for *Abie's Irish Rose*.

Hop Harrigan, an adventure program for kids, was handled by Glenn Riggs.

The punny *It Pays to be Ignorant* started on WOR and would move to CBS the following year. Tom Howard was the quizmaster, and Ken Roberts and Dick Stark played it straight as the announcers.

A wartime serial drama called *Lonely Women* lasted for only one year. Marvin Miller announced.

Radio Reader's Digest leaped off the magazine's pages to the airwaves. Conrad Nagel, Richard Kollmar, and Les Tremayne shared the narrator-MC duties during its six years.

Rainbow House was emceed by "Big Brother" Bob Emery.

Stage Door Canteen was service-oriented with Bert Lytell serving as the master of ceremonies: "Curtain going up for victory."

The renowned mystery thriller *Suspense* made its appearance in 1942. Paul Frees was the narrator, and Truman Bradley announced.

The serial drama *We Love and Learn* was first heard that year under that title. Previously, it had been called *As the Twig Is Bent*. The announcers were Dick Dunham Fielden Farrington, and Adele Ronson.

Counterspy started its fifteen-year stay. Bob Shepherd and Roger Krupp fulfilled the announcing requirements.

Arthur Godfrey did a brief stint as announcer for Fred Allen's *Texaco Theatre* in 1942. Wally Butterworth left *Vox Pop*. Parks Johnson was joined on the program for a short time by Neil O'Malley before Warren Hull filled the co-host slot. Lou Crosby became the announcer on the *Bob Hope Show*. That fall Ken Niles got the Hope job. Niles also was hired for the *Lady Esther Serenade*. Harlow Wilcox, who was still announcing *Fibber McGee & Molly*, succeeded Bill Goodwin for *Blondie*. Goodwin remained with the *Burns & Allen Show*. Bill Bivens, former announcer and advance man for *Vox Pop*, was named announcer for *Fred Waring Pleasure Time*, succeeding Paul Douglas.

Jack Lescoulie, one of the originators of the early morning *Grouch Club* idea, joined WNEW, New York to assist Stan Shaw on *Milkman's Matinee*. Later in the year, Shaw went to WINS, and Lescoulie became the head man on *Milkman's Matinee*. Franklyn MacCormack, former narrator for Wayne King, became the commentator on *Hymns of All Churches*. Dick Joy received two new assignments: the *New Old Gold Show* and *Those We Love*. Verne Smith was named to share the announcing assignment with Gayne Whitman on the *Bob Burns Show*. Larry Elliot replaced Andre' Baruch on *The American Melody Hour* when Baruch went into the Army. Elliot was also the announcer for *Saturday Night Bandwagon*.

Other 1942 announcer situations: Harry von Zell was on *Time to Smile*. Tom Breneman was the MC of *Breakfast at Sardi's* (later to be called *Breakfast in Hollywood*). Frank Gallop was handling the broadcast of the New York Philharmonic Orchestra. Louis Roen announced for *The Guiding Light*. Ken Niles was exposed to the antics of the *Abbott & Costello Show*. Buddy Twiss handled the *Edgar Bergen-Charlie McCarthy* get-together. Ken Roberts was the announcer for *Big Town*.

After the Blue Network began operating independently, its announcers were appointed: Ray Diaz (chief announcer), William Abernathy, George Ansbro, Milton Cross, Jack Frazier, George Hays, George Hicks, Jack McCarthy, Hugh James, H. Gilbert Martin, Ray Nelson, Charles Nobles, Glenn Riggs, Bill Spargrove, and Bob Waldrop. Reginald Stanborough was named supervisor of night announcers.

The announcer station-to-station and network-to-network and station-to-network and network-to-station trek continued in 1942. Bill Baldwin, former director of special events at KFWB, Hollywood, joined the announcing and production staff of KGO, San Francisco. Jack Bailey, chief announcer at KGB, San Diego, went to KHJ, Hollywood. Henry J. Taylor, correspondent for the North American Newspaper Alliance, returned from Europe and began broadcasting for WHN, New York. Jack Brinkley went from free lance status to the staff of WLS, Chicago. Johnny Olson went back to the scene of his former announcing work, WTMJ, Milwaukee. Future Hollywood movie actor Cameron Mitchell joined WSRR, Stamford, Connecticut. Lee Bennett, a former vocalist for Jan Garber's Orchestra, joined the announcing staff of WGN, Chicago. Mort Lawrence finally left Philadelphia and WIP and moved to WHN, New York. Bill Ring, announcer at KWTO-KGBX, Springfield, Missouri, was hired for the staff of NBC, Chicago.

Actor Mel Ferrer, who had formerly been with Hollywood Playhouse, became an announcer at KFRO, Longview, Texas. Dorian St. George and George Gunn transferred from WRC-WMAL, Washington to Blue, New York. Bill Crago went from NBC, Washington to Hollywood to pursue some movie offers. Jim Bannon went east from KFI-KECA, Los Angeles to KMBC, Kansas City. Charles Woods, news announcer at WFIL and WCAU, Philadelphia, went to WOR, New York. Les Vine moved from WCAU to CBS, New York. Jay Sims joined WABC, New York to take over the CBS news schedule of George Bryan when he joined the Army Air Corps.

Other announcer positions in 1942: Lyle Van was on the staff of NBC. Alan Freed was at WKST, New Castle, Pennsylvania. Dick Dunham was with WITH, Baltimore. Sandy Becker was at WBT, Charlotte. Jay Jackson worked for WBNS, Columbus.

Red Barber continued to handle the Brooklyn Dodger games in 1942. They were heard on WHN. Red again received the *Sporting News* baseball award for play-by-play. Paul Douglas was selected by the publication for the top award in the baseball commentator category. Mel Allen took on a new assistant for the Yankee broadcasts. Connie Desmond, who had been at Toledo for eight years, became his number two man. In St. Louis, France Laux did the Cardinals and Browns baseball games on KXOX. Don Dunphy was a sportscaster for MBS and WINS, New York.

Walter Winchell's news broadcast received the top Hooper rating in the listener survey that was released in September 1942. He pulled a 22.1. Winchell held the rank of lieutenant commander in the Naval Reserve and reported for duty in the public relations office in New York while still doing his radio and newspaper work.

The *Movie-Radio Guide* annual listener poll selected a "Star of Stars" in 1942. Don McNeill of the *Breakfast Club* was given the outstanding honor.

Other results of the poll:

Announcer—Don Wilson, Milton Cross, Bob Brown, Ken Carpenter, Harry von Zell, Harlow Wilcox, Bill Goodwin, Durward Kirby, Richard Stark, and Jim Ameche.

News commentator—Lowell Thomas, H.V. Kaltenborn, Fulton Lewis, jr., H.R. Baukhage, Raymond Gram Swing, Boake Carter, and Cal Tinney.

Sports Announcer—Bill Stern, Ted Husing, Bob Elson, Red Barber, Guy Savage, Hal Totten, Fort Pearson, Paul Douglas, Clem McCarthy, and Jim Britt.

Howard Petrie of WEAF and NBC, New York was the 1942 winner of the H.P. Davis Memorial Award.

Martin Block was named vice-chairman of the Dance Orchestra Leaders division of the Committee for the Celebration of the President's Birthday for the National Foundation for Infantile Paralysis, which was observed nationally.

It was the year that Henry Morgan made his famous crack on WOR about the shoes he was advertising: "I wouldn't wear those shoes to a dogfight." After an emphatic sponsor objection, the next day Henry relented: "I would wear those shoes to a dogfight."

Regardless of the success of the CBS news department in covering the war, some dissension arose in 1943 when news director Paul White emphasized that editorial opinion by news analysts would not be permitted. The network bought a full-page newspaper ad to explain it's position. This was too much for CBS correspondent Cecil Brown. He resigned after White criticized a statement he made on a broadcast: "A good deal of the enthusiasm for this war is evaporating into thin air."

The Association of Radio Analysts was disturbed by the CBS policy. The organization's founder, H.V. Kaltenborn, a former CBS commentator, stated: "No news analyst worth his salt could or would be completely neutral or objective." Bill Henry was brought from the West Coast to take over Cecil Brown's newscasts. Henry was also appointed chief of CBS correspondents in Washington.

The star CBS correspondent in 1943 was Charles Collingwood. At the age of twenty-six, after only two years of radio reporting, he was given a George Foster Peabody Award for his reports from North Africa. Collingwood came up with several news beats. By the sound of his voice during broadcasts, he was able to convey certain unfavorable conditions. He explained, "I honestly didn't try to avoid censorship, but sometimes I'd get so upset at the news that I guess my voice was affected." He returned to the United States in October after four years overseas. He made a two months' lecture tour around the nation.

By the summer of 1943, Eric Sevareid felt that he wasn't doing enough by staying in the U.S. He headed toward a China assignment in August, but an Army plane he was riding over the Himalayas from India developed engine trouble. The twenty people aboard had to bail out into a remote jungle. The group was fortunate to make friends with a head-hunting tribe of savages. It was twenty-six days before they were able to make their way on foot to civilization and notify the United States that they were safe. Sevareid worked in the China-Burma-India area until November, when he came back home.

John Daly went to London in February 1943 to join the CBS staff. Douglas Edwards replaced him on *Report to the Nation*. Daly went on to North Africa in July and then landed with the first Allied troops in Sicily. During the remainder of the year, Daly covered Sicily, North Africa, Malta, and the Middle East.

Ed Murrow came back from London for a rest. Winston Burdett, CBS correspondent in Cairo, also returned. Bob Trout presented a program called *Calling America*, which was a report to the American people about their folks overseas. Allan Jackson came from WMC, Memphis to join the CBS news staff in New York. Jackson would stay for thirty-two years. Chet Huntley, a member of the special events staff of CBS in Hollywood, started a ten-minute news analysis program on CBS Pacific Coast stations.

Larry Lesueur made a "fluff" during a news broadcast in March, which resulted in considerable kidding from associates. Referring to a statement an admiral made about lend-lease materials sent to Russia, Lesueur said it had "created a teapest tempot." Ed Murrow sent a cable from London to Paul White: "Please purchase suitably inscribed, old-fashioned, enameled, single-handed teapest tempot and present it to Lesueur on behalf of his admirers in Columbia's London office." In June, Lesueur asked for another overseas assignment and was sent to join his admirers in the London office.

W.W. Chaplain had a good news background as a correspondent with International News Service. He served in the Rome and Paris bureaus and later covered the Ethiopian-Italian war. After World War II began, Chaplain was assigned to the British Expeditionary Force in France. He remained with them until just before the Dunkirk evacuation. Next he did a survey of Pacific Theatres of war. In April, he was sent to India and later to Moscow. Chaplain joined the NBC staff of news commentators in 1943.

Don Hollenbeck, formerly with the staff of the U.S. Office of War Information in London, joined NBC's London office.

The Blue Network was still making good headway in developing a competent news staff. Martin Agronsky and Henry J. Taylor joined the chain as news commentators. John B. Kennedy became a member of the group, also. Newspaper columnist Drew Pearson was heard on Blue on Sunday nights. Walter Kiernan, former writer for INS, began a news commentary on WJZ, Blue's New York outlet.

OWI chief Elmer Davis began a quarter-hour weekly news broadcast in March 1943, which was carried by all four networks.

The march of the mikemen from civilian radio facilities to military services continued in 1943.

ARMY

Mel Allen, New York sportscaster, private (Before reporting, Allen made his radio name legal, changing it from Melvin Israel.); Bob Elliot, WHDH, Boston; Jack Lescoulie, WNEW, New York; Frank Goss, Los Angeles announcer, first lieutenant; Hal Moore, WNEW, New York; Arthur Van Horn, WOR, New York; Jay Sims, CBS, New York; Alan Freed, WKST, New Castle.

NAVY

Mike Wallace, Chicago radio, ensign, submarine duty; Dick Joy, CBS, Hollywood; Fort Pearson, NBC, Chicago, lieutenant.

ARMY AIR CORPS

Cameron Mitchell, chief announcer, WSRR, Stanford.

NAVAL AIR CORPS

Ben Alexander, Los Angeles announcer.

Henry Morgan joined the Army Air Corps Reserve and resigned at WOR to wait for his call. He was replaced at WOR by Budd Hulick, former member of the team of "Stoopnagle and Budd." Morgan grew tired waiting and joined WHN to conduct the *Gloom Chasers*.

Walter Winchell was placed on inactive duty by the Naval Reserve.

Lieutenant James L. Carroll, Jr., former sports and special events announcer for WCDC, Charleston, South Carolina, was killed when the plane he was piloting crashed in Florida.

In the South Pacific, Jack Paar was getting entertainment experience he would use in his post-war career. Jack was performing for troops and earning a reputation as a comedian by using officers as his targets of humor.

Bert Parks was serving in the infantry in China, engaging in reconnaissance and establishing underground radio stations behind Japanese lines. On one assignment, Bert spent three weeks in enemy territory working with a wire recorder.

One U.S radio star during the period was not heard in the States, but she was enjoyed by a large and loyal listening audience. She called herself "G.I. Jill." She broadcast her show, *G.I. Jive*, over the Armed Forces Radio Service from Los Angeles. Her real name was Martha Wilkerson. Her bright, breezy style appealed to servicemen from Kodiak to Canberra. A typical opening to sailors: "Hiya, fellas. This is Jill again, all set to rock the bulkheads on the old jukebox and shoot the breeze to the sons of Mother Carey." Her closing was something like: "Good morning to some of you, good afternoon to some more of you, and to the rest of you good night." Her fan mail and gifts from overseas were received in tremendously abundant amounts.

After Garry Moore proved himself with a morning network show, officials began considering him for a nighttime slot. They decided to give him the support of an established entertainer— Jimmy Durante. Howard Petrie was again brought along as the announcer.

Art Linkletter, who had been on the first six *People Are Funny* shows the previous year, was named the regular MC in 1943.

Arline Francis Kazanjian (who would be known professionally as Arlene Francis) was born in Boston in 1908. Her maternal grandfather was a Shakespearian actor and taught her how to recite. She attended grade school in Boston and the Academy of Mount St. Verson in Riverdale, New York, where she displayed ability as an actress. Her parents reluctantly let her attend the Theatre Guild School for a year. Changing the spelling of her first name to Arlene and dropping her surname, she headed for Hollywood and landed a role in a 1932 movie. Her father ordered her to come back home. Hearing about a bit part in a radio show, she applied and wound up doing various imitations, which included barking, crying, cooing, cackling, and clucking. She did so well she was selected for the program *45 Minutes from Hollywood* to do impersonations of movie stars such as Greta Garbo. This led to assignments on *March of Time, Cavalcade of America*, and other programs.

Miss Francis went on the Broadway stage, appearing in several recognized plays including *The Women*. In 1941, she had radio roles in *Portia Blake, Amanda of Honeymoon Hill. Mr District Attorney, Betty and Bob*, and others. She also continued her stage work. In 1943, she was assigned to the hostess role in a new radio fun show called *Blind Date*. Her wit and sparkling appeal was a hit as she arranged dates between strangers.

A light family comedy entitled *Archie Andrews* appeared in 1943. Ken Banghart and Dick Dudley were the announcers.

Women were urged to help in efforts to win the war by a program entitled *American Women*. Eloise Kummer and Charlotte Manson were the narrators.

Joseph Dunninger read the minds of participants on *The Dunninger Show*. Don Lowe, Glenn Riggs, and Roger Krupp were there to read the copy.

Frank Graham was the announcer for *The Electric Hour*, which featured baritone Nelson Eddy.

A musical quiz show called *Grand Slam* was announced by Dwight Weist.

Movie actor Jack Carson was featured on the *Jack Carson Show* beginning in 1943. Del Sharbutt and Howard Petrie would be the announcers.

Jackson Beck narrated *The Man Behind the Gun*, a program that told stories of the actions of men in World War II.

Michael Fitzmaurice announced a "who-done-it" entitled *Nick Carter, Master Detective*.

Tales of the West were presented on *The Cisco Kid*. Marvin Miller and Michael Rye (real name Rye Billsbury) vocally set the scenes.

The daily quarter-hour of *Amos 'n' Andy* ended in February 1943, but the pair came back with a weekly half-hour version in October. Harlow Wilcox drew the announcing assignment. Bill Goodwin announced a summer run of *Paul Whiteman Presents*. Dick Joy went on Groucho Marx's *Pabst Blue Ribbon Town* and the *Nelson Eddy Show*. Durward Kirby was the MC of *Club Matinee*. Jim Ameche narrated *Manhattan at Midnight*. John Reed King was the MC of *Double or Nothing*. Carlton Kadell announced for *Red Ryder*. Del Sharbutt handled the *All-Time Hit Parade*. Lou Crosby took listeners to Pine Ridge for *Lum 'n' Abner*. Bill Bivens handled the *Harry James Show*. Michael Roy announced *Spotlight Bands*. Harry von Zell was there for *Silver Theatre*. Don Dowd became the announcer for the *Breakfast Club*.

Hugh Downs returned from the service in 1943 and joined WMAQ, Chicago. Steve Allen spent a brief time in military service before being released on a medical discharge. He returned to KOY, Phoenix and joined the cast of *Love Story Time*. Roy Rowan moved from WKBW-WGR, Buffalo to WGN, Chicago. Olin Tice made two moves—first, from WBT, Charlotte to WJSV, Washington and then to CBS, New York. (WJSV was changed to WTOP in March.) Allen Freed, who had been in the service, went to WIBC, Philadelphia. Jay Fix heard that announcers were needed on the West Coast and made the transition from WLW, Cincinnati to CBS, Hollywood. His radio name became Jay Stewart. Art Ford, formerly of WBYN, Brooklyn, went to WPAT, Patterson, New Jersey, and later joined WNEW, New York, taking over *Milkman's Matinee* when Jack Lescoulie went into the service.

Bill Cullen was working at KDKA, Pittsburgh as an MC for a variety program, making $250 a week. He resumed his study at the University of Pittsburgh and earned a B.A. degree. His early illness did not prevent his flying for the Civilian Air Defense as a patrol pilot.

Curt Gowdy was born in Green River, Wyoming, in 1919 and moved to Cheyenne when he was six. As a five-foot-nine high school basketball player, he was the leading scorer in the state. He was also selected for the National Honor Society. At the University of Wyoming, Curt continued his basketball activity and was in the college Reserve Officers Training Corps. After graduation in 1942, he was commissioned in the Army Reserve and called to active duty. Gowdy obtained a transfer to the Army Air Corps; but before he began flight training, he injured his back doing exercises. He was given a medical discharge in the spring of 1943.

After a back operation at Mayo's Clinic, Gowdy took a part-time job covering high school sports for a Cheyenne newspaper. He also did color for the play-by-play football broadcasts over KFBC. In November of 1943, Curt Gowdy broadcast his first football game, a district championship game between two six-man teams. This was followed by an assignment by the station to do play-by-play of high school basketball games. Soon he was employed by KFBC as a full time announcer.

Lt. Bob Elson was the first serviceman to broadcast a major sports event. While he was on leave from the Navy, he and Red Barber handled the 1943 World Series between the Cardinals and Yankees.

Harry Wismer broadcast the *Football Game of the Week* that year. For his endeavors, he was given a *Sporting News* award.

Russ Hodges was assisting Arch McDonald with the Senators games in Washington in 1943.

Arthur Millet, a free lance announcer and formerly with WRR, Dallas; WGN, Chicago; and CBS, died at his home in New York at the age of thirty-four. His programs had included *The Album of Familiar Music, The Goldbergs, Famous Jury Trials, Rich Man's Darling*, and *Our Gal Sunday* (which had developed from *Rich Man's Darling.*)

Norman Brokenshire joined an Alcoholics Anonymous group in Forest Hills, New York. It would be his first step back toward radio distinction.

Arthur Godfrey was still having his physical difficulties. During the winter, he suffered a crushed foot when he slipped on ice and the log he was cutting rolled on his foot. In July, Arthur went to the hospital for an appendectomy.

Blue Network's George Hicks was aboard the invasion flagship *Ancon* on the evening of D-Day, June 6, 1944, which was in a convoy approaching the Normandy beaches of the French coast. Previously, recordings had not been used for reports from war zones, but the policy had recently been changed. Hicks had a film recording machine lent to him by the Navy. Just as he started to give a description of the action along the coast, the convoy was attacked by German bombers, which strafed and bombed the ship. His report of the attack was punctuated by sounds of the ship's warning system, the planes' motors, the gunfire, and voices of ship crew members:

> Our ship is just sounding the warning, and now flak is coming up in the sky with streamers from the warships behind us.... Now the darkness has come on us. Those planes you hear overhead are the motors of the Nazis coming and going in the cloudy sky.... That was a bomb hit. Another one! Fire bursts and the flak and streamers going out in a diagonal slant right over our head.... Flares are coming down now. You can hear the machine gunning... .. Here's heavy ack-ack.... Look's like we're gonna have a night tonight. Here we go again! Another plane has come over.... The cruiser alongside is pouring it up.... Something burning is falling down through the sky and circling down. It may be a hit plane. Here we go. They got one!....(Voices of the gun crew: "We made it look like polka dots!") The lights of that burning Nazi plane are just twinkling now in the sea and going out.... Now it's ten past twelve, the beginning of June 7, 1944.

All four networks worked together on radio coverage of the invasion. Headquarters for the combined effort consisted of one of the small windowless, badly-ventilated rooms deep in the basement of the huge Ministry of Information in London. On hand were many of the networks' reporters. For CBS, Eric Sevareid landed with the first wave of American troops in Southern France. He would accompany them through France and cross the Rhine into Germany. Charles Collingwood would also follow the Allied advance, Richard Hottelet gave a description of the many ships in the harbor and along the invasion coast.

NBC was also well represented. Merrill Mueller, in his report, captured the sight and mood of General Eisenhower's headquarters. Wright Bryan carried a recorder with him on a transport plane going in with the paratroops. He described the tension that was prevalent just before the jump and picked up the "clinks" of the paratroopers hooking up their automatic release belts. W.W. Chaplain and John W. Vandercook also made contributions.

Mutual's Larry Wright described a landing. Ted Malone, who conducted *Between the Bookends* for Blue, had joined the network's London news staff in April.

The newsmen back home were also doing their jobs well. CBS listeners first heard of the invasion from Bob Trout. He stayed in Studio 9 for twenty-four hours, making thirty-five reports. During one period, Trout was at the mike for seven hours and eighteen minutes consecutively. NBC's Robert St. John also exhibited great broadcasting endurance.

John Daly covered the war in Italy for CBS until May 1944. He reported the fighting on the Anzio beachhead and was the first to report on the air bombardment of Cassino. Daly also gave an eye-witness account of the fall of Messina. Eric Sevareid participated in the Italian campaign. He also spent some time with Marshall Tito's followers in the hills of Yugoslavia. CBS's reliable Edward R. Murrow won the George Foster Peabody Award for news in 1944.

One day in late June after the Allied troops had pushed into France, George Hicks, exhausted, was taking a nap alongside a road in Normandy. An army truck came by collecting bodies of dead soldiers for burial. George was about to be loaded aboard when an officer passing by noticed who he was.

Death came to two Mutual newsmen during the year. Raymond Clapper was killed in a plane crash over the Marshall

Islands. Veteran commentator Boake Carter died at the age of forty-six, shortly after one of his daily broadcasts, which had emanated from KHJ, Los Angeles.

Early in the year, Bill Baldwin, special features director of the Blue Network in San Francisco, was sent on a special mission with the Navy. He was assigned to the overseas staff of the network's news and special features division in the Pacific. Later, Baldwin was awarded the Navy Commendation for reporting under fire.

Announcers who reported for active military duty in 1944:

ARMY

Verne Smith, announcer for *Kay Kyser's Kollege of Musical Knowledge*; Hugh Conover, announcer for *Right to Happiness* and *Life Can Be Beautiful*; Olin Tice, CBS, New York.

NAVY

Bob Cunningham, supervisor of announcers at WBBM, Chicago, lieutenant (jg).

ARMY AIR CORPS

Henry Morgan, WHN, New York.

Navy lieutenant Al Helfler was in command of a submarine chaser. NBC's *Cavalcade of America* used the heroic exploits of Helfler as material for a drama.

Ralph Edwards was drafted in the spring of 1944, and a search was launched to find a replacement for *Truth or Consequences*. Harry von Zell was chosen from a large list of potentials. After he did one show, Edwards was rejected by the military. Both MC's shared a couple of broadcasts. A financial settlement was reached, and Harry went on his way to other assignments.

The Adventures of Ozzie and Harriet came to radio in 1944. It's popularity would assure longevity. Announcer Verne Smith would be with it much of the way.

There was more time for comedy when *The Alan Young Show* debuted. It would also mean more work for announcers Jimmy Wallington, Larry Elliot, and Michael Roy.

The *Dreft Star Playhouse* provided more drama for a year. Terry O'Sullivan and Marvin Miller announced.

Ethel and Albert began six years of amusing small talk, which also lasted through six announcers—George Ansbro, Fred Cole, Don Lowe, Cy Harrice, Glenn Riggs, and Herb Sheldon.

Along came two more serial dramas. Larry Elliot announced for *Evelyn Winters*. Joe O'Brien, Fran Barber, and

212

Bob Dixon did the job for *Rosemary*.

The enduring *The FBI in Peace and War* was announced by Warren Sweeney, Andre' Baruch, and Len Sterling.

Outspoken Jack Kirkwood had started *Mirth and Madness* the previous year, and it became *The Jack Kirkwood Show* in 1944. Announcer Jimmy Wallington and later Bill Baldwin played parts in the skits.

A children's adventure program, *Land of the Lost*, used Michael Fitzmaurice as the announcer.

Quick As a Flash was one of the most entertaining quiz shows to come on the air. During its seven years, the MC's were Ken Roberts, Win Elliot, and Bill Cullen. Frank Gallop and Cy Harrice were the announcers.

The Roy Rogers Show brought the western movie group to the air in 1944. Lou Crosby was signed on as the announcer.

A scrambled-word quiz show, *Scramby Amby*, had been on WLW in 1941 and KFI and some other stations in 1943. It was placed on the Blue Network in 1944 with Perry Ward as the MC and Larry Keating as the announcer.

The mystery *Two on a Clue* was aired with Alice Youngman announcing.

A musical quiz called *What's the Name of That Song?* premiered in 1944. It would be popular enough to last for five years. Dud Williamson was the originator and first MC. Bill Gwinn would handle the final year.

Quiz shows were very much in vogue during that era, and Ken Murray emceed one called *Which Is Which?*

The Listening Post dramatized stories from *The Saturday Evening Post*. Bret Morrison served as the host.

The Coronet Storyteller presented stories from *Coronet* magazine with Marvin Miller working as the narrator and doing all the voices. The announcer was Vic Perrin.

Existing shows: Jim Ameche was the MC of *Here's to Romance*. Toby Reed announced *The Bob Burns Show*. Roger Krupp, who had been working at WHN, New York, was assigned as the announcer for the Lowell Thomas newscast.

Announcer Bill Goodwin was making a thousand dollars a week on the *Burns & Allen Show*, but he wanted to be a comedian. Apparently, Bill decided to start by being funny on the show. One week he sang the show's sign-off: "This is CBS. . .the Columbia Broadcasting. . . System," in a high-pitched whine that ended in a hysterical giggle. The next week he concluded with a painful

213

"OUCH!" His final sign-off effort was a distasteful "Ughh!" Goodwin decided to look for work as a comedian and found it on *The Frank Sinatra Show*, with the swooner acting as his straight man. For this he received his usual one thousand weekly.

Meanwhile, back at the *Burns & Allen Show*, Harry von Zell was hired as the announcer.

George Hay, the "Solemn Old Judge," resigned from WSM, Nashville and went to the West Coast to do some movie character parts, but he would be back.

Steve Allen moved from KOY, Phoenix to KFAC, Los Angeles. Bill Cullen left KDKA, headed for New York, and landed a job within a week on the CBS wartime shortage staff. Garnett Marks returned from the Army and went to work for KNX, Hollywood. Roy Rowan also joined KNX, coming from WGN, Chicago. Rod O'Connor also went west from WGN and joined KHJ. Jack Eigen, former WMCA, New York record MC, was released from the Army and resumed his *63 Club*. Chicago free lancer Russ Davis went to work for WBBM. Norman Brokenshire switched from WMAL, Washington to WBYN, Brooklyn. Alan Freed moved from WKBN, Youngstown back to WKST, New Castle. Dick Joy was released from the Navy and resumed his Hollywood announcing duties. Fred Vandeventer, newscaster at WJR, Detroit, went to WOR, New York and replaced Ed Thorgersen on six quarter-hour newscasts weekly.

Ben Grauer copped the H.P. Davis Memorial Award in 1944.

While Jimmy McClain performed at the microphone as *Dr. I.Q.*, he was also studying such subjects as Old Testament history, philosophy, prayer-book history, and comparative religion at Seabury-Western Theological Seminary in Evanston, Illinois. His purpose? In the future, he planned to leave the radio quizmaster role and enter the pulpit.

Russ Hodges, WOL, Washington sports announcer, was named as sportscaster for the entire Mutual network in 1944. Lt. Col. Bill Slater was discharged from the Army in time to join Don Dunphy on broadcasts of the Giants and Yankees games over WINS. Sportscaster Jack Brickhouse returned to WGN after release from the service. Sgt. Mel Allen was transferred to Armed Forces Radio headquarters in New York to broadcast sports programs overseas via short wave. Harry Wismer, a member of the Blue sports staff, won the *Sporting News* award for the second straight year.

Dr. James F. Bender of the National Institute for Human Relations made a survey of announcers working in 1944 to attempt to draw conclusions concerning their ideas about the profession and their educational backgrounds. Many experienced announcers were in military service, a fact that could have altered the results. Nevertheless, Dr. Bender received 204 completed questionnaires. Ninety-eight per cent of those who responded had finished high school, fifty per cent had attended college, and forty-one per cent were college graduates.

Sixty-one per cent of the announcers favored adoption of a single standard style of pronounciation and recommended most frequently the General American dialect, sometimes called Middle Midwestern, as the most useful for nationwide network broadcasters. Only twelve per cent found Oxford English, the standard of the British Broadcasting Corporation, suitable for American stations. They recommended, almost unanimously, that announcers on local stations use the dialect that was spoken by local educated listeners. The greatest phonetic sin an announcer could commit, according to the vast majority, was affectation of voice and pronounciation.

As for personality, the senior announcers mentioned certain traits that made for success—friendliness, sincerity, self-confidence, fairness, and enthusiasm. They felt that egotism was the most frequent cause of failure as an announcer as far as personality was concerned.

And speaking of personality, showmanship-style newscaster Paul Harvey brought his talents to WENR, Chicago in 1944 after various stops along the way, which included Tulsa; Salina, Kansas; and St. Louis. Harvey would find a longtime broadcasting home in the Windy City. It seemed to be the appropriate spot for him.

John Daly interrupted a children's program on CBS at 5:49 P.M., Eastern War Time, on April 12, 1945: "We interrupt this program to bring you a special news bulletin from CBS World News. A press association has just announced that President Roosevelt is dead. The President died of a cerebral hemorrhage. All we know so far is that the President died at Warm Springs in Georgia."

Daly previously had served as CBS White House correspondent for four years and had known the President well. It was appropriate that he was the first to make the announcement. Roosevelt had been the first real radio president, the first to utilize its potential power to the fullest extent. He made almost three hundred broadcasts while in office. Radio's tribute to him from the time of the announcement of his death until he was buried was inclusive. Reports were picked up from many foreign points. Programming was drastically changed. Omitted were commercials, comedy shows, soap operas, violent dramas, and lively music. Arthur Godfrey broadcast a personal and emotional description of the processional down Pennsylvania Avenue:

> The drums are wrapped in black crepe and are muffled as you can hear. The pace of the musicians is so slow. Behind them, these are Navy boys. And now, just coming past the Treasury I can see the horses drawing the caisson. And most generally, folks havin' as tough a time as I am trying to see it. And behind us is the car bearing the man on whose shoulders now falls the terrific burdens and responsibilities that were handled so well by the man to whose body we are paying our last respects now. God bless him, President Truman. (Crying) We return you now to the studio.

For one minute at 4:00 P.M. on Saturday April 15, all radio was silent.

Blue's H.R. Baukhage was given an award by the National Headliners Club for his broadcast of President Roosevelt's funeral services.

U.S. radio had covered the war in Europe since the beginning, and it was there to broadcast the finish after V-E Day in May 1945. Among those to report the German surrender was Charles Collingwood: "General Jodl, Chief of Staff of the German Army, signed the last document. He sat there very straight with his head bent over the papers, and when he signed the last one, he put the cap back on the pen and looked up at the men sitting across the plain wooden table. Opposite him sat General Bedel Smith, Eisenhower's Chief of Staff. . . ."

Lieutenant Frank J. McGlogan, former newscaster and announcer for WJR, Detroit, was killed in action over Germany on one of his first missions as a bombardier. He had come to WJR from KSTP, St. Paul in October 1941. He enlisted in the Army Air Corps in January 1943 and was sworn in on the air. After two years at bases in the U.S., he arrived in England less than a month before he was killed. Upon his arrival, he had written to his former news editor at WJR: "Well, I'm finally at a station where I can at last see some action."

Milton Chase, staff correspndent in the Phillipines for WLW, was commended by the Army for excellent reporting of the Battle of Manila and the fighting elsewhere on Luzon.

216

National Headliners Club awards, in addition to the one given to H.R. Baukhage for his coverage of President Roosevelt's funeral, went to Blue's George Hicks for his reporting on the evening of D-Day and to CBS' Bill Downs for a vivid account of the surrender of German Armies in Northern Germany, Holland, and Denmark to English forces in Hamburg.

In August 1945, when it was thought that the Japanese might surrender, Robert Trout stayed at CBS headquarters in New York for four days. When V-J Day seemed a certainty, he moved out of Studio 9, just outside the door where the news machines were and where a direct telephone from the White House hung on the wall. The word came on August 14:

> 7:00 P.M., Eastern War Time. Bob Trout reporting. The Japanese have accepted our terms fully. That's the word we've just received from the White House in Washington.The United Nations on land, on the sea, in the air and unto the four corners of the earth are united and are victorious. . . .

Marine Captain Steve Cisler, a former announcer and manager, gave an account of his coverage of the Japanese surrender:

> I covered the surrender ceremonies on the *USS Missouri* in Tokyo Bay with about 10 hours notice, using a wire recorder. I was a Marine captain on the initial occupation to get sound recordings for the Marines and the Armed Forces Radio Service as we opened the prison camps and took the surrender of the military Naval posts. We used two GE wire recorders, powered by 6-volt batteries, which had to be hauled up and down ships' ladders with the help of my enlisted helper or convenient Naval and Army personnel. Logistics were hell!
>
> In the Bay, I was based on the Naval communication ship *USS Ancon*. I got word the night before the surrender to be prepared to record the ceremonies alongside the Army team.
>
> On the *Missouri*, we set up just aft of the ceremonial table, behind General MacArthur and the Allied generals. We were to put the wires on the short wave circuit back to the States. The RCA people in California were going to use the best signal from either the Navy relay or the Army short wave out of a Jap station near Yokohama. They had recorded on a Presto disc machine but had to take it back up the Bay to get to the station. (MacArthur had ordered any broadcast held up 40 minutes to give the press a chance to file.) I rewound my first wire reel in the control room of the *Ancon* and the damn wire jumped off the reel and flew over the cabin. Imagine a hair net unraveling! Luckily, the backup reel

could be rewound slowly, and we put the signal on when it was due. I understand that our signal, relayed through Guam and Hawaii, was the best level in California. Ours was used by the networks that historic day. "But why," I often would ask, "was a momentous moment handled so casually in its official scheduling and broadcast with hit-or-miss equipment I just happened to have on hand!"

Edward R. Murrow found an important position waiting for him at CBS after the war. He was named vice president in charge of public affairs, but this title wouldn't keep him off the air.

Elmer Davis, having completed his work as head of the OWI, resumed his news reporting, this time for the American Broadcasting Company; which, as of June 15, 1945, was the new name of the Blue Network.

Norman Brokenshire was doing some air work and making talks to Alcoholic Anonymous groups. One day he received a call telling him to come to the United States Steel Corporation for an interview. The Theatre Guild was going to produce a dramatic radio show for the steel company, and they were interested in talking to Broke about being the announcer. On the day of the meeting, he shaved and put on his best suit. He didn't try to put up a front for the assistant chairman of the board. He didn't attempt to conceal his irresponsible background. The company decided to take a chance on him. *The Theatre Guild on the Air* was first heard September 9, 1945. A review by the New York *World-Telegram* reported that the announcer was "Norman Brokenshire, long absent from big-time radio. . . . He still has a fine, easy way of announcing, mercifully lacking in the phoney exuberance we have too much with us these days." George Hicks, his war reporting finished, was assigned to do the commercials for U.S. Steel.

While one radio veteran was getting another opportunity to make good, another was retiring from the microphone. Major Bowes announced that he was retiring from *The Original Amateur Hour*.

Tom Breneman's *Breakfast at Sardi's* was renamed *Breakfast in Hollywood*. John Nelson and Carl Webster Pierce worked as announcers on the very popular ABC feature.

Art Linkletter gained more radio exposure when he started *House Party* on January 15, 1945. Jack Slattery served as his reliable announcer.

It was a good year for audience participation shows. Another, *Queen for a Day*, made its debut. For a short time, Dud Williamson was the MC, but soon Jack Bailey was signed to a long-term contract as the head man. Gene Baker announced.

The Andrews Sisters finally got their own show—*The Andrews Sisters Eight-to-the-Bar Ranch*. Marvin Miller announced.

Bob Hawk started a quiz show called (what else?) *The Bob Hawk Show*.

Larry Elliot announced the serial drama *Barry Cameron*.

Break the Bank was quite a successful quiz show. Its capable lineup of MC's aided that success—John Reed King, Johnny Olson, Bert Parks, and Clayton "Bud" Collier.

During its five-year stay, about a thousand couples were married on the program *Bride and Groom*. John Nelson was the MC. Jack McElroy did the announcing.

Bob Hite was the announcer for the short-lived drama, *Cimarron Tavern*.

Win Elliot and Jack Bailey were the MC's for the audience participation show *Country Fair*. Lee Vines announced.

The mystery *The Falcon* came from the movies to radio in 1945 with Ed Herlihy as the announcer.

The Gay Mrs. Featherstone, a sitcom, lasted for one year. Marvin Miller was the announcer.

The quizzes kept coming. John Reed King emceed *Give and Take*.

His Honor, the Barber featured delightful actor Barry Fitzgerald in the leading role. Frank Martin announced.

Maisie, played by actress Ann Sothern, was a movie series that went on radio in 1945. Ken Niles was chosen as the announcer.

Meet me at Parky's was a comedy announced by Art Gilmore.

One more soap opera came on the radio scene. *The Second Mrs. Burton* was good enough to last for fifteen years, even with its late start. Harry Clark and Hugh James were the announcers.

The Saint provided adventure for radio listeners. Dick Joy was the announcer.

This Is Your FBI was first heard in 1945. Milton Cross, Carl Frank, and Larry Keating were the announcers.

Those Websters brought more situation comedy to the airwaves. Charles Irving drew the announcing assignment.

219

The *Whistler*, a real thriller, had first come on the air on the West Coast in 1942. Bill Forman had the title role, and Marvin Miller was the announcer. When Forman went into the Army in 1945, Miller became *The Whistler*.

Other 1945 announcing assignments: Dick Joy was on the *Danny Kaye Show*, *The Telephone Hour*, and the previously mentioned show, *The Saint*. Kenny Delmar doubled as the announcer and the character "Senator Claghorn" on the *Fred Allen Show*. Del Sharbutt was assigned to the *Jack Carson Show*.

Arthur Godfrey finally got his wish. He had been mostly a local man with only sporadic network assignments. When the network's *School of the Air* went off for the summer in 1945, Arthur persuaded CBS brass to let him try the time slot from 9:15 to 9:45 A.M. His show proved to be so successful that when fall arrived, *School of the Air* was moved to 5:00 P.M., and Godfrey's time was lengthened to forty-five minutes.

Steve Allen moved over to KMTR, Hollywood as an MC and writer. Bill Baldwin came back from an overseas news assignment and resumed his announcing work in San Francisco. Robert Q. Lewis was discharged from the Army and went back to the mike and turntables. Howard Duff turned mostly to radio acting after he got out of the Army. When Rex Marshall put aside his uniform, he headed back to WJTN, Jamestown, New York. Ernie Ford didn't head for Tennessee after his discharge. Instead, he decided to try West Coast radio, working as an announcer in San Bernardino and later in Pasadena. George Fenneman was transferred from KGO, San Francisco to the ABC staff in Hollywood. Pierre Andre' moved from ABC, Chicago to ABC, Hollywood. Cy Harrice left WGN, Chicago to free lance in New York.

Pioneer announcer Tommy Cowan was still working for city-owned WNYC, New York, announcing and interviewing artists, conductors, and personalities from the stage of the Center Theatre in Rockefeller Center.

Martin Block contributed to the nostalgia of returning servicemen by writing the lyrics for the popular and timely song *"Waiting for the Train to Come in."*

Ted Husing did the play-by-play of the Orange Bowl game for the tenth year, and it would be his last time for that assignment. In post-war radio, Ted would become a highly-paid disc jockey.

Sportscaster Harry Caray made the jump to major league baseball broadcasting by convincing a sponsor that he was the

220

man to handle the games of the St. Louis Cardinals and Browns on WIL.

Sportscaster Van Patrick went to WPEN, Philadelphia.

One day in August 1945, the manager of KOMA, Oklahoma City was driving through Cheyenne, Wyoming. He heard Curt Gowdy doing a re-creation of a major league baseball game on KBFC. Gowdy was hired as sports director for KOMA.

Gary Breckner, veteran Pacific Coast announcer who was handling *Maxwell House Coffee Time*, was killed in an automobile accident in June 1945.

Uncle Don Carney, veteran children's MC on WOR, formed the Uncle Don Institute of Child Guidance and Recreation, a non-profit organization to help solve child delinquency and recreational problems.

Andre' Baruch signed off Mutual's *Leave It to the Girls* by saying, "This is CBS, the Columbia Broadcasting System." Phillips Carlin, Mutual's vice president in charge of programs, sent CBS a bill for $11,630.55, the full half-hour rate.

Ed Murrow returned to the air with a regular nightly newscast after he bacame acclimated to his position of vice president in charge of CBS public affairs. For a period of time, Ernest Chappell worked as his announcer. When Chappell decided to leave the program, Murrow used the occasion to pay a tribute to announcers:

> Now I would like to talk about radio announcers, particularly those who announce news programs. Maybe many of you think they just announce commercials supplied by advertising agencies, but this is not the case. Often the announcer is the only tangible audience the commentator has, for he is the man across the mike, the only one you can see. You walk into the studio when the big red hand is sweeping the face of the clock for the last time. A good announcer is likely to say: "What have you got tonight?" and you reply: "It's a turkey, there is no news, and what there is has been written badly and the end result will probably be merely a contribution to confusion." And the announcer says: "It can't be that bad. Sit down and give it a reading," and while you read he listens and seems interested.
>
> When you fluff a line or get a backlash on a sentence and it begins to strangle you, he grins and shrugs his shoulders and says with his eyes: "Go on, let it alone. If you go back for a second try, it would be worse anyway and it wasn't as bad as you think." And occasionally, not too often, this good announcer, when the big hand has gone around the clock fifteen times and the program is off the air will turn to you and say: "You had a couple of minutes of good stuff in that show tonight." With a good announcer you always feel

221

that if your throat closes up or you go crazy, you can throw him the copy and penciled notes and he will carry on and get you off on time. That's the kind of announcer Ernest Chappell is. After tonight, he will not be announcing this news broadcast and I wanted to take a minute of your time to say my thanks to him. Thanks, Chappie, carry on.

At radio's twenty-five-year mark, some announcers had already enjoyed their greatest success; for others, the peak of popularity was yet to come. With the rapid acceleration of commercial television ready to begin and the radical change in popular music style only a decade away, for traditional radio programming, it was the beginning of the end. Some announcers would adapt to the TV camera—some would find a place in format radio. Others would leave the profession. One thing was for certain. It would never be the same.

Index

Collier, Clayton "Bud", 131, 152, 163, 182, 184, 219
Collingwood, Charles, 187, 188, 197, 204, 211, 216
Collins, Ted, 141
Compton, Walter, 183, 185
Connelly, Vincent, 118
Conover, Hugh, 133, 140, 183, 212
Conrad, Dr. Frank, 6, 7
Conte, Bill, 163
Conte, John, 163, 172, 174
Cook, Dick, 144
Coolidge, Calvin, 46, 48, 52
Cooper, Jack L., 134
Cooper, Robert, 18
Correll, Charles, 49, 68
Costello, Jack, 113, 142, 153, 175, 176, 192
Cowan, Tommy, 14, 15, 16, 21, 22, 34, 37, 41, 144, 195, 220
Cox, James, 6, 8
Crago, Wm. T., 153, 203
Craig, Ken, 155
Cronkite, Walter, 107, 138, 149, 159
Crosby, Bing, 90, 91, 142
Crosby, Lou, 133, 163, 184, 201, 208, 213
Crosley, Powel, 13, 18
Cross, Milton, 21, 22, 30, 37, 41, 42, 60, 65, 78, 90, 94, 97, 121, 141, 144, 145, 153, 156, 182, 183, 194, 195, 202, 203, 219
Crowley, Matt, 195
Cruger, George, 34
Crummit, Frank, 162
Cullen, Bill, 171, 192, 209, 213, 214
Cunningham, Bob, 156, 212
Cunningham, Glenn, 195

—D—

Daggett, John, 55, 105
Dahlstead, Dresser, 103
Daly, John Charles, 147, 148, 165, 185, 189, 205, 211, 215
Damrosch, Dr. Frank, 21
Damrosch, Walter, 66, 71
Daniel, John B., 41, 60
Darrow, Clarence, 50
Davis, Elmer, 166, 167, 181, 187, 188, 194, 197, 206, 218
Davis, H. P., 194, 204, 214
Davis, John, 39
Davis, Meyer, 44

Davis, Russ, 143, 154, 214
Delmar, Kenny, 105, 132, 220
DeMille, Cecil B., 105
Dempsey, Jack, 10, 12, 17, 33, 62, 195
DeRose, Breen, 66
DeRose, Peter, 66
Desmond, Connie, 134, 174, 203
Devine, Otis, 122, 143, 193
Diaz, Ray, 202
Dixon, Bob, 163, 213
Doggett, Jerry, 164, 185, 193
Donaldson, Dan, 112
Douglas, Jack, 105
Douglas, Paul, 104, 144, 145, 192, 200, 202, 203, 204
Dowd, Don, 109, 113, 122, 192, 208
Downs, Bill, 217
Downs, Hugh, 170, 171, 185, 198, 209
Dreier, Alex, 190, 198
Dudley, Dick, 208
Duff, Howard, 129, 191, 220
Duke of Windsor, 149
Dunham, Dick, 201, 203
Dunn, Eddie, 162
Dunninger, Joseph, 208
Dunphy, Don, 203, 214
Durante, Jimmy, 207

—E—

East, Ed., 162
Echlin, Erland, 179
Eddy, Nelson, 208
Edison, Thomas, 14
Edwards, Douglas, 105, 133, 142, 163, 185, 194, 197, 205
Edwards, Gus, 73
Edwards, Ralph, 76, 90, 113, 125, 130, 138, 153, 163, 172, 182, 194, 212
Edwards, Webley, 129, 164, 180
Ehmke, Howard, 77, 195
Eigen, Jack, 214
Eisenhower, General Dwight, 211, 216
Ellers, Richard, 122
Elliot, Bob, 206
Elliot, Larry, 106, 153, 163, 184, 202, 212, 219
Elliot, Win, 213, 219
Ellis, Kenneth, 105
Elson, Bob, 65, 70, 77, 106, 130, 154, 174, 186, 194, 199, 204, 209
Elton, David, 122

226

227

231

232